"FEAR, FUN & FAITH"

John Flanner with John Cheek

BRUNO WELLS PUBLISHERS part of Impact for Life Ltd.,
Cheltenham Film and Photographic Studios, Arle Court,
Hatherley Lane, Cheltenham, Gloucester GL51 6PN

Published 2009 by Bruno Wells Publications part of Impact for Life Ltd.

A catalogue record for this book is available from the British Library.

ISBN 9780954495756

Typeset in 10/12pt Minion by
Steven Levers Design & Typesetting, Sheffield.

Printed in Great Britain by
Digital Book Print, Milton Keynes

Front cover *(clockwise, from bottom-left):*
• Scenes from Birmingham past, including a derby match at Villa Park, and the
  city-centre, by New Street station;
• John Flanner aged 11;
• John receiving the Outstanding Achievement Award from Sir Gus O'Donnell in 2006

Back cover
• Civil Service Diversity Awards in London – (left to right) TV broadcaster Rageh Omaar,
  John Flanner, Sir Gus O'Donnell: Cabinet Secretary and Head of the Home Civil Service,
  Paul Gray: former Chair of H.M. Revenue and Customs

"Fear, Fun & Faith"

The Remarkable Story of a
Diversity Award Winner

John Flanner
with John Cheek

Foreword

by Lord Taylor of Warwick

AS THE one-time US President Franklin D. Roosevelt once said, "the only thing we have to fear, is fear itself". Sometimes the fear of something can be more destructive than the thing in question.

With my background of a career in Law, I have sadly encountered many people experiencing fear. Some of it justified, some not. But if we are honest, there is not one of us, over a certain age who can say that fear has never impinged upon our lives at some stage. Many adults are acutely aware of the phobias and hang-ups which they carry daily with them; often these fears are personal, trivial and have no legal implications - they are not rooted in dramatic injustices, but perhaps are simply grounded in long-term aversions, which have sadly developed over time.

This book is not a Self-Help Guide and doesn't pretend to be. Instead, it is a frank revelation from someone who began to struggle with a host of fears from within, before being afflicted with unexpected disability from without. What followed, was plenty of tears and no-little dearth of embarrassing moments, before the process of overcoming such fears eventually proved triumphant.

What became John's experience, may not be replicated identically in the experience of others. The path for life which he proposes, will be greeted sceptically by some. But many of us have known what it is like, to wake-up in the morning and immediately dread the day ahead - whether it will be one spent at home, at work or in education. Some reading this, are people who feel apprehension and inadequacy, at the thought of certain social situations and activities. This book does not claim to have all the answers. But it shows that (deeply entrenched) feelings are not uncommon; that there is hope that *it doesn't always have to be this way.*

Diversity is a modern buzzword, and through these pages you'll get a flavour of Midlands' life; a reminder of how things were, growing up in the Birmingham of the 1960s and '70s - a time of industrial and racial strife, dimpled beer mugs and Love Thy Neighbour on ITV - and a hint, at best, of what it must be like to live with near total-blindness. During his story, he even attempts to take an honest look at perhaps the root of all fear: fear of death.

John Flanner and I go back a long way. Like me, he's a Brummie with Solihull connections. We used to go to the same church, years ago. We love music and support Aston Villa; both Villains!

I fully endorse John Flanner on a personal and professional level. I hope you enjoy his story but more importantly, gain from it.

Rt. Hon. Lord Taylor of Warwick
House of Lords
Palace of Westminster
London

Introduction

Easter Monday, 25 March 2005

As I sit at my computer today, I realise that I am at a crossroads. I am approaching 58 years of age; in theory I can retire in just over two years' time - however, from both a financial and conviction point of view, I need to continue working. From a career perspective, I am more interested in 'refirement', than retirement.

I cannot escape the thought that I was put on this planet for a purpose, and with a specific destiny to fulfil: my life has been interesting, varied and challenging to date, but there is no sense whatsoever, that it is a case of 'mission accomplished'. On the contrary, I feel that the best of me (and for me) is yet to come.

In the course of living your life, you will no doubt come across people who are 'multi-talented'. They seem to be expert at a wide variety of different things. I have often felt intimidated by such people; at times wondered where I was, when God was dishing out the talents. I class myself as a one-or-two talent person. It has taken most of my life to begin to appreciate what those talents are.

I am told that I possess the ability to encourage and inspire people of all ages, thanks to the gift that I have been given of being able to communicate, both orally and in writing. I will explain later how these talents/gifts were released to me. For the moment, however, it has been confirmed to me just how powerful these gifts are, thanks to a project I have undertaken as part of my job at the Inland Revenue over the past couple of years.

It all began when I wrote a Disability-related article for our office magazine, and to my surprise, one of our Area Directors, John Dolan, picked up the phone to thank me for the article and to congratulate me on the way it had been written. He was also enlightened by its contents, which highlighted a disability email forum that had been set up nationally across the then Inland Revenue, now Her Majesty's Revenue & Customs (HMRC). The same Director then followed up by recommending that I enrol on a Personal Development programme, which the Department were hosting in Coventry.

Typical of me, feeling somewhat insecure about all this, I said I felt it would be great if I was 25 years of age, but as I was 56 maybe it was too late for me! Thankfully, he would have none of that, saying that I had an obvious gift in the field of communication and would like to see it being developed. I can honestly say that I have rarely come across anyone who was so positively on my side, and wanting me to succeed, as much as John did at that time. So it was, that I duly applied to go on the programme and was accepted.

It was called "Breakthrough". It covered such topics as "Making Positive Personal Affirmations", "Dreams & Visions" and "The Power of Forgiveness". Those early seminars were dynamic; and left me with the feeling, "I wish I had been taught these things at school – they would have changed the course of my life". The ethos behind Breakthrough can be summed up in the following affirmations, which we were encouraged to speak out and begin each day with:

"My future is in my own hands - Change is possible - I have the ability to make the necessary changes."

Why not write down those three statements and begin to speak them into your life on a daily basis? You might just find that something amazing starts to happen!

As a result of what I learned on the Breakthrough programme I now believe I could have achieved my desire to become a sports journalist. However at the tender age of 15, when I was informed by the Careers Officer that I had to gain five GCE 'O' Level passes I gave up on my dream, thinking I was not intelligent enough for that. My mind was telling me lies. A little bit of encouragement at that stage may well have worked wonders.

Breakthrough also taught me that every person has a genius inside of them, just waiting to be released in some way. I go along with the Biblical view that says we are all created in the image of God, who is Himself a genius, and has put part of His genius inside each of his superb creations.

I realise that many children have their dreams stolen by well meaning, but sceptical adults who in turn, had their childhood dreams stolen by sceptical adults. It's a cycle which keeps on being repeated. Some kids are strong-minded enough to press on with their dreams regardless ,but many have them crushed and go on to live their whole lives with a feeling of what might have been, if only… "Dear God, please don't let me become a stealer of dreams, but allow me to encourage and help people of all ages realise their potential".

Two other necessary ingredients of Breakthrough, were to establish a mentoring relationship and to undertake a project which would benefit the business overall. My mentor, Ruth, an Area Director from Merry Hill in the West Midlands, was very good for me because she held me accountable for suggestions and ideas which I came up with. I have never been short of ideas, but have often lacked the confidence or discipline to put them into action.

As far as a project was concerned, Ruth came up with an idea that I should put together a talk under the umbrella of Diversity Awareness. I protested, mildly, that I did not know anything about Diversity, but she insisted that I was 'diverse'. I think that that was the word she used - and not 'perverse'! Ruth said that I had dispelled a lot of the preconceptions she had about blind people, and, in terms of my attitude to life, I certainly brought a different approach compared to many other people.

I gave the matter some thought, and once I had put down in writing what I wanted to say, I then had to actively seek out opportunities to go and talk at team meetings, around the building. I had worked for the Inland Revenue for twenty two years as an audio typist, never doing anything else. However, if I was going to develop some of this talent for communicating, I had to make a start somewhere. In City Centre House where I work, in the centre of Birmingham, there is a workforce of approximately eight hundred staff, so plenty of teams to approach.

I fired-off an email to all Line Managers requesting an opportunity to attend team meetings, to give a short presentation on the subject of Diversity Awareness. I gave the matter further thought as the invitations started rolling in.

My first talk to our Business Support Team was for a15-minutes duration, and thinking that the title of *Diversity Awareness* sounded a bit dry, I subtitled it 'Fear, Fun & Faith'. The meeting went well and, at one point several people were wiping tears from their eyes, whilst a moment or two later they were laughing heartily at some of my stories. At the end of the talk there was a steady stream of questions, followed later by a flow of congratulatory and appreciative emails.

After that initial meeting, others followed and slowly but surely my time was increased to the point where I am now being invited to speak for an hour at meetings. The response from people has been truly amazing and I have since taken this talk across the country to HMRC staff in places such as Peterborough, Southend, Norwich, Leeds, Coventry, Lincoln and Milton Keynes, speaking to some of the senior management within HMRC. Even since starting to write this book, I have been honoured by the Department with an invitation to attend a champagne dinner at the (London) Park Lane Hilton, to celebrate with others the work which has been done in advancing the Diversity and Equal Opportunities cause.

The feedback from staff has said that my talk is humorous, inspiring and highly motivational. Numerous people have suggested that I should write a book, that others may benefit from my experiences and insights.

What follows is the expanded version of the 'Fear, Fun & Faith' talks that have taken Revenue & Customs by storm and me by surprise. I have endeavoured to incorporate many of the suggestions that people have written to me about; things they want to hear about or learn more of. I sincerely hope you enjoy it, have a few laughs along the way and feel inspired enough to grab your life by the scruff of the neck, so that you begin to walk more purposefully into your God appointed destiny.

John Flanner, *Birmingham, West Midlands*

Preface

I didn't realise that the job of knocking into shape John's story, would be such a long or, indeed, absorbing one for me. Although I'd already met him when I first offered to help, and had witnessed one of his many presentations, it didn't fully dawn on me that I would be editing a text, many thousands of words long, which had been written by someone who was largely blind. Whilst it proved to be more of a challenge than I had first anticipated, it was one I thoroughly enjoyed from the start. Even if the grammar wasn't perfect, the story often had me riveted; and it proved to be a 'journey' for me, on several levels.

As well as having to work full-time as a Civil Servant, the editing process was also dogged by inexplicable 'technical difficulties', right up to the end. If you come across any problems with the content or layout of this book, don't be surprised! By the time my wife and I had to invest in a new home computer, I'd long since reached the conclusion that something, or 'someone' didn't want the book to happen.

It was also disrupted by my having to deal with a considerable amount of personal loss. During a twelve-month period, Fiona and I lost eight people known to us; not least the untimely passing of my mother at a relatively young age, after a short struggle with cancer. Each time, when I was able to return to the text I immediately picked up the story at a stage when it 'spoke' directly to me, and to what I was experiencing; periods and incidents from John's past seemed to be waiting for me, to bring encouragement and insight as I progressed along an emotional (and difficult) part in my own journey through life. I like to think that perhaps you, the reader, may take something from his story as well, which will prove inspiring or, at least, leave you with hope.

The quotations from the Bible in this book, are usually from the New International Version (NIV) unless otherwise stated - scripture taken from *The Message* Copyright 1993, 1994, 1995, 1996. Used by permission of NavPress Publishing Group.

Many thanks, regarding other copyright permission goes to Allan Dann and David Jacome at Peer Music; Lee Thomas at Imagem Music; Mark Thompson at the Communications and Media team of H.M. Revenue and Customs; Steve Dyson at the Birmingham Mail. Repeated attempts to contact other copyright holders did not illicit a response - the holders are invited to contact John Cheek at **JohnCheek@hotmail.com**

In some parts of the book, certain names have been changed, and some events and details omitted, out of respect for people's privacy.

Sincere thanks go to Elizabeth Webb - and Heather Hannant and her mother, from the Gateway Community Church, Kettering - for all their tremendous support, for both this book and John's activities in general; to Elizabeth - and John's wife Sylvia - for their time spent going through old photographs.

Expressed gratitude goes to Jon Stanton and David Elcock for I.T. assistance and help with the cover design, respectively. Thank you to Phillip Allen; Doug Ellis; Carl Chinn; Graham Pearce; Sir Gus O'Donnell at the Cabinet Office; Anna Rogerson; Martin Power and anyone else, who helped in any way.

John Flanner is a special person. I feel pleased and honoured to share his story with you.

John Cheek

'Rose Of My Heart'

The words to this song are dedicated by
John Flanner to his wife, Sylvia

We're the best partners this world's ever seen
Together as close as can be
But sometimes it's hard to find time in between
To tell you what you are to me

You are the rose of my heart
You are the love of my life
A flower not faded nor falling apart
If you're tired, rest your head on my arm
Rose of my heart.

When sorrow holds you in her arms of clay
It's raindrops that fall from your eyes
Your smile is the dun come to earth for the day
You brighten my blackest of skies

You are the rose of my heart
You are the love of my life
A flower not faded nor falling apart
If you're cool let my love make you warm
Rose of my heart.

So hard times are easy times, what do I care
There's nothing I'd change if I could
The tears and the laughter are things that we share
Your hand in mine makes all times good

You are the rose of my heart
You are the love of my life
A flower not faded nor falling apart
You're my harbour in life's restless storm
Rose of my heart.

(words and music - Hugh Moffatt)

This book is dedicated to Sylvia,
*and John's late parents, **Francis ('Frank')***
*and **Marjorie ('Marge') Flanner***

Chapter One

Heroes and Villains
(1947- 2007)

"I'm sorry Mr Flanner there's nothing more we can do. John will have to be registered blind".

The Eye Consultant, Mr Vernon-Smith at Birmingham Eye Hospital, was talking to my Dad after I had been attending the outpatients' clinic for around six months. I was currently employed at Fort Dunlop, part of the Dunlop Rubber Co in Birmingham, as a sales clerk in the Motor Cycle Tyre Sales Department. One morning, I was checking a balance sheet and found it difficult to read some of the figures. I took the balance sheet back to the typist and said, "I'm sorry Pam, but this will need to be retyped because some of the figures are blurred."

Pam, looked up and took the balance sheet from me and then, rather quizzically said,

"But John, this is perfectly clear".

She gave it back to me and I looked again saying, "No it isn't, look at these", and in that moment my mind went back to a Sunday football game I had played a week or two earlier, when I experienced blurred vision during a rainstorm and then to another occasion, when I had sustained a slight bang on the head during a game, again leaving me with temporary blurring in the left eye.

Now I knew something was seriously wrong. "Don't worry Pam, I'll sort it", I said in a worried tone.

I went straight to my boss, explaining the situation and he gave me permission to go and see the firm's optician. I did, and on examination I was referred to the Birmingham Eye Hospital immediately. By now, my eyes were the talk of the office and when I returned to explain that I had been referred to the hospital there were a few worried faces around. Despite the offers to accompany me to the city centre, I decided to go alone catching the Number 66 bus from near the office. Tests on that first visit confirmed a significant loss of sight in the left eye, though at that stage the right eye was perfect. After several tests I was told that I could go home, but would need to return at the same time the following week. That was the pattern for the next six months up, until now.

In that time, my sight had deteriorated week after week to the point where both eyes were now affected and, for my own safety and that of others, I needed to be escorted. I could not do my job any more and was effectively on long term sick. Funnily though, having got over the initial shock, I was quite enjoying my afternoons at the hospital and any time now I thought, they would give me some tablets, put in some drops or perform a minor operation and then I would be okay. So now, therefore, to hear these words being spoken to my Dad in response to his question, "When are you going to do something?" was, as it usually is, a bolt from the blue.

"What do you mean, there's nothing you can do?" Dad protested.

"John is suffering from a very rare hereditary condition, called Leber's Optic Atrophy - and there is no cure" said Mr Vernon-Smith.

My mind went back to a movie I had watched only a couple of days before. Reach for the Sky starring Kenneth More as Douglas Bader, the World War II hero who had to have both legs amputated. One particular scene in the film stayed with me.

Douglas is lying in his hospital bed in a state of semi-consciousness when he overhears two nurses talking at the foot of his bed.

"How is he doing?" asked one nurse.

"Not good, I think he's given up" said the other.

Apparently it was at that point that Douglas Bader said to himself, *"I'll show them"* . The same attitude rose up inside of me, as I listened into this conversation between the consultant and my dad on that spring morning in 1967.

Completing the necessary forms, we eventually left the hospital in something of a daze. Mum waited anxiously at home, but dad and I delayed the inevitable by going for a coffee at the Kardoma coffee shop, in Colmore Row. The shop was not especially busy and dad left me at a window seat while he went up to the counter. There was a radio playing behind the till. The news headlines came on. I was to be shocked and saddened by what I heard.

"Donald Campbell has been killed in a crash on Lake Coniston, while attempting to break the world water speed record," read the BBC newsreader.

"Here's your coffee, son…" said dad, as tears streamed down my face.

Dad reached out, touched my hand and said, "I'm sorry".

"That's okay dad", I said. "But what about Donald Campbell? That is terrible…"

The fact was, that at that moment I was far more upset about the death of Donald Campbell, than I was about the fact that I had just been registered blind.

Dad and I eventually arrived home; a ground floor maisonette, on the Wyrley Birch Council Estate in Erdington, Birmingham. Mum was devastated at the news of course, especially as the diagnosis was that the condition had apparently come from her side of the family.

Mum and dad were to have two further crushing blows, because my sister Joan and brother Paul were later to go blind also. I don't think mum particularly ever fully got over those emotional hammer blows and like many kids, I live with the regret that I did not treat my dear mother with the love, respect and understanding due to her, while she was alive. She was the kind of mum who waited on us hand and foot and I took her so much for granted. I take great comfort in the fact however that before she died of cancer on 23 August 1986, she had some ten weeks beforehand put her trust in Jesus Christ as her Lord and Saviour, so I am confident that I will see her again one day, to let her know that there are no hard feelings from me to her. She gave me life. For that I will always be grateful.

*

I am the eldest of four children. My parents, Francis (Frank) and Marjorie were married in St Paul's Church in the Lozells area of Birmingham, on 20th April 1946 and I arrived at Heathfield Road Maternity Hospital, Handsworth, on 29th July 1947. Almost two years later my sister Joan was born.

Some two years after that, my parents moved from their house in Aston, in the north of the city, to a back-to-back council house in Scott Street, Vauxhall. Our house had an attic, which was my bedroom and across the road was the London Midland Scottish (LMS) main railway line; when the high-speed steam trains went through to Vauxhall & Duddeston station, the bedroom windows would rattle. It was a great room for train spotting, so I quickly developed that hobby. When hearing the sound of a train coming along the

Track, I would dive out of bed, train spotting book in hand and peer out of the window. I would make a note of the train number or name, and then find it in my book and underline it very neatly in red ink.

It was not too long after moving to that house, that my brother Paul was born and then my sister Susan followed a little while after that.

We had great fun growing up in that neighbourhood - despite the fact that we did not have a lot of the luxuries we enjoy today. The lavatory was situated in the back yard, which we shared with our neighbours at the rear. Bath time was once a week and consisted of a tin bath in front of the living-room coal fire! Mum had to pour in several saucepans full of hot water before it was deep enough to get into. We also had a 9-inch black & white television with just one BBC channel to look at. I do remember ITV starting and the first programme we watched was *Sunday Night at the London Palladium*.

As kids we played lots of street games with many other children. The girls would be out playing with their dolls and prams while the boys, if not play-ing cowboys and Indians, would often be playing football in the middle of the concrete road or cricket against the lamppost, which we used for the wickets.

Like thousands of others of that generation, it was in such an environment that I developed my love of association football. The games in the street would sometimes last for hours at times and occasionally we would carry the game over to the next day or two, if necessary. The tackles would fly in hard and fast and there was many a cut knee to prove it – I have the scars on each knee to this day.

I attended Loxton Street Infant & Junior School where I was very happy, apart from a few glaring exceptions! The first of these came in my very first day at the age of five. I will never forget that smell as long as I live. I don't know whether it was the polish on the desks, the bleach on the floors or a horrendous cocktail of a few things. It was horrible. I came to identify it as the "school" smell. Somehow, it was austere and scary and I cried to go home. But I had to stay and eventually, as you do, I got used to it to the point that I didn't notice that smell any more, until I came across it unexpectedly that is.

The other two bad experiences? Both took place in school assembly, which incidentally I used to enjoy. It was the singing of the hymns that I found inspiring, even though I had no idea what most of the words meant. One morning I was singing heartily away, probably *Onward Christian Soldiers*, a particular favourite of the school, when suddenly one of the bigger boys in front elbowed me in the stomach, and said, something along the lines of "Shut your foghorn Flanner".

I was stunned (not to say winded) and as it turned out, deeply hurt. I say that because from then on, even though I still loved the songs, I only ever mimed the words. I have been very self-conscious about my voice ever since. I have since learned that God loves it when we make a joyful noise, so at least as far as he is concerned, I'm 'okay'. Another powerful illustration of the power that words can have over us for good or bad, for positive or negative! I trust that, like me, you no longer believe the old rhyme that says, "Sticks and stones may break my bones but names will never hurt me…"

The final thing I recall from school assembly was the morning when we were asked to bow our heads for prayer. I looked down and to my horror, I was still wearing my slippers. I suddenly felt hot with embarrassment. The end of that day could not have come quickly enough for me.

One of my most vivid and wonderful memories of school took place when I was just turned eleven years of age. By this time I was attending Hastings Road Secondary Modern Boys, Perry Common, after my parents had moved house to a first floor modern maisonette: it was luxury by comparison to Scott Street and we overlooked a lovely park, by the name of Witton Lakes. By now I desperately wanted to be in the school football team but until then, had never made it as a regular. On this particular Friday lunchtime I was walking along the corridor and I stopped to check out the notice board. On it were printed the names of all the people who would be in the various school teams the next day. I stared and could hardly believe my eyes. My name was there: 'Number 10, J. Flanner'. As I looked I could feel my chest swell with pride and excitement. I ran all the way home to tell mum. "I'm in the team, mum" I shouted. There I stayed. Right up until I left school at the age of fifteen.

Just to be picked for the team gave me so much confidence. For a few years I cherished a desire to become a professional footballer. That's what happens when someone chooses and approves of you. You actually do believe that you are accepted and that you have a worthwhile contribution to make. Once realising that I was not quite good enough to make it professionally, I then conceived the ill-fated dream of becoming a writer – or maybe it was not so ill fated, after all!

At this point I want to place on record my love and passion for Aston Villa Football Club. This is an affair which was fanned into flame at a very young age when I attended matches with my dad. I first attended our magnificent home ground of Villa Park in 1956, to watch Villa reserves play. I fell in love with the place immediately. It's a ground of incredible history, character and charm. For me there has always been something magical about the atmosphere of the place. Aston Villa was born out of a young men's Bible Class in the mid-19th Century; part of Aston Villa Wesleyan Chapel. In fact it was our first Chairman, a Scotsman by the name of William McGregor, who was the main inspiration behind the formation of the Football League and its inaugural twelve clubs.

Apart from the ground itself, there's been the many great characters who have worn the claret and blue shirt with pride, regardless of their ability. I have so many wonderful memories as a Villa fan and I intend to encapsulate these in a separate book, but one of the most enduring and emotional ones was in the last Cup final at the old Wembley Stadium, in 2000, before it was demolished. The game was between Villa and Chelsea and even though we lost a very poor match by a single goal, I will always remember singing (not miming) the FA Cup Final hymn *Abide with Me*, turning to my son Ian and giving him a hug. We both had tears in our eyes. Only a few years before, Ian had almost died when he went down with encephalitis (a virus on the brain) and was within a whisker of death. On that May afternoon in London as over 70,000 people sang Abide With Me, I got to the line which says "In life in death/Oh Lord/abide with me" and I said thank you to God, for sparing the life of my dear son. Interestingly, God did not spare his own son. Jesus Christ freely died upon a cross, so that we who believe in him, would live for ever.

By then, my own life-journey had not been without it's fair share of heartache and emotion.

Chapter Two

Fear, Fun & Faith
SECTION ONE – FEAR

"They call me Mr. Pitiful/That's how I got my fame…"
Fear is an emotion which every person experiences at some time in their life.

Sadly, however, for some people fear is something that grips them on a daily basis. Many lives are paralysed by fear. Some fears are quite understandable of course; whilst others are totally illogical and phobic in their manifestation.

I have often been asked, especially by schoolchildren, who enquire with great enthusiasm and excitement in the voices, "John, what does it feel like to be blind?" With those kids I often feel like adding the word "wow" at the end of their question, because they sound rather envious and would probably love to try being blind for a while. In some cases I have actually blindfolded the children and allowed them to walk around with my white stick, so that they can get a feel of what it is like. They usually love it.

However, to answer the question properly I have to take myself back to that time when, at the age of nineteen I was first registered blind. Once the reality had hit home and that I was not in fact Douglas Bader reaching for the sky, then fear became the overriding emotion. Day by day, a variety of fears assaulted my mind. Before I tell you about them, however, I must confess that I had a number of fears even before losing my sight.

The bogey Man

As a child were you ever told about the "bogey man"? I can remember people saying things like, "Don't go down there, the bogeyman will get you". Sometimes on a Saturday night at about 6.30, dad would ask me to go out and buy a newspaper called the Sports Argus, a well-know local favourite, which contained all the nation's football scores and reports, from the matches which had only just finished a short while ago. My reward was always to have a little money to buy some sweets. However, I would be very nervous about going for the Argus, particularly on a dark night, and would delay and delay until mum would say, "Hurry up John, they'll soon be closed".

I would then reply, "But the bogey man might get me."

"Don't be silly", said mum, "there's no such person."

I would eventually go out into the dark on a winter's evening, and with the railway wall on the one side, and the high garden walls on the other I would run as fast as I could in the middle of the road, so that I could keep an eye open for the bogey man (in case he came over either wall). I guess I was about nine or ten years of age at the time. When I was not far from home I would stop running so that I would not be out of breath when I got home but look really 'cool' and relaxed. Nevertheless it was a very real fear for me, then.

Fear of Failure

The fear of failure was something I was aware of from a young age, though of course, I would not have articulated it in those terms. It manifested itself, in me being ultra cautious in whatever task I was given to do. School exam results were always published on the school notice board - starting with the number one right down to the bottom, a bit like the pop charts. My big dread was seeing my name at the bottom of the list and so my heartfelt prayer was, "Please God don't let me finish bottom of the class." My thinking was, "If only I could finish bottom but one, that would be enough". I usually managed to finish up somewhere between sixth and tenth from the bottom; I was enormously relieved when that happened.

In maths I would work slowly and methodically, trying hard to get each answer right first time. The teachers often encouraged me to go faster..but that might have meant making more mistakes. Years later, after losing my sight, I went for an interview to be trained as a computer programmer. I had to sit a Braille test, containing twenty sequential mathematical questions. At the end of my one hour exam I'd completed six questions and to my delight, I got all six right! Guess what, I didn't pass and never did become a computer programmer. Those old fear-filled attitudes certainly do stick around, don't they?

Fear of Death

The fear of death is something common to many people. Someone once said that the fear of death is the route of all fear. Whilst I can't say that this fear gripped my life as a young person, I did think about it and it would send a cold shiver down my spine at times. This wasn't helped when a friend of mind told me after losing my sight, "My sister (a nurse) thinks you may have cancer of the eye". Now isn't that just what friends are for!

I was coming home from school one night, when I was ten and saw a headline on the newspaper stand, "England Stars Killed in Plane Crash". I soon discovered that a plane carrying Manchester United players, staff and journalists had crashed on take off from Munich Airport. I could hardly believe it. I had seen many of those same players only a short while before, in an exciting game at St Andrews when Birmingham City had held Manchester United to a 3-3 draw. I'd stood by the halfway line that day, right at the front and the likes of the legendary Roger Byrne, David Pegg, Duncan Edwards and Tommy Taylor, who were almost within touching distance, were now dead.

Then about the same time, I'd been watching an Aston Villa reserve game with my dad when our brilliant young goalkeeper, Arthur Sabin, had been injured and carried off on a stretcher. That was a very sad sight indeed, but nothing compared to the shock I was to receive a few days later when again on my way home from school and on that same newspaper hoarding, I read with disbelief, "Young Villa Keeper Dies". I think he broke his neck and later died in hospital.

In my teens I had some great mates and often on the way home from tenpin bowling, we would buy fish and chips and walk the two miles home late at night chatting away about issues of life and death. Often the stars would be shining brightly in the sky, and we would discuss how they actually got there; was it an accident or was there some genius called God who was behind it all? Those times of open discussion and debate were, I believe, really healthy for me; don't know about the fish & chips though!

Fear of the Dentist

As children in school we used to get regular visits from the dental nurse. Her visits were always greeted with a great deal of apprehension. As our names were called out we would join the queue and wait with 'butterflies in the stomach' to have our teeth examined. The fortunate ones would come back with nothing, but others would return carrying a form, which had green print on it, together with a stamp mark declaring either '20 minutes' or 'D'. Apparently the former meant a filling or two was needed, but the dreaded 'D' stood for decay and signalled a trip to the school dental clinic for an extraction.

After several successful visits to the nurse, my date with destiny came around. Sure enough, I received the dreaded 'D' stamp. Within a few weeks I was at the Clinic, accompanied by mum and I don't know who was more scared! I had to have several teeth removed. Still shaking with fear, mainly from the smell of the place, I was sat back in a chair, and a metal clamp-like device was put on my mouth so that it could be stretched uncomfortably wide open. A mask was then placed on my face and the gas sent me to sleep. Even to this day, the horrendous dream I then had, is so vivid in my mind. I was taken high into the sky, and then dropped, and before I hit the ground I was lifted up again by a hook from my mouth and I could sense it pulling and ripping my mouth apart. Then I came back to consciousness, with blood everywhere and a gaping hole in my gums. It was a nightmare that I vowed even then, never to repeat. I was about eight, then. I didn't return to a dentist for many years. I know that many children of my generation can tell similar horror stories, involving the school clinic. I'm happy to say that, many years later, I faced up to and overcome this fear. But I'll come to that, later.

Fear of Water/Swimming

As far as the fear of water goes, my earliest memory is my sister Joan falling into an open-air swimming pool in Blackpool when we were very small children. As she fell-in and screamed, I ran for my dad who jumped in and saved her. It really was that dramatic.

My real dislike of the water, however, came about when I found out that swimming was on the school timetable. We would arrive at school on that day, with our towels and swimwear, then head off in an orderly fashion (er…) and march the half-a-mile or so to the public baths, with teacher marching alongside to keep us in order. Entering the building, the 'bleach smell' got right up my nose, conjuring up a very negative emotion for me. The boys and girls went off to their respective communal changing rooms. I felt incredibly embarrassed getting undressed in front of the other boys, because I was so thin compared to most of the others. It was a really tricky operation trying to get my trunks on, without anyone seeing my private parts. Added to that, it was freezing cold. I was always shaking like a leaf in a gale.

As a non-swimmer I would look at the boys and girls having such fun, swimming up and down the pool and though it looked very appealing, and indeed easy, I just couldn't pluck up the courage to let go of the rail and launch out. The cold water didn't help matters much. I was shivering, just as much if not more, than in the changing room! The whole experience was an absolute nightmare for me. It seemed like the ordeal would never end, and relief only came when we were marching back to school; although I must confess that I felt much fresher for actually being in the water. It didn't stop me from week-after-week, begging mum to write me a letter, excusing me from swimming due to ear-ache, a cough or whatever else I could pathetically come up with.

I have come to realise, that God knows all about the 'inner-child' within each one of us, and loves to set people free from their fears - one at a time, he's dealt with all of mine, but never in a pushy or pressurising way. Swimming, to me, looked so easy when I watched other people doing it and it looked so refreshing, especially on a hot day. As I grew into adult life and had children of my own, who themselves learned to swim, I found myself praying and asking God to help me overcome this fear. See the 'Faith' section of this book.

One day I was told that in Solihull, where I was living, a new club had been formed, 'Seals'. This was a group of people who were giving their time freely, to take and teach disabled people to swim. I felt that God was on my case and providing an ideal opportunity for me. I went along to the Tudor Grange swimming baths for several weeks on a Monday night, and was introduced to a Dr.

McKenzie, then a local G.P. I immediately felt confident with him, in a way that I never did with the teachers at school. I trusted him, that he would not let me drown. Within a few weeks he had me swimming and the 5 metres badge on my shorts was for many years, one of my proudest possessions! Another fear was met head on and overcome.

Fear of Girls

This was undoubtedly the worst of all my fears. I don't really know how it came about, because as I said earlier, I had two sisters with whom I got on well.

Back in my infant and junior school days there was a girl I always liked the look of, and thought she was beautiful – let's say her name was 'Gail' – but I don't think she ever spoke to me. As I grew older I still liked to look at girls, but I just lived to play football every moment of every day.

As I grew into my teenage years I found myself becoming ever more self-conscious. Often, and especially before going out in the mornings, I would stand in front of the mirror and tell myself how ugly I was. I had beady eyes, stick out ears, big nose, a big gap in the front of my teeth, scruffy hair that blew all over the place and to top it all, I was very skinny. The fact that I was in the "A" stream at school, was a decent footballer, in the school PE team and had some good friends, counted for nothing in my eyes.

The girls' school was just a few hundred yards down the road from the boys', so I would often see groups of girls standing together talking, laughing and invariably pointing in my direction. "No doubt mocking me", I thought to myself.

This to me, was a terrible handicap. There were times when I took a fancy to a certain girl but could never pluck up the courage to ask her for a date, because I was convinced she would reject me.

I've always loved the magic of the cinema. Sometimes, when watching a film I would study hard to see how men and women kissed each other. After all, these are the paid professionals so they ought to know how to do it. However, it occurred to me that even if I did get to go out with a girl, I didn't think I could kiss properly. How do you practice something like that, until you get it right on the night?

I've already mentioned that I worked at Dunlop in a tyre sales office. Part of my job was to take the invoices that were to be typed each morning to the typing pool. This was a large pool of around forty typists; all of them female, of course. That was a really scary business for me – a bit like Daniel in the lions' den, except that I was no courageous Daniel! I tried hard to look relaxed and unperturbed as I walked briskly across the office, not saying a word to anyone. I hastily handed over the invoices to the supervisor and hurried out again, convinced that there were a few derogatory remarks being formulated behind my back. An experience of truly terrifying proportions at the time.

Later on, imagine the horror: after going blind and having gone through a period of rehabilitation, I was then told that I would need to attend a college in London to be trained as an audio typist. This was after I had already been turned down for the computer programming training. Even though I did get six out of six!

The thought of spending my life as a typist and working with all of those women didn't bear thinking about; but at least that, was way off in the future…

What Does It Feel Like To Be Blind?

I have said that fear was the major emotion and in those early days as a registered blind person the fears came thick and fast. If you've never had any problems with your sight, it's understandable that you wouldn't really know what fears can be experienced with blindness - or how they can be overcome. Prominent among them are:

> **Fear of never going out alone again in case of accident.**
> **Fear of having to hold onto someone else's arm (particularly if it was a man). After all, what would people think?**
> **Fear of eating in public.**
> **Fear of what would be going in my mouth when eating.**
> **Fear of never working again.**
> **Fear of never getting married and having children.**

Fear of Never Going Out/Accidents

Newly registered as a blind person I arrived home from the hospital with dad, still with the death of the great Donald Campbell uppermost in my mind. As was my custom I entered the maisonette, said "Hi" to mum and having discarded my coat over the handrail at the bottom of the stairs, headed off upstairs to the sanctuary of my bedroom. I shared the room with my brother Paul, who was then thirteen. Like innumerable teenagers before and since, sadly I didn't communicate a great deal with mum and dad at that time, but I took refuge in my large record collection. I'd been buying records for about five years, starting with Things by Bobby Darin, followed soon after by The Swiss Maid, sung by Del Shannon. I proceeded to buy singles at a rate of about three a week, costing the princely sum of £1. I also got into buying albums (or LPs as they were called) though not as often as singles, because of the price. Apart from catchy tunes I used to love listening to the lyrics of songs and often drew strength and encouragement from them. Oddly enough it was the sad songs that brought me most comfort, particularly those with a soul and Tamla Motown point of reference. One exception to this was the Beatles' song, *Nowhere Man*. I loved the tune and the words:

> *"Doesn't have a point of view/Knows not where he's going to/Isn't he a bit like you and me/Making all his nowhere plans for nobody…"*

The song made me feel that there could be somebody else out there, who feels like I do. So many songs too, made me feel happy inside and gave me strength. A particularly enjoyable album at this time was, *I'll Take You Where The Music's Playing*, by the Drifters. I don't know what it was exactly, but that record had such an aura about it; I felt that I was there at the party with them. Each track was so full of atmosphere.

For around three months I spent hour after hour in my room, playing music all day long. The noise must have driven my family and neighbours almost to the point of distraction, but I was too wrapped up in myself to realise. The Searchers, Jim Reeves and Otis Reading were three of the acts that kept me company during these unnerving days of adjustment to my new (and rapidly Changing) world.

My world of music and tears was interrupted rather abruptly one day when mum knocked on my bedroom door. "There's a lady here to see you, she's from the Social Services".

I hurriedly followed mum downstairs.

On entering the living room I was greeted by the person who was to become a regular companion in my life for the next few months.

"Hello John, nice to meet you. My name is Miss Clews." They were more formal in those days.

Mum and I sat down on the settee, whilst Miss Clews began her discourse from the comfort of the armchair opposite.

"Well John", she said, "you've been registered for quite a few weeks now, so maybe it's time to draw up a plan to aid your rehabilitation. Have you given any thought as to what you might do in the future?"

"Not at all", I replied, "what is there to do?"

"Well there's quite a lot really", she answered in a warm, reassuring tone, "and that's why I am here: to look at our options."

Mum was sitting anxiously beside me, puffing deeply on a cigarette, wondering just what our young lady from Social Services was going to come up with.

It transpired that I was first going to be offered some mobility training. That is, learning to get around outside with the use of a white stick. Then plans would be made for me to attend a rehabilitation centre in Torquay for three months. I recall taking a very deep breath at that point, as fear raced through my senses. It was bad enough having the thought of walking the streets of Birmingham whilst carrying a white stick, let alone leaving home for three months. I had never been away from home in my life. I know that it came as a big blow to Mum. I quickly realised however, that both of these challenges had to be faced and overcome if I was ever going to do anything with my life.

Miss Clews began by visiting our home for four mornings a week, where I was given two hours of mobility training. I was introduced to the symbol cane. This was a flimsy, plastic coated aluminium stick that actually folded away into four smallish sections so that it could be put in a pocket if say, I went out to the pub. I remember thinking, "that won't give me much protection…", but least it wasn't as big and ugly as I had imagined. Miss Clews, who by her fourth visit had said that I could call her by her first name, which was Janet, began to teach me some of the skills that blind people use when getting out and about. These included becoming aware of the surface under my feet, so as to distinguish things like concrete, tarmac etc. In addition I learned to listen for traffic as it passed in and out behind bus shelters, even lampposts and stopping at traffic lights. Then there was the sense of smell and I discovered that it was possible to distinguish different shops by their unique aroma. Places like fish and chip shops, chemists, hairdressers and hardware shops were pretty easy, even to a novice like me.

After a couple of weeks of training, it was clear to Janet that my confidence was not really increasing to the point where I would attempt to go out unaided. It was at that point that she told me of a new revolutionary mobility technique for blind people, which had just come in from America . Called 'The Long Cane Technique', they were looking for someone to trial it in the Birmingham area. Somewhat nervously, I decided to give it a go.

So it was, that on her next visit Janet introduced me to Miss Hulme, who I immediately thought was much more vivacious and outgoing than her predecessor. I was told that Miss Hulme was the person who had been chosen to pioneer the 'Long Cane' training in Birmingham. I was thanked for 'agreeing' to be her first pupil. I was also told that she had rosy cheeks and long blonde hair. She was from Devon and loved horse riding.

Miss Hulme (now to be called Mary), full of infectious enthusiasm, went to fetch the long cane from her car. She actually arrived back with three canes because as I was about to discover, each cane had to be made to measure to suit the needs of each user. I was surprised at how big the canes were, but the requirement was that each one had to come up to the breastbone of its owner.

"Goodness me", I mused, "if I thought I wouldn't ever come across as being self conscious, then I've got no chance now, with this great thing".

Mary soon had me out on my local streets learning the 'Long Cane Technique'. It was at this time that I started my tradition of naming my sticks. This first one was called 'Elsie' for the simple reason that it was a Long Cane (L for long and C for cane – LC, otherwise known as Elsie). Every other long cane I have used since then, I have called Elsie!

If you're interested, I'll introduce you to the names of my other two sticks. The flimsy symbol cane I spoke about earlier, I call Arthur (or more precisely, 'Arfer'). This is because one day (many years later and by now more confident) I was running for a bus as I was late for work, and using my symbol cane. I arrived at the bus stop, out of breath, but just as the bus arrived. I placed my stick on to the platform of the bus at the same moment as a lady jumped on to the bus with all of her weight and snapped my stick in half. I held it up and looked at it rather sorrowfully and said "Oh dear, half a stick" or words to that affect, and in that moment 'Arfer' was born - every symbol cane I have had since then, has gone by the same name.

More recently I have 'Eileen'. This is what is called a 'Guide Cane'. It's much sturdier than a symbol cane, though not quite as long as a 'Long Cane'. This guide cane is so strong that I can (and often do) lean on it, hence the name 'Eileen'. Not exactly rocket science, but kids in school (and some childlike adults) love to meet Elsie, Arthur and Eileen.

Anyway, back to long cane training. Mary taught me to hold the cane in the correct way: I am left-handed and have to hold the cane with my left index finger pointed down the flat side of the rubber grip. I then have to hold the cane out in front of my chest, and as I walk forward with my left foot, I have to swing the cane to the right and then, as my right foot goes forward, I sweep the cane back to the left with the tip of the cane fractionally above the ground. In this way I am covering the ground where my next footstep is going to be. This was hard work at first, particularly on the left wrist; however, as I became more confident I was able to relax and when 'Elsie' did locate an object on the pavement I had enough warning to be able to pull up in time and walk around it. It was not long before I was being trained in Birmingham city centre, around the main streets, in and out of New Street Station, up and down the escalators and around the Bull Ring shopping centre.

During this training I did encounter several scary or humorous moments. I was undertaking a test which involved catching a bus. I was waiting at a bus stop on a busy road, near to some traffic lights. It was at a particularly busy time of the day and the traffic kept on stopping, near to the bus stop. I heard what I thought was the bus pull up, right by the stop and I attempted to get on. I was waving Elsie around all over the place trying to locate the platform on the bus when eventually Mary, who had been watching me from a short distance away, came up to me and told me I was trying to board a big lorry.

On another occasion, Mary had given me an assignment. I had to go into a local shopping centre (about a mile from the training centre) and take a bundle of her washing to the launderette, where she would meet me. I negotiated the bus journey successfully and proceeded to the row of shops, somewhat cautiously. I thought to myself that even with my blocked up nasal passages I should be able to sniff out the launderette, without much difficulty. Gradually, I stepped out with more confidence, until I located the smell of the chemist where I knew I was drawing near. Passing the tobacconist, the launderette slowly but surely came into smelling distance. Arriving at where the fragrance of wet washing was particularly strong, I turned into the shop. Locating the counter, I placed Mary's bundle of washing on there and waited for assistance. Or at least to hear the reassuring sound of Mary's "Well done". Instead, all I got was a man's deep voice enquiring, "Can I help you Sir?".

"Yes", I said hesitantly, "I've brought the washing".

"Sorry Sir, you've come to the wrong shop", said the man with what sounded like a smile on his face, "The launderette is next door".

Somewhat hot with embarrassment, I promptly left the premises and then arrived safely, but sheepishly at the launderette. Mary was there to greet me and say well done.

"But I blew it", I said.

"No you didn't", replied Mary, "You arrived at the right place, just going via the Midlands Electricity Board. But it's mission accomplished and that's what it's all about".

Mary was so positive and encouraging. Just what I needed in my life at that particular time.

I completed my long cane training and, because I was one of the first blind people to be trained in this revolutionary new technique, I was invited down to London by the BBC to give a demonstration at Broadcasting House and take part in an interview for a radio programme, In Touch. It was an experience I really enjoyed and a mild flirtation with broadcasting which later developed into an affair which has blossomed, on and off, ever since.

Then news came through that I had to go away from home for three months. Printed indelibly in my memory is the date of 8th June 1967. That was the day I packed up and left home for the very first time, in order to attend the Manor House Rehabilitation Centre in Torquay. I was dreading this day. It was so sad saying goodbye to my family, especially mum. Dad came with me and we boarded the train at New Street Station, in Birmingham. I think we sat quietly for most of the journey, which lasted for what seemed like an eternity. On arriving in Torquay, we took a taxi to the Manor House and I remember feeling how Julie Andrews must have felt in *The Sound of Music* when she arrived with luggage and guitar in hand, at the palatial home of Captain Von Trapp - except I didn't have a guitar. I wasn't about to burst into song.

Upon entering this mansion of a place, we were greeted warmly by one of the administrative staff and taken to an office. We were informed of a meeting for myself and eleven other new entrants at 4.00pm; for now I would be shown to my room. Dad and I were led up the wide central staircase to the first floor and along a corridor which smelt well-polished and possessed a wooden floor. We came to a room on the left and were shown in. Inside were four beds. One for me, and the others (who'd already been there a couple of weeks), allotted to Alf and Len, and Les, due to be arriving later in the day. I placed my bags on my designated bed and dad helped me unpack. I had a locker and a wardrobe to use.

With the prospect of tea and coffee served downstairs in the lounge, we quickly finished unpacking and left the room, only to bump into a very cheerful sounding guy on the landing outside.

"Hi, nice to meet you, I'm Les". It sounded like a Cockney accent.

We shook hands. "I'm John and this is my dad".

"Meet my wife", Les replied. "This is Jill".

Les was around forty years old. From Loughton in Essex, we were destined to become great friends - even though, of course, he was old enough to be my dad! For those three months I was in Torquay, Les was to keep a fatherly watch on me. Partially sighted, but always chirpy and quick witted, his favourite word was "astounded". At least I presumed it was, because he was often astounded at something or other!

My first evening at the Manor House saw us polish off fish and chips in the huge dining room that catered for seventy-two residents, not to mention visitors and staff. It was on that first evening too, that I experienced the first of many embarrassing moments that I continue to have to this day. I reached out to put salt on my chips, only to discover that I'd covered them in sugar, leaving me asking for a replacement meal. Others around the table, except for Dad, laughed at my predicament. The trouble was, was that I'd not yet arrived at a place where I could laugh at myself. That lesson was to come later, in the rehabilitation process.

After tea, when all of the new residents had arrived, there was a traditional barn-dance to welcome and help integrate the newcomers. Enjoying the music, I had my introduction to west country national anthem, *Drink Up Ye Cider* recorded by a certain Adge Cutler and the Wurzels, later to have a gigantic number one hit single with *I've Got A Brand New Combine Harvester*. It was a good, fun way to launch my time in Torquay.

As the clock approached 10.30pm, it was time for dad to leave and go to his hotel for the night. Back in the reception area, dad shook me warmly by the hand and drew me into a tight hug and I felt him begin to sob in my arms. We both began to cry and through his tears he said, "Good luck son, keep in touch". It was a moment of realisation, about something which perhaps I'd previously taken for granted; my dad truly loved me. It was so powerful. I'll never forget it. I determined there and then to make a success of this course, for mum and dad's sake as much as my own.

I became more competent with my mobility, learnt the basics in Braille and typing skills as well as turning my hand to a bit of pottery. A model I made of a cottage I still have to this day. In terms of developing social skills, we went out to restaurants, discos, dinner-dances, football matches, tenpin bowling and variety shows. It was a great life and a great summer, in fact.

The 'Summer of Love' of 1967 was also a time when the offshore pirate radio stations were forced off the air under the then Labour Government's Marine Offences Bill. Listening to Radio Caroline and Radio London had become a passion of mine. Though they were rebels, somehow the music, the disc jockeys and even the adverts of the time brought a joy, freedom and excitement that was lacking in mainstream broadcasting. I became a big fan and friend of Johnnie Walker, on Radio Caroline. I loved his theme tune, *Because They're Young* by guitar legend Duane Eddy; Johnnie's regular features 'Kiss in the Car' and his 11pm 'Warm &Tender Love' feature, when he played that great song by Percy Sledge every night. Laying in my bed at the Manor House in Torquay, with my transistor radio under the bedclothes, I somehow felt a kindred spirit with those pirate broadcasters, out on the high seas. The thing about Johnnie Walker was that he came from the West Midlands like me, and I remembered him from his days at the Locarno in Birmingham, when he was then known as Peter Dee, because his original name was Peter Dingley.

*

An amazing August evening began at midnight when the Marine Offences Bill became law and Walker and Robbie Dale stayed on board ship with Radio Caroline continuing on air in defiance of the Bill, as the civil rights song *We Shall Overcome* rang out across the airwaves, sung by Joan Baez, together with The Beatles' *All You Need Is Love*. Under my bedclothes that night I shed more than a few tears as together in heart we 'took our stand' for freedom on that historic night!

My three months in Devon passed very quickly and I had a wonderful time during that long, hot summer. I grew to love the county, not least the seaside resorts of Paignton, Brixham and Goodrington. The local beach to the Manor House was Meadfoot, and I discovered the very quaint model village at Cockington, where a few years later I would have the thrill of taking my own children.

Despite becoming pretty confident in the mobility stakes, I have, over the years, had my share of accidents...please indulge me, as I fast forward into the future, briefly...

I crossed a road at some traffic lights late one night when a big van swerved around the corner and headed straight for me. The screech of his brakes and the brightness of his headlights full in my face caused me to walk backwards and on impact, the van sent me cart wheeling backwards into the gutter. Thankfully I was only bruised and shaken. After the accident the driver was very caring and considerate, stating that he hadn't even seen my white stick. He did drive me home when we'd both recovered our composure, and he later returned to see how I was doing and to invite me to his wedding! Though I wasn't able to attend, it did make me think; after all, it could have been him being invited to my funeral.

On another occasion I was taking my daughter Beverley to nursery. She was just about four years of age, and walking happily with me, hand in hand on my right side. It seemed very quiet that morning, with the usual chatter of little children talking excitedly with their guardians strangely absent. Thinking that we be a little on the late side, I did a very irresponsible thing. I folded my stick away (must have been Arthur therefore) and put it in my jacket pocket. I then picked up Beverley in my arms and hurried along the pavement for the quarter mile or so, to the nursery. However, we'd probably only gone about 50 yards down the road when I trod on a mound of earth and disappeared down a six foot hole. Thankfully, Beverley fell clear of my arms and landed on the dirt on the other side of the hole, but I went straight down, tearing my jacket and bruising my pride in the process. Quickly, one or two of the neighbours had gathered around and were giving Beverley and I a helping hand. Some gas workers had left the hole unattended for a minute or two, just enough time for me to come along and perform one of my stunts! I later received some compensation to enable me to buy a new jacket, but more importantly I learnt a very painful lesson and thankfully, Beverley was not emotionally scarred by the experience.

One dark November night, I was returning from London by train to Market Harborough. As it pulled into Market Harborough station I gathered my small suitcase together with a box of literature and records which I happened to have with me. I opened the door and together with my stick and two cases stepped off the train. Through the heavy mist on that winter's night I vaguely heard my wife calling me from the platform, but as I was stepping off, my descent seemed to last for ever and ever! Eventually I hit the ground with a thud and found myself face down on what was the railway track. I heard my wife screaming, "Are you all right?"

Mercifully I was okay. Again a few bruises, but more embarrassment than anything. I was later told that it had been a long train and a short platform, but no announcement had been made to inform the passengers. Subsequently that was rectified, but it was to be another hair-raising scrape to add to my already painful collection.

My final story also involves a train. I was travelling into Birmingham to go to work, as the train pulled into Moor Street station. I got up from my seat to leave the train, as I had done so on numerous occasions in the past. On this occasion however, I stepped off the train only for my leading right foot to go down the gap between the train and the platform. My left foot became trapped under the weight of my body and the pain was excruciating. Despite being smaller than me, a young teenage boy, on his way to school was quick-witted enough to not only pull me out, but was able to get me to a bench. I was in agony and my left ankle had ballooned up to an enormous size. Soon, the paramedics had arrived and I was whisked off by ambulance to the City Hospital with a suspected broken ankle. It turned out to be only ligament damage, but it was still extremely painful and uncomfortable for many months to come. I'll be forever grateful to the lad who came to my rescue - I dread to imagine what would've happened to me, had nobody came to my assistance at that moment.

In all of these chaotic situations, perhaps with the exception of the van driver, were accidents which could have been avoided if I'd been using the mobility techniques which I'd been taught. The trouble is, when we do anything repetitively and we become good at it, there's a danger that we might also become somewhat blasé about the whole thing. Somehow it seems to be human nature. I am reminded, not for the first time of some words in the Bible which state, "Pride comes before a fall". In the Good Book it's also recorded that a man by the name of Job once said, "That which I feared has come upon me".

Fear is a powerful force and if we believe our fears long enough and hard enough, they can sometimes become a self-fulfilling prophecy.

Fear of Having to Hold on to Someone's Arm

It's strange how some fears can stick around and blight us for life, whilst others are dealt with and overcome at fairly short notice. The fear of having to hold on to someone else's arm when going out was a very real fear, but it only lasted for a short while.

I have already mentioned my love for football and for Aston Villa in particular. Well, to say I was an avid supporter is a massive understatement. My dad first took me to the games back in the *Rock Around the Clock* days of 1956, but it was in 1959 that my support of Aston Villa took off. The 1959/60 season, under the managership of Joe Mercer, saw Villa go storming to (the then) Division 2 championship with some gargantuan performances. I didn't miss a home game all season. Most memorable in that immensely memorable season came in November 1959, when Villa beat Charlton Athletic 11-1 at Villa Park. The game was notable because Gerry Hitchens, Villa's talented, blonde haired centre forward, who went on to play for England, scored five times and Charlton fielded three different goalkeepers during the game. It was a wonderful season and for me it commenced a run where I didn't miss a Villa home game for fifteen years. It was all so nearly different, however.

The last game of football I actually saw perfectly, was England's World Cup Final against West Germany in July 1966. What an occasion to go out on! By the time the new domestic season had started at the end of August, I can vaguely recall seeing Villa lose 1-0 at home to Arsenal. Even then however, there was a 'thick mist' in the ground and I couldn't see clearly, the play at the other end of the pitch. I then went with a friend to watch Villa play against Stoke at their Victoria Ground. Again, it was to my mind very 'misty'; it certainly was for the Villa players, as we were humiliated in a 6-0 thrashing. The defeat was made all the more galling because one of our former players and a big favourite of mine, Harry Burrows, scored a hat-trick against his old team mates.

The following week Villa were at home to Tottenham, but by now I was starting to realise what was happening to my eyes and I decided that I wouldn't go. However, at 2.30pm, half an hour before kick off, a friend from schooldays (who, a little while earlier, had actually eloped to Gretna Green and married his Cornish girlfriend) arrived unexpectedly and expressed his shock at the news that I was to all intents and purposes, losing my sight. He cajoled me into going to the game. I'll always be grateful to Brian for that, because not only was it a great match which Villa won 3-2, but I thoroughly enjoyed his ahem, highly animated commentary on the game, as well as the mutterings of the fans around about me! So I was totally persuaded that even losing my eyesight wouldn't keep me away from my beloved Villa Park. My unbroken record was intact for a few more years yet, and crucially, a link to the outside world in the midst of my increasing 'darkness' was maintained.

Of course, what it also did for me was to break that fear, or stigma that I felt about having to hold on to somebody's arm, particularly a fellow male. After that one game Brian went back to Cornwall to rejoin Lyn, but in no time at all I found other arms to hang on to. Included in those of course, were my family plus my very good friends Ronnie and Graham, to whom I owe another debt of gratitude for their friendship, particularly during those early traumatic months of blindness.

Apart from going over the football matches with Ronnie, I'd also be found with them in pubs, discos and even the cinema on one occasion, to see The Sound of Music on the huge Cinerama screen, in Birmingham's Gaumont. Ronnie said, "It's a massive screen, so you may be able to see something..."

Sure enough, at that stage I could make out a lot of the activity on the screen. Well, it was reputedly the largest cinema screen in Europe at the time! Ronnie, rugged of reddish hair and complexion, was definitely the more macho of the two but Graham, with blonde hair and glasses, nicknamed "The Milky Bar Kid" and "Joe Ninety", was a bit of a showman. He was into amateur dramatics and it showed, whenever we went into a pub or disco with me on his arm; he liked being the centre of attention when people stared at us. Sometimes at a disco, he would deliberately walk across the middle of the dance floor with me in tow, so that people would move aside for us and he would then let out a shriek of excited and satisfied laughter at his sense of importance. Had I been able to see what was going on I would probably have cringed with embarrassment, but somehow I was able to enter in to Graham's enjoyment of the whole scene.

Graham and I sadly lost contact with each other, for many years so it was a real thrill to be able to meet up again recently, and would you believe it, he was then Sheriff of Toronto. If I'd never let go of his arm, would that now make me Deputy Sheriff I wonder!

From an early age, I was a very finicky eater. I was particularly fussy and disparaging about fat on meat, especially boiled ham, bacon or chicken. Likewise with any skin on rice pudding or custard. Then there was the slimy stuff that comes on top of a fried egg. All of these things turned my stomach over. I would make my feelings known to mum and often I sat at the table picking at my food with "a face as long as Livery Street", a well-known Birmingham expression for being miserable.

Now my mum is no longer with us, I'm sorry that I hardly, if ever, told her that she did a wonderful job of cooking for us, especially bearing in mind that her own sight was far from brilliant either. I urge you, if your mum is still alive, to give her lots of praise and encouragement, for she has one of the most difficult jobs in the world.

Now with that in mind, can you possibly imagine how nervous I would feel at having a plate of food put in front of me but not being able to see what was on the plate? After all, there might be a lump of fat, a piece of skin or something vile to the taste buds - not to mention those highly dangerous fish bones? I tell you, something as simple as eating had suddenly become a very dangerous and scary occupation.

Then there was the business of having to eat in public; how daunting was that! Even with my family in toe, at first it was a psychological hurdle that had to be overcome. Eventually I think they just got used to me leaving more food on the table and on the floor than went into my mouth. Sometimes I would get so frustrated that I would just pick up the potatoes, meat, vegetables with my fingers. "What the heck", I would think to myself, "cavemen did it this way didn't they?"

Time can be a great healer, for it allows you to adjust to new circumstances. In this case I became more relaxed when eating with my family and as they saw me beginning to enjoy my food again, if at times a little ungainly, the more at ease we all became with each other. Gradually I grew in confidence, to the point where I could ask for someone to cut up my meat and roast potatoes, or anything else for that matter, which would not fit easily into my mouth. Okay then, that was at home, but what about if I was eating out at a friend's place, or at a restaurant? Well, the same process applied. At first I'd struggle and try to manage by myself, often getting into a mess in the process. In that way I would feel embarrassed and equally so would those eating with me. They were probably thinking, "I wish I could just cut it up, in order to make it easier for him."

I came to the realisation that I wanted to enjoy my meal, rather than endure it as a trial. Those eating with me also wanted to enjoy their food and to watch me struggle was painful for them. So began a practice which continues to this day in requesting that any awkward items be cut up into bite-sized chunks. Now everyone is more relaxed about it, and we can all get on and enjoy what is, after all, God's gift of food.

With normal eyesight of course, people make choices based largely on what they can see. That's certainly true of food. When you're without sight, there's a depending to a large degree, on what other people tell you. On many occasions I allow people to make up my mind for me, and of course that's not necessarily a good thing, especially when it comes to 'independence'. One of those areas for me, was food. For instance, people close to me would sometimes say, "You wouldn't like that…" and I would just accept it.

One day I was staying at a house in Devon. On arriving for breakfast, my host said to me, "John, I'm terribly sorry but I've run out of breakfast cereals. But I do have some grapefruit."

"That's okay," I said, "I'm not much of a breakfast person."

"But I feel really bad about this", replied the lady, "won't you please have some grapefruit?"

"No honestly, I don't like grapefruit", I responded firmly. Sitting next to me at the table was my blind friend Peter Jackson, a full time 'Gospel pianist' and preacher. Peter, never short of a word or three, entered the conversation by saying to our concerned host, "Knowing John, he's probably never tried grapefruit."

"That's right, I haven't", came my instant reply.

"Well in that case, how do you know you won't like it then?" said Peter, while chuckling at the same time.

I knew I was beginning to lose this little debate as I responded feebly. "Because other people have told me I won't like it".

Now Peter, ever the opportunist to make a spiritual point, came back with, "You're just like the people who say they have no time for Christianity - when they've never given Jesus a chance with their lives. It's nonsense. Give the grapefruit a try for yourself and then, if you don't like it, fine. But really, it's very refreshing."

"Will you have some, John?" said our kind host, now an amused bystander in this light-hearted discussion.

"Yes, okay then, but just a little" I said, with Peter choking back the giggles at my side.

Well, as you'll probably realise by now, although the grapefruit tingled initially on my tongue, I have to confess that it was not anywhere near as sour as I'd been led to believe. In fact it was rather nice and as Peter had rightly said, very refreshing. These days I love grapefruit, but to think of all those years of missing out, just because I was allowing myself to be controlled by other people's ideas and opinions, instead of looking into it for myself, so that I could make an informed judgement. Oh yes, and Peter was correct that many people do make the same mistake when it comes to the big questions in life. We often mimic other people's opinions or experiences instead of thinking it through for ourselves. I still think that some of the most important questions are, "Where will I go when I die?" or "Is there such a place as Heaven or Hell, and if so, how do I get to one and avoid the other?" These are important questions to be asking and unlike the grapefruit, which is far more trivial (sorry grapefruit worshippers) the matters of life, death and eternity are far too important for me to rely on someone else's opinions. I have to know for myself. I've discovered a little verse in Psalm 34 of the Bible which says "Oh taste and see that the Lord is good…" which thankfully I now have and I've discovered He's even better than grapefruit; in fact He made the grapefruit!

I'm still fussy when it comes to certain food, but by no means as bad as I used to be. I'm now prepared to try all kinds of things that I would've turned my nose up at, if I'd been offered them as a young lad by mum. Nowadays, for me eating is an adventure. My outlook has totally changed and far from being ruled by fear, I'm now excited by the anticipation of what might be on the end of my fork or spoon.

Fear of not working again

To be truthful, this was more of a lingering, negative thought than an outright fear because there were other things much more pressing at the time. However, as I became more used to life as a blind person I realised, particularly in the late 1960s, that there weren't many job opportunities available to people with sight loss. If I said to you basketwork, light engineering, typing, telephony, physiotherapy and computer programming, then it's a comprehensive list of what was available. The first two on the list were probably the most common and the last two the most exclusive. My early interest in computer programming came about because I used to enjoy working out logical mathematical problems in my head and I thought that it would be a prime requisite for a computer programmer. I hadn't taken into consideration the need to be a proficient Braille reader.

It was at Torquay however, during my three months of rehabilitation that I really took to the typewriter keyboard and discovered just how much I enjoyed communicating in that way. I sent letters home to the family fairly frequently, and found it to be a great and therapeutic way of expressing my feelings. Having shown such an aptitude in this way it was no surprise that I was recommended to undertake further training in London, at a commercial college for the blind, to be trained as an audio typist.

At first I felt insulted by this assessment, because the only typists I ever came across were women. Apart from my fears of that particular species, there was the nagging thought that this was a particularly effeminate job for a man to undertake.

Ultimately, I did commence training, on 1st January 1968 at Pembridge

Place near Notting Hill Gate. For the next eight months it was my home. Whilst there I made some really great friendships, one of which has lasted to this day.

On my very first day I gingerly climbed the stairs to get to my second floor bedroom, which I was to share with three other lads. Partway up the second flight, I collided head-on with someone much more robust than me. I fell backwards down the stairs. As had always been my way, I quickly mumbled, "Sorry mate".

"That's okay. It was probably my fault", replied the man I was to come to know as Neville, in his broad Norfolk accent. It turned out that Neville was sharing a room just across the landing from me. We got to know each other and it transpired that he was suffering from a similar eye condition to me. We discovered a shared love for sport: his football team was Norwich City and he liked cricket. Like me, he'd been a keen listener to the pirate radio stations and we went on to have many a conversation about our favourite disc jockeys.

Following on from Torquay, it was my second time away from home and just as I had enjoyed my three months in sunny Devon, I also had a wonderful time in the capital. I made some really good friendships. The food at the college wasn't bad, either!

I remember one day in the dining room when this quite pompous guy sat opposite me. New to the college and the area, he blustered, "How does one find the Post Office?"

I replied, "The same way that two does!"

Everyone around the table, except the guy in question, erupted in laughter and I was left surprised, at quite where the put down had come from! The little joke went around the college for days, but I did apologise to the man concerned, in case his feelings had been irreparably damaged!

Whilst thinking about my time at Pembridge, two other events stand out.

Firstly, it was June and I'd returned home to Birmingham by train for the weekend. On travelling back to London on the Sunday teatime, it was really hot with temperatures in the high 80s, Fahrenheit. I arrived back at the college to eventually discover that most of the residential students had disappeared off to the King George VI pub on the Bayswater Road, a regular haunt for some of them. I wasn't an habitual pub-goer. But on that hot and steamy night I headed off there, in search of some much needed liquid refreshment. I was about to have a rude awakening in more ways than one.

It was about 8 o'clock as I entered the packed, oldie-worldly pub and going into the lounge area, headed off to the right-hand side where I knew that the blind and partially sighted contingent gathered. Amid the noisy chatter, I picked up the sound of a voice I recognised. It was Frank, a man with a very posh accent, kind of a Hugh Grant-type, thirty years ahead of his time. Frank was quite a bit older than most of us at the college.

"Frank is that you?" knowing very well it was.

"Ah John, my boy", he replied as if he was really glad to see me, "Chris is up at the bar, if you want me to take you up to place your order."

Frank did have some sight and I accepted his offer to weave me through the crowd to the bar.

"Flanner's back and he's gasping for a drink" said Frank, once he'd located Chris, still waiting patiently to be served.

Chris broke off from a conversation he was having, and turned to me saying, "John - I would like you to meet Julie".

"So you're John", the lady chipped in.

"Yes…" I said "and you're Julie?"

"Of course" she responded, in a rather beguiling tone. "I've not seen you here before."

"I've only been here twice and never on a Sunday" I nervously gabbled.

"What are you drinking?" she asked and I replied, "I'll have a shandy".

Julie evinced surprise that I wasn't drinking anything stronger, but I explained that I was very thirsty, especially after a long, hot train journey and I wanted something thirst-quenching.

Chris, still at the bar, piped up, "He likes rum and coke as well, though".

With that Julie said, "George, get my friend John a pint of bitter-shandy and a large rum and coke, on me".

Out of politeness more than anything else, I stayed at the bar with Chris and Julie, together with her friend George who, by now had introduced himself to me. I remember wondering, "She might be old enough to be my mother, or maybe not", when she flawed me with a question.

"What do you think I look like, John?"

Somewhat flustered by a question from someone I'd only met a minute or two earlier, and wanting to be complimentary to this mystery woman who'd just bought me a couple of drinks, I said, "I think you're a cross between Sophia Loren and Elizabeth Taylor."

Seizing her moment, and my free hand, she said "You're not far wrong. Just feel that…" as she slapped my hand on one of her ample breasts.

In a state of shock I pulled my hand away as if I'd touched an electric fence. I spilt some of my drink in the process. It was a hot evening and now I was sweating profusely and my heart was thumping full of nervous energy.

Julie proceeded to tell me how much she liked me, and would I like to go round to her flat in Bayswater, one evening?

George, with his strong Cockney accent, chipped in. He won't come, he's chicken! After all, he's only a boy!

"Of course he'll come, won't you John" said Julie, in what I realised was a well-rehearsed routine.

Whilst having no intention of ever meeting Julie or going within a country mile of that pub again, I did say that I'd meet Julie there, at 7.30 the following

Wednesday. As we parted and I left with Chris to go to our table, she shouted assertively, "Don't let me down now…"

I arrived at the large oval-shaped oak table, where my fellow students were sitting. There was much laughter and jibing at my expense. I hastily finished my shandy and my rum and coke and promptly left the pub with Frank. We walked the short distance back to the college. Frank was keen to know if I was going to take her up on her offer. Despite my pleading that in no way was I going to do so, Frank tried everything in his power to persuade me that this would be good for my manhood. However, I was scared. I didn't mind admitting it. Exasperated with me, Frank eventually said that if I didn't turn up for the date then he would go in my place, which is exactly what happened. I won't go into the details, but that night cost Frank a fair few quid. Being a shy young man with sight problems, I found it all quite bewildering, as you can imagine.

Talking of Chris, I was in the classroom one day whilst we were waiting for our Typing teacher to arrive. There were only four of us to a class and Chris used to sit behind me. He'd been blind from birth, was the same age as me, short of stature, liked a beer and had a great sense of humour. Like me, he gave a name to his cane. He said he'd had the same long cane for years. However, because he was very short, so was his cane and so he named it Arthur Conley, after the diminutive soul singer of Sweet Soul Music fame. Towards the end of the audio-typing course, Chris and I were to go on an amazing hitchhiking trip to his parents home in Poole, Dorset. We set off one Friday evening, carrying our cardboard signs. One of them said, "To Bournemouth Please" and the other, "To Poole Please". It was a great experience, getting lifts all the way. On the return journey on the Sunday afternoon, we got picked up by a very interesting gentleman who turned out to be a Brigadier. We enjoyed a great conversation.

Anyway back to the classroom, where Chris and I had been given a toffee by Barbara, the only female student of the four of us. Still waiting for our teacher, Mrs. Craig to arrive, I unwrapped my toffee and put it in my mouth. I then screwed-up the paper and threw it back over my head, hoping to hit Chris. At that moment, Mrs. Craig walked in and thankfully didn't see my uncharacteristic behaviour. We proceeded through our typing lesson, during which we had to type out some audio dictation, which lasted about twenty minutes. At the end of the class we left our work on Mrs. Craig's desk and went off for our tea break. On returning to the class for the continuation of the lesson, Mrs. Craig, a disciplinarian of the old school, began by saying that on the whole, the work was of a very high standard, with the exception of Chris - whose two sheets of paper were totally blank. She walked over to Chris' Olympia typewriter. She was able to see why. A piece of toffee wrapping-paper had become lodged on the roller where the typewriter keys would make contact. I knew that Chris was about to be lambasted; so with trepidation, I owned up to the fact that I had, er, thrown the toffee paper…

Mrs Craig expressed surprise and disappointment at my behaviour. Both Chris and I were in for detention that night, to undertake the work again. Thankfully Chris didn't hold that against me and neither did Mrs Craig, who went on to be instrumental in helping me make the most important decision of my life.

I went on to leave the college gaining Distinctions in RSA Audio Typing, Elementary and Intermediate levels. I was really enjoying living away from home and I wanted to stay working in London. So I secured a position as an audio typist with the Ministry of Overseas' Development in Clerkenwell. I've gone on to work for over two decades performing the same typing role, for the Inland Revenue. It's a job that I've really enjoyed, meeting some fantastic people in the process, even women! So, as far as never working again, I needn't have had any worries at all.

Fear of Never Getting Married or Having Children

As a teenager I became an avid cinemagoer, which meant going alone to the many cinemas in our locality, as well as in the Birmingham city centre. One Sunday afternoon when I was about fifteen, I took myself off into Birmingham to the Odeon in New Street, for the opening day showing of The Young Ones starring Cliff Richard and The Shadows. Being a fan of theirs, I'd already bought the single of the same name which had topped the charts. In the film there's a scene where Cliff walks along a beach with his girlfriend, and as they move in and out of the many children playing and building sandcastles, Cliff is singing the title song. Contained within it is the lyric, "…and some day when the years have flown/Darling, then we'll teach the young ones of our own".

Being sensitive and sentimental, it brought a lump to my throat and I so desperately hoped that one day, that might be me, too. But seriously I doubted that I would ever be in the same position.

As I got older and my fear of girls intensified, the dream seemed to drift off almost into oblivion. It wasn't that I didn't like girls. It was just that I never had the courage to actually ask someone out. Fear of rejection, which perhaps could be included in this list of fears, was perhaps the overriding factor. Then of course, going blind just 'capped it' as far as I was concerned. For what girl in her right mind would ever want to go out with a blind person?

One Friday night in December 1968, I was travelling back from London to Birmingham for the weekend, on the Midland Red bus. As well as seeing my family, I wanted to watch Aston Villa play. On the journey, as we meandered slowly through the streets of London, heading towards the M1 my mind began to unwind after a week of audio typing. My thoughts turned to the matter of, "Will I ever get a girlfriend?" As I turned this matter back and forth inside my head, I felt an aching in my heart. After all, I was twenty-one years of age and had never had what you would call a real girlfriend. I'd been out a couple of times with Pamela, a girl from Dunlop but she really had her heart set on a disc jockey friend of hers, and she just liked me as a friend; I did start going out with a blind girl from Pembridge, but I always felt ill-at-ease with myself when we were together. Now, on the coach, as we sped up the motorway I had this intense longing for a steady girlfriend. A few weeks earlier I'd become a 'born again' Christian, while attending Westminster Chapel and I was still having some struggles concerning that whole experience. In that moment of agonising on the bus, I found myself mouthing a prayer from deep within my heart.

"Oh God, if you *are* real, and you have come to live inside me, then would you please give me a girlfriend. Amen."

Prayer uttered, I enjoyed the remainder of the journey, rehearsing the football game I'd be attending the following day, trying to work out the Villa team, who would score the goals and so on.

Two weeks later, I was back in Birmingham again (yes, another football match). On the Saturday night of 28th December 1968, my mum and dad had gone to a local pub, The College Arms, where they used to have a bit of a sing-a-long. I joined them there for the night. My sister, Joan, also came along, with her fiancé and a friend from work, Sylvia.

We'd been there for about an hour. The singing was getting into full swing as the alcohol took effect. More importantly for dad and me, was that the man had entered the pub selling all kinds of sea food which we so eagerly indulged in. Back then, it was common in pubs and working-men's clubs for a guy to come in, or to have a stall outside, selling sea food. A bit like the way that girls now go around town-centre pubs nowadays, selling single-roses for charity. That fateful Saturday night, I politely offered my cockles around.

Sylvia was sat on my right, and the only thing I said to her all night in the pub was, "Would you like a cockle?"

Not surprisingly, it was met with a firm, "No thank you." Little did I know, that in that most romantic of settings, she was destined to become my wife.

History recalls that we left the pub at 11 o'clock that night, but not before dad had invited a crowd of people back to the house for a bit of a party. He often played the piano at the local pub, needing a few beers to get him in the party mood - unlike me, who really hated parties because I equated them with girls and dancing, both of which I felt distinctly uncomfortable around, although something was about to change in me for ever.

A dozen people came back to our home and I quickly volunteered to sit in the corner of the long, rectangular living-room, by the record player and my large collection of singles. In those days I had Braille labels on most of my singles.

My sister Joan came over to me and said, "Would you play something especially for my friend Sylvie, as she's desperately unhappy with her boyfriend? One of her favourite artists is Otis Reading".

I quickly searched through my collection, all strictly in alphabetical order, until I came to the Otis Reading section! I picked one out and shouted above the din of lively conversation, "This is *Mr. Pitiful* especially for Sylvia".

The record had hardly started when Sylvia came across. "How did you know? That's one of my favourite songs, thank you. Would you like to dance?"

I could hardly believe my ears. Before I could take it in, this young woman (who'd earlier refused my generous offer of a cockle) was taking me by the hand and leading me around the dimly lit living-room, in a bit of a slow dance. She held me close and I loved it. But was this really happening to me? I felt a little awkward in terms of the dancing, if that's what you could call it, but it sure felt good. I just didn't want Otis to stop singing. Feeling Sylvia's body next to mine, was sensational. I felt amazingly proud and chuffed with myself. Remember that great song by the Bellamy Brothers, *If I Said You Had a Beautiful Body Would You Hold It Against Me?* It would've been somewhat appropriate, at that moment!

All too soon the record stopped. I had to get back to my duties of playing the music. That was it for me, though - my night had been made. I would cherish that moment for the rest of my life.

On Monday I was back at work, typing away for the Ministry of Overseas Development at their Clerkenwell office in London. From time to time during the day, my mind would drift back to that sensational Saturday night and the slow dance. After work I travelled by bus as usual, back to my digs in Stoke Newington. Smalley Road was located in a fairly run down, working class area but the home in which I lived, was warm and friendly. Ron and Rose saw to that.

They were a lovely, jovial couple and were parents to Mike, one of my room mates from Pembridge. We'd struck up a good friendship at college. When Mike knew I was planning to stay in London, to work, he told his parents. Typical of them, they immediately offered me a room in their home. Mike himself was a great character. A year younger than me, redheaded and extrovert, Mike was always the life and soul of the party. A talented guy, blinded by a firework at the age of ten, he left college as a fully-trained shorthand typist and obtained a job at what was then, the Board of Trade. Not surprisingly Mike didn't stay there too long, before further studies and qualification as a Social Worker, where he quickly rose up the promotional ladder.

Mike has gone on to represent the UK in athletics, skiing and what's known as 'blind cricket'. I'm not sure of the rules, but it involves having something like peas, or ball-bearings inside of a (larger than normal ball) so that the batsman can hear where the ball is pitching. In the early 1980s, Mike was the subject of *This Is Your Life*, presented by that great Irish broadcaster, Eamonn Andrews. My wife and I were privileged to be in the audience as guests.

Mike, I understand, has more recently been part of the successful Committee which campaigned to bring the 2012 Olympic Games to London, thus resulting in him being honoured with an OBE.

I was relaxing in my room at Smalley Road, listening to *The Archers* as I did in those days, when Rose shouted up the stairs, "John, there's a phone call for you".

I leapt off the bed and hurried down the winding staircase. I picked up the phone to find that it was my sister Joan.

"Hello John, sorry to bother you, but you made quite a hit at the weekend" she said, with some amusement in her voice.

"In what way", I replied coyly.

"With Sylvia, of course! She's written you a letter, which she wants me to read to you over the phone". Joan sounded just a little excited.

Of course I couldn't wait to hear what Sylvia had to say, judging by Joan's tone! My sister read it to me and in essence, Sylvia was saying that she was desperately unhappy and locked into a relationship with her fiancé, in which she felt trapped. She said she enjoyed meeting me and would love to meet up again for a chat. Once again, I could hardly believe my ears. A girl, *a member of the opposite sex* no less, was actually asking to meet with me! This was unheard of, but I was up for it. My only concern though, was this boyfriend. What about him?

That night I went off to a Civil Service folk club in London with Mike, but through the evening all that my mind could concentrate on, was Sylvia…and what it was about me, that had apparently impressed her so much.

Next morning, and I purposely got into work particularly early so that I could type a letter, to be delivered via my sister. I arranged to meet Sylvia the following Friday, explaining that my coach would be arriving at Birmingham Digbeth Coach Station, around 8.30pm. If she was there to meet me, then perhaps we could go for a drink and a chat somewhere?

As anybody who has even attempted to conduct anything approaching a long-distance relationship will tell you, the time spent looking forward to meeting up with each other can take on an entirely different perspective, compared to 'normal time'. It can seem like an eternity. Or as in this case, the week flew by - in no time at all, I was getting off the coach in Birmingham and there was Sylvia to meet me. We walked hand in hand through Birmingham city centre, to the bus stop. Whether it felt romantic or not, it felt so natural. As we talked, there was more time to take things in now, and whilst I was 5ft 10ins tall and very skinny, Sylvia seemed about 5ft 3ins. I later discovered that she had short, light brown hair and big sparkling brown eyes – still a feature to this day.

We jumped on the number 5 from Corporation Street and headed back to my parents home in Erdington. Just took a few moments to say "Hi" to my family, drop off my bags and then head off just across the road to our local pub called The Chase. We chatted at length for an hour or so, before it was time for

Sylvia to head off home. We talked about a number of things, but in the main it centred on how unhappy she was; she was experiencing a certain amount of abuse at the hands of her boyfriend and that she needed to summon up the courage to put an end to the relationship. I'm glad to say that in the following week when I was back in London, I received a phone call from Sylvia to say that she'd made it clear to Kenny that she didn't love him and that their relationship was over. I breathed a sigh of relief and congratulated Sylvia for having the courage to do what must have been a very difficult thing.

"I'll see you on Friday at the same time then" I said.

"Yes, of course, I can't wait" responded Sylvia enthusiastically.

It was beginning to look as if my heartfelt prayer, uttered on the Midland Red coach just a few weeks beforehand, had been answered in spectacular fashion. I remember, on my way to work the next morning saying, "Thank you God, for answering my prayer in such a surprising way". I think this was the first time that I'd became aware that God is the God of surprises . I have come across Him on many occasions since.

I know it's amazing what a woman can do for a man and, in Sylvia's case she certainly unlocked a romantic poet in me. In a letter I wrote to her that week, I said to her that the letters of her name, Sylvia Lloyd stood for "Sexy, Youthful, Lovely, Vivacious, Intimate and Attractive, plus, Lovely Legs Of You Darling". I also said that my surname Flanner stood for "For Loving And Never Never Ever Rowing"; a nice ideal but not one I've managed to live up to.

After our first meeting I was in Birmingham every weekend, but I confess that it was only four weeks after our first meeting that I did something totally out of character for me at that time. We started attending a Saturday night disco held at a club called "The Heartbeat" which was located on the same complex as the Silver Blades Ice Rink and Bowling Alley, in the centre of Birmingham. We loved the music there, which was mainly soul and Tamla Motown, with a few chart songs thrown in for good measure. It was a bit 'Mod'. We danced a little - clumsily in my case - and talked a lot. Sylvia used to wear this black velvet dress, with a scooped neckline and just above the knee, which I used to like. To me, she looked magnificent and elegant in this. She was wearing it on the night of 25th January 1969. We were sat talking, sipping on our drinks and as *Ob-La-Di Ob-La-Da* by Marmalade played in the background, I found myself saying, "Sylvia, I love you so much, will you marry me?"

I was shocked at the words coming out of my mouth. But even more shocked when Sylvia said, "Yes I will, of course I will".

WOW! Could it really be that after four weeks and four dates with my first girlfriend, I was now about to become engaged to be married? Was the same Lennon & McCartney song, about Desmond having a barrow in the market-place, destined to have a special place in my affections for the rest of my life? You bet it was!

Following that, Sylvia and I enjoyed a very pleasant courtship, actually waiting until the June to become officially engaged and then getting married at St Margaret's Church, Erdington, Birmingham on 29th November 1969, just eleven months after our first meeting in the College Arms.

We'd originally planned to get married the following year, but we couldn't wait for that. It was made possible to bring our wedding forward, thanks to Sylvia having an accident at work.

From the moment we decided we wanted to be married we opened a Building Society savings account, putting money away each week. It was exciting to see the amount build up as we made progress towards our goal of marriage.

From time to time Sylvia would accompany me to Villa matches, home and away. One occasion we went down to London, to see them play Fulham at their Craven Cottage ground, right alongside the banks of the Thames. It should be noted that there was plenty of room on the terraces, with no need for segregation of rival fans in those days. Watching football was an altogether more pleasant experience than it is today. A Villa player whom Sylvia liked was David Rudge, a diminutive guy with chunky thighs! I soon discovered that Sylvia rarely does anything passively, not even watching football. She shouted with all her lungs, especially when an opposing player tackled little Davie Rudge.

Typically she would bellow, "Leave him alone you filthy bully, he's smaller than you."

Some of the Fulham fans nearby got a bit exasperated with this particular visitor, and one shouted back at her, "Go back to Birmingham, Marlene, you haven't got a clue what you're talking about", and with that, many people roared with laughter. It was all good natured fun and the reference to Marlene was because the Birmingham-born actress Beryl Reid used to play a 'Brummie' barmaid called Marlene, in television advertisements for many years. So the Brummie accent became synonymous with 'Marlene'.

Not long after, there was an away game at Blackpool and we discussed the possibility of going to the match and staying overnight in my favourite English seaside resort, having gone there many times as a child with my parents, for family holidays. WE, or should I say Sylvia, decided that we couldn't justify the expense as we were saving hard for the wedding. It turned out that Sylvia was called into work on the Saturday for overtime. At the time she worked for IMI Kynoch Works at their factory in Witton, a stone's throw from the Villa ground. Sylvia worked with my sister Joan on the inspection of zips. It was very hard work, but well paid and it was here that you might say fate took a hand in our relationship. Or more precisely, a thumb.

I was at home that Saturday morning, probably wishing I was in Blackpool for the game. The telephone rang in the hallway and Dad went to answer. I could hear by the concerned tone in his voice that something was seriously wrong. I'd no idea it was Sylvia.

Sylvia had had an accident at work and was at the General Hospital in Birmingham. She'd apparently had part of her thumb ripped off, when she got it stuck in one of the machines. The message conveyed was not to go to the hospital but to await further messages. Eventually I received a phone call to say that Sylvia was back at home with her parents, and so I made my way hastily across Witton Lakes, our local park, and then the other mile or so to the home of Denis and Ada Lloyd: Sylvia's parents.

I found her lying on the settee with her left thumb heavily packed and bandaged and with her arm in a sling. She was very emotional as she recounted the accident, the pain she endured, the loss of blood and of losing the end of her thumb. She endured discomfort from that injury for many months afterwards and we pursued a compensation claim. We settled out of court, receiving a cash sum of £500, which enabled us to pay for the wedding and accordingly bring the date forward. It was "thumbs up" all round, on the big day!

The night before our wedding, Sylvia spent a quiet evening at home with family. I went to a favourite local pub called The Lyndhurst, mainly because I liked the band which played there at weekends, with their mix of Irish, country & western and pop music. It was just a few mates having a nice time, or so I thought. They were doing things to my drinks and if I asked for a rum and coke, they would make it a double rum and so on. When the pub closed I thought I was going home, but I remember going through a turnstile and thinking in my semi-drunken state, "I must be at the Villa".

I then found myself standing next to loads of people, probably all men, who were cheering and applauding. Then came the shouts of "Off, off, off". No, there wasn't any footballers receiving the ubiquitous red-card. I was at a strip club. Now I ask you, fancy taking a blind man to a strip joint!

I awoke on my wedding day with no hangover but loads of nerves. The wedding was set for the hallowed hour of 3 o'clock, just at the time Villa were due to kick off. It was bitterly cold and icy that November morning and there was still snow on the ground from an earlier snowfall - the match just might be called off! The football match that is. I had made myself unpopular with a number of people for arranging the wedding to coincide with a Villa home match, not least Reverend Power, a Villa fan too.

Just minutes before I was due to leave for the church, mum and I were sitting in the kitchen, with the Johnnie Walker show (my old friend from Radio Caroline days) on Radio 1 in the background. Johnnie mentioned that he'd received a request from Neville Howes in Norwich, saying that his friend John Flanner was marrying Sylvia Rose Lloyd, that afternoon and could Johnnie play a record for them? He duly obliged and sent his good wishes by playing the Everly Brothers' song, *All I Have To Do Is Dream* by Glen Campbell and Bobbie Gentry. When Sylvia and I awoke next morning on our honeymoon at the Great Western Hotel in London, and turned on the radio the first song we heard was

All I Have To Do Is Dream; not surprisingly, it's now our special song.

The wedding service was a pretty traditional affair. Sylvia looked lovely in her white dress and she had four bridesmaids – Linda and Joyce, two of her own sisters and my sisters, Joan and Susan. In the black and white wedding photographs they all look absolutely frozen. We had three hymns, all of which we knew from school assembly days. They were *Immortal, Invisible, God only Wise, Love Divine All Loves Excelling* and *The Lord's My Shepherd*. You'll be glad to know that when Sylvia arrived at the front of the church to join me in my light grey suit, just before the Vicar said "Dearly beloved, we are gathered here today in the sight of God…", he whispered to me those immortal words, "Good news John, the match has been postponed" and from that moment on, I knew it was going to be a good day.

The reception was a fairly low-key affair, with the speeches just about the briefest I have ever heard, because all participants were so nervous. My best man was Brian, who ran away to Gretna Green and who persuaded me to continue going to the football even after losing my sight. We sat down for a simple chicken meal and the party afterwards was good fun, but incredibly tame by today's standards. We just took a mono record player along and people played singles or LPs. One person did get too drunk and caused a scene, but that was after we had left to go off on honeymoon.

Heaven for me arrived at 6pm when Graham (alias the 'Milky Bar Kid' or 'Joe Ninety') drove us into Birmingham to catch our train. Sitting on that railway carriage with my bride was indeed one of the very proudest moments in my life. I really never thought it would happen to me, but it had.

A fear of never having children? After about a year of married bliss, Sylvia was feeling that she would love to have a baby. I didn't really want a child coming along and disturbing what was now a very pleasant way of life. By this time, it'd been a good eighteen months since I'd moved back from London to a job working as an audio typist at the Inland Revenue, Birmingham 16 Tax District, as it was then, at King Edward House in New Street. Sylvia was working at Dunlop as a cashier in the staff canteen. Eventually, as men tend to do, I relented and as a 'first wedding anniversary present' we decided that we would start trying for our first child.

In the spring of 1971, I returned home from work to an empty flat. Sylvia had gone to see the doctor, as she hadn't been feeling at all well and, as she had already missed one period, we were thinking that she just might be pregnant. I'd been home for about half an hour, when the doorbell rang.

It was Sylvia. She flung her arms around me and said, "Congratulations, you've done it. We're going to have a baby".

I was so amazed and excited, I embraced Sylvia in a tight bear hug and swung her around with glee. Another one of those proud, chest expanding moments and my confidence levels rose dramatically and possibly went way off the scale!

Our beautiful daughter, Beverley Jane weighed in at 7lbs on 8th October 1971. It was a Friday night at Dudley Road Hospital, when she was born after Sylvia had endured a long period of labour. I was honoured to be present at the birth, to witness this miracle of creation.

God really does have a sense of humour, because he was beginning to deal with my fear of girls, and not having children, in an amazing way. Having Beverley around was wonderful; however, something extraordinary and deeply challenging was about to break forth in our lives.

It was February 1972 and Beverley was just four months old. I was busy typing in my Birmingham office, when a lady popped her head around the door and said, "John, there's a phone call for you in the main office."

Why the call had come through in the main Pay As You Earn Office, I never did find out. I was surprised to find Sylvia on the other end and her tone immediately told me that she wasn't happy.

"John, you are never going to believe this," she stated "…but I'm pregnant again." There seemed like an eternal silence before she went on more forcibly. "You and your bright ideas. I'm so embarrassed." With that she broke down in tears and conscious of many colleagues around me, I just said that I would come home early so that we could talk, and Sylvia put, or rather slammed the phone down.

As I walked back to my office I tried to look calm, but really I was trembling inside. "How could this be?"

I remember stopping off at the gents in an attempt to recover my composure and reflected, "Malcolm Muggeridge, it's all his fault, if only I hadn't listened to him."

At this time in our lives, Sylvia and I were still very young and immature as Christians, and seeking to grow in our understanding of the faith and in obedience to God's word, the Bible. We were attending St Martin's Church, a notable edifice, located in Birmingham's Bull ring. We used to attend the Sunday morning and evening services there, but since the arrival of our baby daughter we only went in the morning. On Sunday evenings, BBC television were conducting a series of debates on the rights and wrongs of birth control for the Christian. We watched the anti birth-control debate presented by Malcolm Muggeridge a highly respected writer and broadcaster, well known for his conversion to Christianity from atheism, late in life. We'd heard him preach at St Martin's Church and been very impressed. We were equally impressed by his anti birth-control stance, and decided (or was it I decided?) that we would now live and make love by faith, using the self-control method. Great idea, we wanted to honour God in all areas of life, but now we were expecting another child, so soon after the joy of welcoming Beverley into the world.

The journey home was a tense one. What would Sylvia's reaction be to me? We talked and, of course, as you have to do, we accepted the situation and got on with our lives. On the whole Sylvia enjoyed being pregnant, apart from the fact that she developed some very unpleasant itching, through the duration of each pregnancy.

As the months passed, we moved from our 15th floor Council flat to a first floor, three-bedroom maisonette, near to where my parents lived and where I'd lived from the age of eleven. We also changed to a more local church, this time a lively Pentecostal Church that had been recommended to us by a friend. Each Friday night we would have a crowd of teenagers come to our house, mainly friends of my brother Paul, who himself was a lively seventeen year old, at the time. These kids, usually between twenty and thirty of them, would come with their musical instruments and we would sing modern Gospel songs, pray and read the Bible together.

It was on a Friday night in August, when Sylvia was coming up to eight months pregnant and we were having such a good meeting and singing heartily, that during one of the songs Sylvia turned to me and said, "I have a pain in my back and don't feel well. I'm going to bed to have a lie down. Tell the kids the refreshments are all out in the kitchen."

Sylvia made her exit and a few minutes later I went up to see how she was. Seeing that she was clearly in a lot of discomfort, I didn't know quite what to do. She'd been to see the Doctor earlier in the afternoon and he'd done some poking and prodding around - so maybe the baby was lying on a nerve?

I called the midwife who quickly arrived and ascertained that Sylvia had actually gone into labour. The midwife, named Pat, normally very pleasant, wasn't amused by the sheer number of people in our home and, in no uncertain terms, told me to clear the house because this was no kind of atmosphere in which to give birth.

When I'd picked myself up after the shock of it all, the youth meeting came to an abrupt end, but not until they had insisted on saying a prayer for Sylvia. After making some preliminary arrangements, the midwife undertook a more thorough examination of Sylvia's anatomy and exclaimed, "Has Dr Griffiths said anything about twins?"

A startled Sylvia gulped, "No, only that I have a big baby".

"Well I'm not convinced," responded Pat, "I'm sure I can feel several arms and legs in there. I know we agreed that you could have this baby at home, but to be on the safe side I'm going to ring for an ambulance".

By now, I think my anxiety levels had gone through the roof. As Sylvia continued further on into labour, my mum and sister Susan arrived from the maisonette just below ours. The whisper had gone around that we just might be having twins. For some strange reason, the ambulance took ages to arrive and by the time it did get to us, Sylvia's labour had advanced to the point of no return and she was just about to give birth. I was waiting anxiously outside the bedroom door, sitting on the stairs with mum. Suddenly I heard a baby's faint cry. Without further ado the midwife had opened the door and thrust this baby into my arms saying, "Congratulations, it's a girl. Everything's fine, she has all her bits, but as I suspected, there's another baby on the way".

I was in a daze as I held our new baby daughter, born at 11.50pm. Would the other baby be born the same side of midnight?

Beverley was sleeping soundly through all the commotion. Mum was making the ambulance crew a cup of tea downstairs. Dr. Griffiths was just entering the house as the second baby arrived, another daughter at 12.10am. It was an identical twin, born on a different day. Unlike giving birth less than a year previously to Beverley, Sylvia's comment this time was that it was easy, just like shelling peas. The twins were born six weeks or so premature, but just ten months and ten days after our first child.

Dr. Griffiths sat for a few moments at the foot of Sylvia's bed, and bemoaned the fact that he had, once again just missed the birth of twins. He expressed his surprise at it being more than one child, and observed, "I bet you haven't got two lots of names chosen..."

"No" I replied, "...we only have Allison Marie".

The doctor thought for a moment. "I know it's none of my business, but maybe you should name the second baby Allison Marie, as she was born after midnight and her initials are AM".

Well, that really appealed to my mind and so I quickly obtained Sylvia's agreement, who was weary and in no state to debate the issue. Dr. Griffiths and I then went through the process of trying to find names with the initials PM, for the firstborn twin. With the occasional nod of approval from my very tired wife, the only name that really appealed to us was Sara Louise and so we settled on that.

Because the babies were born premature they had to be taken off to Sorrento Maternity Hospital in Birmingham. It was quite emotional for us, especially for Sylvia, to let Sara and Allison go, after all the hard work and emotion of the evening. She found it very upsetting to think that these two beautiful identical babies were being taken away so soon and in particular, that we had only one carry cot for them. This had taken us and the medical profession by surprise. To add to the sense of anticlimax that Sylvia was feeling, not only had her precious new born babies been taken away for a while, but at about 1am the local fish & chip shop was closed, when she really fancied tucking into roe and chips!

Not many people can claim that Malcolm Muggeridge had a hand in the conception of their twins, as we hadn't made a conscious decision to have a baby quite so soon the second time around. Nevertheless I truly believe that God himself decreed and purposed the birth of Sara and Allison and together with our son Ian, who came along six years later, no four children could be loved by their parents any more than ours. There's been tests and trials along the way, as well as much joy and I thank God for these wonderful gifts that He saw fit to entrust into our care. I just hope we've done a half-decent job in parenting them the way our Heavenly Father would want.

Some words from *The Young Ones* with Cliff Richard:

"Some day, when the years have flown/Darling, then we'll teach the young ones of our own".

It was just a dream, one I never thought could happen to me. But it did and Sylvia and I now have nine young grandchildren; how appropriate Johnnie Walker's choice of song was for us, on our wedding day. All I Have To Do Is Dream.

*

How amazingly wonderful it is to be free of all of these fears. From the bottom of my appreciative heart, I thank God for setting me free to enjoy life and have, even in the midst of difficult circumstances, a fun-filled life. I'm serious about my fun, and there was plenty of it to come - along with some truly embarrassing moments, as my dual responsibilities of being a husband and a father were to be sorely tested by my sight problems. Moments which would reveal themselves in often humorous, but sometimes alarming ways.

Fear, Fun and Faith
SECTION 2 - FUN

I love the Beach Boys' song, *Fun, Fun, Fun*. For me it captures the essence of fun, with it being so light of spirit and conveying a glorious freedom and the feeling that all is well with the world. Maybe other songs, movies or situations do the same for you.

Deep down, fun really is important. Take fun out of your world for any length of time and you do so, at your peril.

Amidst all of those fears, there were also times of fun, such as going on family holidays to Blackpool, playing and watching sport, going to the cinema or just a favourite television programme. Fun, however, only became an integral part of my life after losing my sight. I realised how easy it is to take even fun for granted; I also realised how important it was going to be, to learn to laugh at my own expense. In this section I want to share with you some of the experiences that have made me and others laugh.

Tenpin Bowling

It was one of the most profound and lasting influences in my life. It took place within the first week of arriving at the Manor House in Torquay, for my three months of rehabilitation.

Brian Varley was a stocky, muscular man; a member of staff. It was his job to provide us with a series of social events to help towards developing our social skills which, certainly in my case, had been crushed by the onset of blindness.

My first sortie with Brian was in a mini bus with five others to a bowling alley in the town centre. When I could see, I loved Tenpin Bowling and bowled for a team in a league; we were called 'The Kinksmen', after the '60s pop group The Kinks. Since then, in my misery I didn't want to go bowling as a blind person, when you couldn't have the thrill of seeing the pins go down. Perhaps nearer to the truth would be that I didn't want to go through the embarrassment of bowling the ball down the gutter. Or even worse, down the wrong lane. Oh, I was very self-conscious at that stage!

That particular evening, it was mercifully fairly quiet and it wasn't long before the six of us, fully decked-out in our bowling shoes were choosing the most comfortable balls and then taking our seats, ready for the first assault on the pins.

Usually when people are excited about something, they can't wait to get started. Even adults, in a childlike kind of a way, will shout, "Can I go first?"

However, on this occasion, someone piped up "Can I go last?"

They were soon followed by someone else saying, "No it's all right, I'll go last. As for me, I most definitely wanted to go last!

We were all relieved when this bloke called Geoff interjected. "Okay guys, I'll go first".

As Geoff picked up the ball and stepped back, we were all ears. There was a hush around the lane. Geoff moved forward to bowl, with me at least, hoping the ball went down the gutter. Then, there would be nothing to live up to!

Suddenly Geoff gave out a loud shriek of anguish. Almost as one we said, "What's the matter Geoff, have you fallen?"

"No. One of my eyes has fallen out," came his eventual reply, "...and I think it's gone rolling down the alley".

It was my introduction to the world of artificial eyes and I've had quite a few encounters with them since, but at that very moment none of us knew whether to laugh or cry. There was a long, awkward silence. Shattered when Geoff continued, "But don't worry chaps. I'll be okay. Once I get my eye in."

Something broke in me. I laughed so much the tears ran down my face. In fact, on several occasions throughout the evening, I would just break out into laughter.

I reflected. There was Geoff, scarred from an explosion at work, no real eyes and yet he's able to laugh at himself and seemingly enjoy having other people have a laugh at his expense. It was a liberating experience for me; from that moment on, I know I began to loosen up and not take myself nearly so seriously. I later heard that Geoff had died a few years later, still only a young man. He will always be a hero to me, for that priceless lesson he taught me at the bowling alley in the heart of Torquay, all those years ago.

Years later, I was at a Birmingham bowling alley with my son Ian. It was Saturday morning and fairly hectic with lots of children of all ages playing, many in junior league bowling. Ian and I were sent to play on Lane number one, which was great because it meant that we had a wall on our left and lane two on our right. Sometimes, when people are bowling either side, I find it distracts my concentration. On this occasion we were in a quiet little corner and, as it turned out, it was a good job that we were.

Ian bowled first. True to form he got a strike first ball. For those unfamiliar with Tenpin Bowling, a 'strike' is where the bowler fells all ten skittles at once, in the same bowl. Now it was my turn. I stepped back and concentrated hard, before stepping forward with the ball in my left hand, as usual. I approached the lane and was about to release the ball, when I was filled with a deep sense of panic because I sensed something in my way. But it was too late and I let the ball go with all of its usual force. It had hardly left my hand when I heard a terrific noise of the ball crashing against metal and other things. Ian rushed up to me in a flash. I was full of concern. "What have I done?"

"Dad, you turned on an angle and bowled the ball across the lane. It bounced against the left edge of the gutter, hit the wall, made a hole in it and it has gone straight through" said Ian, with a great deal of alarm in his voice. He continued, "What are we going to do now?"

"Er...let's carry on as if nothing has happened", I suggested.

Exasperated, Ian said, "You must be joking! Loads of people heard the bang. They're staring at the hole in the wall."

"Keep your voice down" I warned, "I just want to carry on as normal."

"But dad, you don't understand", Ian protested. "People are watching and I think you should go to reception and see what they have to say."

After a few minutes I was able to persuade Ian to get on with the game, on the understanding that, at the end I would go and, as it were "confess my sins". Really, in my panicked state I didn't know what I was doing. I did go and explain to the lady on reception at the end. Thankfully she made light of it, said it was only plywood and everybody watched as the man who maintains then lanes, clambered inside the hole and retrieved the ball. We did return to the alley about six months later, for a more conventional game of bowling and would you believe it, the hole was still there!

Washing Up

One of the many hard things I find, as a blind person and particularly as a husband, is that there are lots of things I cannot do, which brings extra pressure and responsibility on my wife and sometimes, my children too. I cannot do the painting and decorating; I cannot drive the car; read or fill in the many forms that come through the post. I did try mowing the lawn; but my career as a would-be gardener came to an abrupt end when I took the electric mower straight over the cable, completely cutting it in two. Mercifully, I didn't even get an electric shock, but it was still a shock, if you know what I mean. I wasn't allowed near the mower again.

Thankfully, one job I did take to, however, was doing the washing up. I was drawn to this task particularly when our three daughters were very small. One evening, it was about 6 o'clock and tea was just about over and done with. As anyone who has ever had children will know, the time leading up to bedtime can be very stressful with small children. At about 4 o'clock they start to get tired, grizzly and argumentative. By this time too, parents are weary themselves and desperately trying to come up with ideas to keep their little angels awake until bedtime rolls around at about 7 o'clock. Bath time is a godsend because the kids usually have a bit of fun splashing around with their toys in the water and it does seem to revive them for a while, but in truth it is very hard work trying to keep them amused and in a good frame of mind. The favourite television programme, a singsong or reading them a story often provide short-term relief! Anyway it was into one of those scenarios that one night I volunteered to go into the kitchen and perform the washing up duties.

I left Sylvia to oversee the bath rota whilst I disappeared into the kitchen to commence my labour of love. This became an acceptable pattern over time. There's no doubt that I got some personal satisfaction from actually doing a job well, in the knowledge that it was one less task that I was saving Sylvia from doing.

To this day I can often be found at the kitchen sink either listening to the radio or more often than not singing away to myself. I have come a long way since those days, miming the hymns in school assembly and now I am just happy to make a joyful noise. I still cannot sing well, but it was wonderful for me one night when my next door neighbour tapped on the kitchen window whilst I was in full flow to say how lovely it was to hear me singing. We used to have a small poster above our kitchen sink which read "Divine worship takes place here three times daily". Although in strictness I did not wash up three times a day I did often find myself singing hymns and some of the praise and worship songs that I had learned from church.

Anyway, there I was, singing away to myself, working in my regular routine of taking the dirty dishes from the left, putting them into the washing up bowl and then putting them to drain on the right side to dry off. As I was scouring a saucepan I became aware of bits of food floating around in the water. I picked a couple of lumps out of the water and began to squeeze them. I held them up, not knowing what they were, when Sylvia walked into the kitchen. Looking at me she said inquisitively, "What are you doing?"

"Sorry love," I replied, "It's not me. You haven't cleared the dinner plates".

Sylvia walked up closer and peered into the bowl and exclaimed, "Oh no, you're washing up the steak for tomorrow's dinner".

We were due to have some friends around for a meal the following day and Sylvia had cut up some braising steak, and left it in a saucepan as she thought, out of reach of my eager hands. She wasn't best pleased, and I tried to redeem the situation by suggesting that I rinsed out the steak, under the cold water tap. That way, no one would ever know. She was even more horrified by this suggestion, and our guests the following evening enjoyed a lovely steak casserole, marinated in something far more pleasurable than washing up liquid.

Mistaken Identity

One couple at the meal that night were Richard and Audrey, friends we'd made through various church connections. Their company was always easy and relaxed. They too, knew what it was like to live with disabilities in the family because their sons, Stuart and Graham, suffered with major hearing loss. On another night we were all gathered in our living room, having a chat whilst Sara and Allison had already gone up to bed. Beverley was kind of hanging around, chatting and delaying bedtime as long as possible. I knew that Beverley was sitting in an armchair opposite me when Richard and I got into a lively debate about football. I became aware of the time and how late it was becoming, so I turned to the chair opposite and said "Come on my love, it's time for bed", only to be shocked to hear Audrey say in a loud, startled voice, "I beg your pardon?"

Richard, sitting beside me, gave a hearty laugh and so did Sylvia. As for me, I was extremely embarrassed, as you would imagine. I tried to apologise, saying that I thought it was Beverley, only to be told that Beverley had gone quietly up to bed whilst Richard and I were in animated football conversation.

More recently at work, someone used to come in and pass my desk and everyone else's, with a cheery "Good morning" and I would respond with an equally cheery "Good morning Carol". I did that for a few weeks until somebody plucked up the courage to tell me that the person I was calling 'Carol', was actually Barry. I do hope Barry is okay and that I haven't damaged him for life!

Luncheon Club

One of the things I enjoy doing is attending luncheon clubs and talking about my experiences. One such invitation took me to a very posh do, at a ladies luncheon club in Stratford-upon-Avon. The meal was excellent. Consisting of three very nice courses of prawn cocktail, a chicken dish in some very nicely flavoured sauce and a fresh fruit salad. It went down very well, just like my talk, which was really well received. I travelled home with a great sense of satisfaction. They'd enjoyed the jokes and somewhat exceptionally, I'd been very well remunerated. It felt like a good day as I arrived home and relaxed in the armchair.

Within a few minutes my son Ian arrived home, bright and breezy as usual.

"Hi dad". He then laughed a little; "What are you doing?"

"Sitting here relaxing", I replied.

"Yes, but why are you sitting like that..." enquired Ian.

"Like what?" I had a somewhat perplexed tone.

"Dad, you haven't been to Stratford like that, have you?"

By this time I was getting a bit impatient. "For goodness sake Ian, what's your problem?"

"I hate to tell you dad, but you have one black shoe. And one grey shoe."

By now Sylvia had come home. "Mum you're never going to believe what dad has done".

She was horrified. She always got my clothes from the wardrobe for me, to make sure they all matched in terms of style and colour. On this occasion however, I'd done it myself, hence the mistake. I just don't know how I'd done it, other than not taking enough care. Sylvia always felt that this reflected badly on her and she was most upset that no one had told me that I was wearing odd shoes. For my part however, I'm glad. If I'd known it may've made me feel far more self-conscious. Definitely a case of ignorance being bliss.

Wallpaper

Sylvia and I were looking to buy a house in Solihull and went to view a particular property. On ringing the doorbell, a Mrs. Jones opened the door and greeted us, reassuringly. After the customary handshakes, we were shown around downstairs and I remember being very impressed by the size of the living room – ideal for our growing family, I thought to myself. However, when Mrs. Jones was taking us upstairs she made what I thought at the time, was a strange remark.

"Oh, I just want to say that the wallpaper in the bathroom is not my choice."

We arrived at the top of the stairs, walked across the landing and looked at the three good-sized bedrooms. I was beginning to get a good feeling about it. We entered the bathroom and immediately I was struck by what I thought was an amazing contrast of colours.

I've often said that I can see light and dark and some bright colours, if they're close up. Well, what I saw here, was the light of the bath, hand basin and toilet which contrasted sharply with what looked to me, like black walls. I had never seen black walls before and my natural instinct was to reach out and touch. As my fingers made contact with the wall, I was impressed by the beautiful texture which was smooth and velvet-like to the touch. There was also an embossed pattern on the paper and I said to Sylvia, "Wow this paper is absolutely gorgeous: such fantastic quality and what a pattern!"

At this point Sylvia nudged me in the ribs, which usually means, be quiet. However, I continued feeling the paper and saying once again, "No, it's really Lovely - and such a pretty embossed pattern, too".

I felt Sylvia's elbow, sharper than ever in my side. I knew I'd overstepped the mark...

Mrs. Jones led us back downstairs and, as we stepped outside both Sylvia and I remarked to her that we liked the house. We would be back in touch, with an offer. With the door finally shut behind us, Sylvia then laid into me.

"Sometimes John, you are such an embarrassment".

"Why, what have I done?" I felt a bit hurt, emotionally and physically.

"Didn't you hear the lady say that the wallpaper wasn't her choice?"

"Yes" I replied, "but I didn't know what she meant".

Sylvia responded. "What she meant, was that the paper was covered with hundreds of topless women and you were feeling them all over and saying how gorgeous they were and "such a lovely embossed pattern". The poor woman was going red from the neck up!" Needless to say we bought the house.

The paper actually stayed on for a few more years. Sylvia said I wouldn't be corrupted by it, and our daughters had a lot of fun at bath times, with their pens and colouring pencils, drawing clothes and moustaches on the ladies.

Two incidences persuaded us to strip them off, so to speak. Firstly, Beverley had a bad dream one night, in which the ladies came off the wall and were chasing her; then a little while later, one of the tops came off a tap in the bathroom and the water was shooting up in the air. Allison was sent to go and get Eddie, a young teacher from a couple of doors away. As Eddie was coming up the stairs, Sylvia suddenly thought of our lewd wallpaper. What would our schoolteacher neighbour think about this, with us being respected churchgoers? Sylvia felt embarrassed, apologised to Eddie as he was fixing the tap and in no time at all, Sylvia had replaced the wallpaper with something a lot more cheaper, but far less controversial - much to the disgust of some of the male visitors to our house, apparently.

Birds

Singing is a lot of fun. It brings refreshment to the one who is singing and spreads joy all around like a smile. Doctors now tell us what I learned from the Bible long ago, that it is a healthy thing to have a song resonating from the heart. In my childhood people such as the milkman or the bus driver would often be singing, or whistling as they worked and as they did so, it spread an aura of joy. People don't seem to do that kind of thing much today, so let's start a campaign to get people singing again!

Have you noticed that if people do speak in the morning, which can be rare, then they might say "Morning". It's led me to ask, "Where has the 'good' gone in good morning?" I now make a point of saying "Good morning", even when it's pouring with rain! One person said to me "What is good about it?" and I replied "Well you are alive, aren't you?" You could be dead". I think it brought them up with a jolt.

In times of hardship, singing has been a great antidote to worry. It has united people and inspired so-called ordinary persons to perform great feats of courage. In the First World War, one of the great songs was *Pack Up Your Troubles In Your Old Kit Bag And Smile*. It's a very hard thing to sing for much more than ten minutes and remain in depression. Something happens on the inside of us, as we sing a joyful song that somehow dispels the darkness all around and we begin to see things from a different perspective. Again, I have had to learn this secret for myself and the revelation has come through reading the Bible and discovering that God is a God of song, dance, exuberant joy and a great deal of fun. I discovered that God loves me so much that he sings over me and dances around me, with great excitement. He loves music because he invented music. God also had fun in creation. Of all of his creation I just love the birds of the air, apart from the pigeons when they drop stuff on my head in Birmingham City Centre, that is! It's a wonderful thing to wake up in the morning to the sound of the birds singing their cheerful song of joy. They just don't seem to get depressed. Many of us wake up, blurry-eyed, saying rather grumpily "Good lord, it's morning" instead of awaking bright-eyed and bushy-tailed with a cheery "Good morning Lord, thank you for a brand new day". Not so with the birds; they appear to be bright and cheery everyday, no matter what the weather.

Budgerigars have been pets in our family since I was a child. When I was at home with mum and dad, nearly all budgies seemed to be called 'Joey' and ours was no exception. Since being married we've had three budgies. The first was yellow-looking, similar to a canary. We called him 'Chico' and he was quite a little character. He bounced up and down to the Tamla Motown song by the Miracles, *Tears Of A Clown* and he used to love coming out of his cage and flying around the room. He would walk on the floor (a dangerous thing to do with a blind man around) and then take off and land on anything he could find from chairs to vases. He also loved landing on the heads of people much to Sylvia's terror. It got to the stage where Sylvia could not stand to be in the room while Chico was flying around. As I had developed a practice of getting up at 6am to get ready for work, and to pray, and to read the Bible, it was an ideal opportunity to open Chico's cage and let him have his fly around before the rest of the family got up.

I remember one Saturday morning. I was sitting in the armchair, concentrating very hard on reading part of my Braille Bible and Chico flew on to my lap and walked across the page I was reading. I found this quite cute and amusing, until Sylvia walked in and said "Do you know that the bird is pecking your Braille dots off the page?"

At this, I hastily flicked Chico off as I wondered to myself how many months has he been doing that? Was this the reason I was finding so many Bible passages hard to read? Braille was difficult enough for me to read, without Chico making it even more so! Pecking dots off here and there can change a word into something completely different. Nowadays, if I go out to give a Bible talk I will sometimes preface the message by saying "If this is heresy, don't blame me. Blame the budgie".

Latterly we have had two budgies – they actually belonged to our son Ian, but because of his job they spent most of their time with us, being fed and watered by Sylvia. The birds (one blue and one green) were named by Ian as Diamond and Denver, by way of a tribute to his two favourite singers, Neil Diamond and John Denver. To help us, and particularly our grandchildren know which one was which, I made up the following rhyme:

"Blue Diamond and Denver green
The most beautiful budgies you've ever seen
They whistle and play throughout the day
Blue Diamond and Denver Green."

Sadly, like his namesake, Denver has now died, but Diamond lives on and to me, he is an inspiration. Despite living his life entirely in a cage (even when the door is open, he won't fly out) nevertheless he is so cheerful. He doesn't appear to like being alone. He loves company, particularly the sound of women's voices and lively music. He whistles away for hours on end and when I come home from work, he always gives me a most chirpy welcome as if he is really glad to see me. Yes there's no doubt about it in my view, birds are a lot of fun. I've learnt so many lessons about life, simply from contemplating these wonderful creatures.

Children

My children have grown up with a blind dad, so they've never known anything different. I'm sure there's been times when they would've wished I'd been able to see, but on the whole I think they've been okay about it, and they have certainly had a lot of fun at my expense, which I think is great.

When my daughters were of infant school age, they would occasionally bring friends to the house and introduce them to me. I think I was a bit of a personality in the area, being that bit different. I remember one occasion when Sara brought a friend into our house. I was sitting in the armchair (probably listening to my radio) and I hadn't realised that Sara was waving her hands up and down in front of my face. She then exclaimed to her friend, "You see, I told you he can't see; look he's not blinking".

I once decided that for my birthday, I would like a photograph album with postcard size pictures of the Aston Villa players to be put into the album.

A few days later, Sylvia made the eight mile trip into Birmingham City Centre. She purchased a nice album from one of the stores, and then went along to the Aston Villa shop, to buy the photographs. She was to be disappointed. They had none in stock - being summer, they were awaiting a new batch before the start of the new season. Sylvia made the journey home feeling more than a little disconsolate, that my requested birthday present was not going to materialise.

Later, that evening, my daughter Beverley rang from her home in the northeast. I was out at the time, and she chatted with her mum, who proceeded to tell her about her unsatisfactory trip to Birmingham for the photographs. Beverley expressed surprise that her dad should want a photograph album for his birthday, when he couldn't actually see the photographs. Sylvia sighed. "But, you know your dad".

Beverley came up with what they both thought was a good idea. "Why don't you fill the album up with family photographs, mum? Dad will never know the difference, if you just tell him the names of each player".

They laughed at the idea, but eventually Sylvia couldn't go through with it. She later told me about it and I roared with laughter, because I thought it was such a marvellous idea and it showed to me that Beverley had a completely healthy attitude towards me not seeing.

On my birthday Beverley phoned to see how I was and if I had received anything nice. "Yes" I replied, "I've had a wonderful photograph album, with all of the Aston Villa players in it". I was winding her up and I could sense some feeling of guilt and embarrassment in her voice, as we continued. Eventually I could stand it no longer and I dissolved into laughter, as I let Beverley know that I was aware of her fiendish idea and I thought it was absolutely great. She said that, at first, she'd felt guilty for suggesting it, but I reassured her that it was okay and that it was a marvellous idea.

Nowadays my grandchildren play me up when they come to stay. My oldest grandchild, Lowenna, together with Allison her Mum took advantage of my washing up job to wind me up recently. I went to do some work on my computer, whilst they got the washing up ready for me. After a short time I received the call from downstairs to say that the washing up was ready, and I dutifully went downstairs and made for the kitchen, not knowing that prying eyes were fixed on me. I plunged my hands into the hot washing up water and reached out for the dirty dishes. I couldn't find them and with a puzzled look on my face I felt around a bit more thoroughly, only to realise, as I heard the giggling behind me, that the washing up had already been done as a surprise for me by Allison and Lowenna.

Fairly recently three of my other grandchildren had been staying the night. Jake, who is only three was fast asleep in bed when Amy, ten, and Libby, seven, went up to bed accompanied by Sylvia. I stayed downstairs for a while to watch a bit of *Match of the Day*. About twenty minutes after, I duly followed them up. Before getting undressed I sat down on the bed, only to be surprised as I clearly sat on a body. The laughter of Amy and Libby, not to mention Sylvia, echoed across the room as they saw the startled look on my face.

Talking of Amy, here's a fun poem that she decided to write about me when she was nine years old and which proudly hangs in our kitchen:

"My granddad is the best, really really funny
Near me all the time, always telling jokes
Dancing and singing all the time
Yes dancing and singing, that's my granddad."

Over the Top

I discovered very early on in our marriage that Sylvia is a wonderful house-keeper. She's one of those rare people (I think) who actually loves housework, though she draws the line at ironing; one of her pet hates. As part of her house-work routine she would rearrange the furniture quite regularly.

I arrived home from work one evening, breezed in through the living room door and had hardly got my usual "Hello sweetheart" out of my mouth when I flew head first over the back of the settee. I ended up with my face where my backside should have been, with my legs up in the air behind me. After that Sylvia decided that rearranging the furniture with a blind person around was maybe not such a good idea after all.

No Smoke without Fire!

Again, quite early on in our marriage, I was sitting down 'watching' the telly whilst Sylvia was in the kitchen, cooking the tea – something with chips I seem to recall. At one point I smelt the whiff of smoke, but thought something had simply been overcooked. Wisdom I thought, said don't interfere, Sylvia will have it all in hand. After a few minutes however, the smell had definitely inten-sified so I went off to the kitchen to investigate.

I poked my head tentatively around the kitchen door. "Everything okay love? I can smell smoke".

Our kitchen was next to the living room. In the space of a split-second, she had the good sense to look into the living room - her cries sent a shiver down my spine. "Oh no, the television's on fire".

Apparently, there was smoke billowing from the back of it and she quickly picked it up wholesale, having disconnected it from the mains of course and carried it straight out on to the balcony of our 15th floor council flat.

Once things had calmed down, Sylvia had some serious talking to do. "Didn't you smell the smoke?"

"Yes. But I thought it was coming from the kitchen and I didn't like to inter-fere while you were cooking".

When I'm Cleaning Windows

George Formby was one of my mum's all-time favourites. I was a bit of a fan, too. I loved his movies going right back to the 1930s and 1940s, with what be-came his very famous catchphrase "Turned out nice again, hasn't it?". They were funny movies, with the ukulele-playing George often playing the shy, clumsy individual who always gets the girl in the end. I could relate to that, sort of.

We were still living in the same flat, back then. Can you imagine what it was like to clean the windows outside, when you're fifteen floors up in the air?

Well it's easy when the windows revolve as these did. The trouble is, as Sylvia discovered, when you're that high up and you revolve such a large pane of glass, it's as though you are being pulled to the ground and you also have the scary thought, "What if the window should drop out and fall to the ground, putting people's lives at risk?" In that situation I came in very handy, being blind. When it was time to clean the outside of the windows, Sylvia would take herself off into another room whilst I revolved the window and cleaned it to the best of my ability. Sylvia would pop back into the room to examine my work, and would let me know if I'd missed any dirt: yes, it was all great fun. For me at any rate, because it was one of those rare times when I actually felt as though I was doing something useful around the house, Apart from washing up the dishes, that is! Feelings of clumsiness were to bedevil me, for a long while. Unlike in the films, there was nothing endearing about those feelings.

Unlucky 13

Still at the same address, I arrived home from work one night. I got off the bus which stopped right outside Warstone Tower, Bromford Bridge, where we lived, on the site of the old Birmingham Racecourse. I entered the block of flats and pressed the button for the lift. On entering the lift I usually counted the buttons, to ensure I pressed the right one. When the lift stopped I got out, turned to the left, through the swing doors and using the handle, I opened the front door to the flat. On entering I walked down the hall towards the living room, saying "Hello love, I'm home". I was greeted by a hefty sounding Irishman. "What do you want mate?"

"Oh…" I said, "am I in the wrong flat?" now knowing that I was, because the smell was different and the carpet under foot was unfamiliar to me. I'd actually got off at the thirteenth floor by mistake, so I made my sincere apologies and beat a hasty retreat.

Mayhem in the bathroom

For many years it's been my practice to get up early in the morning – anything between 5.30am on workdays and 6.30am at other times. Of course, especially in winter, it's dark at those times and I admit that I'm usually somewhat blurry-eyed and not fully with it. It's led to two particularly funny and traumatic episodes.

I don't know about other blind people, but I've developed the habit of squeezing the toothpaste onto my index finger and then putting my finger in my mouth. In that way, I can feel how much toothpaste I have whereas if it were on my toothbrush, I wouldn't know. On the particular morning I couldn't find the toothpaste, so presuming it had all been used I stretched up my hand to the medical cupboard and pulled out a tube of what I thought, was toothpaste. When I started to brush my teeth, the taste in my mouth was extremely bitter. I stopped brushing and began frantically washing my mouth out with loads of water, but I couldn't get rid of the awful taste for ages. Later I discovered that I'd been brushing my teeth with some cream that had been prescribed to one of the female members of my family for the relief of thrush.

Another early winter's morning saw me enjoying a refreshing hot shower. Suddenly my left foot slipped, I lost my balance and fell backwards into the shower curtain, out of the bath and thudding on to the floor. As I lay there in all of my glory wrapped in the shower curtain, the curtain rail fell on top of me as did some of the wall tiles, that the shower rail had pulled off the wall. Sylvia, roused from her deep slumbers, came rushing into the bathroom to find me spread-eagled across the floor in a sorry mess. I will never forget her compassionate response. "Oh no, just look at my bathroom!" In fairness she did follow it up with a concerned "Are you all right?" But the damage had now been done, in more senses than one!

Erection problem

Once, we needed to have an extension on our house. Our children were growing rapidly, my mum was ill and Sylvia and I wanted mum and dad to live with us while she was having regular hospital visits for radiation treatment. A friend of ours from church, Dave Gardner, drew up the plans and submitted them to the local Planning Office. To our surprise the plans for the ground floor extension on the side of the house, to give us two extra rooms, was turned down on the grounds that it may be objectionable to our neighbours.

Dave suggested that we appeal against this decision. First of all we needed to get all of our neighbours to sign a letter from Dave, which read thus:

"Dear Neighbour, Would you please indicate below if you have no objection to Mr Flanner's proposed erection (see drawings attached)."

We had some pretty down to earth neighbours. The wording of That Letter kept them laughing for years. Until I managed to get away, a couple of the men regularly enquired about my erection proposal.

Ready Steady Go

One Wednesday night whilst I was still a student in London, I decided to go with two blind friends, Neville and Mike, to The Flamingo club, 'for some Soul'. Located in Wardour Street, we had to get the tube from Notting Hill Gate. Duly arriving, we weren't quite sure where Wardour Street was, in relation to the tube station. Picture the scene, therefore: three young blind men, walking arm in arm (so as not to all go off in different directions), all carrying white sticks.

It wasn't long before a gentleman enquired as to where we were going and did we need some assistance?

Mike piped up, "Thanks mate. We're looking for Wardour Street and The Flamingo".

"Fine, I'll take you there" said the man, coming in between Neville and me and now making up a foursome. Good job the pavements were wide around there. Picture the seen: four men, arm in arm with three white sticks. Must have looked very interesting. With the aid of our Good Samaritan, we were striding out confidently when, to our surprise, a very confident-sounding lady stopped us in our tracks and asked if we needed any assistance. This time, it was my turn. "No thanks. We're heading for The Flamingo".

To our increasing astonishment, she promptly wheeled us around, linked arms between Neville and the other gentleman, whilst at the same time saying, "You're heading in the wrong direction, so let me take you there."

Our gentleman guide was left speechless; Neville and I were nonplussed at these events, whilst Mike was almost choking trying to hold back his laughter. It was four men and one woman, all arm in arm and three white sticks. Give the mystery lady her due, she got us safely to the hip Mod nightclub, asking the doorman to "Take care of these four gentlemen, would you? They're blind." When safely inside, and sure the woman had gone, we all burst into uncontrollable fits of laughter. Except our male helper, who was clearly embarrassed and, after wishing us a pleasant evening, made a hasty exit. If that woman hadn't come along, where would we have ended up?

Steak restaurant

Whilst still at college in London, my friend Mike had received some particularly impressive exam results from his shorthand typing tests, and as part of his celebration, he invited me to go with him to one of his favourite steak houses. This was at a time when I was still very nervous about eating out, but somewhat reluctantly I agreed. It helped, knowing that Mike was also blind, even though much more confident and extrovert than me.

At Mike's chosen restaurant, I was very much guided by him as to what to order from the menu. We each had a sirloin, cooked rare-to-medium. I just followed Mike's lead as I was a novice in such matters. e were waiting for the meals to arrive Mike decided that he needed to visit the toilet. We were waiting for the food to arrive when Mike decided to avail himself of the toilet. He returned to find the meals had already landed on our table, brought to us by a very efficient and well-mannered waiter. Part of my dread was having a really tough steak and not being able to cut it. However, it was incredibly tender and I managed to cut the steak and savour its delicious juices, along with the chips, mushrooms, onion rings and peas. Mike and I didn't converse much at this point. In fact I was too busy facing up to the delightful challenge in front of me, when I become aware of Mike hacking away at the contents on his plate.

"Tough steak, Mike?"

"It bloody well is. Tough as old boots. What about yours?" came his animated Reply.

"Mine's absolutely fine, really succulent" I responded, blissfully chewing away.

On hearing the sound of the waiter's voice at the next table, Mike called out in a firm voice, "Excuse me, but his steak's very tough".

The waiter quickly drew alongside our table and almost instantly began to chuckle, "Pardon me, Sir" he said, "…that is not your steak you are trying to cut up, but your tie. The steak Sir, is now sitting on the table at the side of your plate."

Maybe when Mike returned from the loo, he'd let his tie dangle on to his plate, but whatever, we laughed so much we almost cried. Mike, however, had the last laugh. They not only brought him a fresh meal but said he could have his steak on the house.

Over the wall

Our car was booked in for a service. Sylvia stopped the vehicle outside the garage and said to me "If you wait by that wall, I'll go and park the car".

I stepped out of the car. I located the wall with my stick. I turned around, putting my feet against the wall and looking out on to the main road. After a minute or so, as you do, I decided to relax and lean back against the wall. To my horror I found myself falling backwards and I couldn't stop myself toppling over the top of the wall, which I now discovered was only about two foot high. Sylvia who, by this time had parked the car and was approaching me, could hardly believe her eyes as she saw my legs and my white stick flying through the air. A group of men in the car showroom were also laughing hysterically at this amazing sight, which had clearly disturbed their flow of conversation. Once the amusement had subsided, all parties expressed appropriate concern as to my wellbeing. They were interested to know how I'd managed to perform such a wonderful piece of agility. Once again, I'd escaped with minor grazing, but major embarrassment.

Blind jokes

A lady living in a flat is relaxing in the bath when suddenly she hears a ring on the doorbell. "Who is it?" she calls out.

"It's only the blind man", comes the reply.

"That's okay then" says the lady, "I'm in the bathroom, first room on the left".

The man enters the flat and going into the bathroom, says to the startled lady "Where would you like me to put the blinds then?"

*

A teacher, takes a group of blind lads to the seaside for the day and sets up a game of football on the beach. (Blind people use a ball with a bell or something else inside it, rattling around so that they can locate where the ball is.) The game had been in progress for a little while, and all seemed to be going well, so the teacher thought to himself, "I'll just nip across the road to the pub for a quick pint".

He'd only been in there a short time when a woman rushed in, and asked the teacher, "Are you supposed to be in charge of those blind kids on the beach?"

"Yes madam, I am" came his reply.

"Well you had better get over there quick, because they're kicking the life out of a poor Morris Dancer."

*

A man with three eyes, no arms and one leg is waiting by a bus stop. Suddenly, a kindly car driver pulls up and says, "Aye, aye, aye, you look harmless, hop in".

True stories

Blind person waiting to cross the road says to passer by, "Can you see me across the road, please?"

The stranger says "Hang on a minute and I'll go and have a look".

A blind man walking along the towpath of a canal. Shouts across to some people "Can you please tell me how to get to the other side?" The reply came back, "You're already there".

Blind person waiting to cross over a busy road when a man approaches and says "Can I assist you in crossing the road? If so, put your hand on my shoulder". The blind person replies "I'd rather hold on to your arm". "So would I..." said the man with the hint of laughter, "but I haven't got any".

*

A teacher of blind students was out for a meal with his wife in Hereford, quite near to the college where he worked. The teacher, who was also blind, was fairly new to the area and this was his first visit to this particular restaurant. "Have you any menus in Braille?" he asked the waiter. "I'll just go and check" said the waiter.

After a short time, the waiter returned saying, "Sir, we just have this one" as he handed it with an air of triumph, to the teacher.

Later in the evening, when the teacher and his wife were towards the end of an enjoyable meal, the couple engaged the waiter in conversation once again on the subject of Braille menus. This time it was the wife who picked up the point by saying, "In view of the fact that you have a large college nearby, for blind and partially sighted students, don't you think it would be a good idea to have more than one Braille menu? Also some in large print?"

The waiter agreed and went off to talk with the manager.

A little while later, the very amiable waiter returned, waving a small batch of large print menus and exclaiming "The manager agrees with you, that we should have more Braille menus and he will arrange to have some photocopies done later".

The blind teacher almost choked on his spotted dick at this well meaning, but nevertheless idiotic suggestion. Because any clear thinking person would realise that you cannot photocopy Braille. It has to be done on a proper Braille embossing machine.

More Fun Stuff

A quick look at the dictionary shows me that the word 'fun' is interchangeable with 'pleasurable', 'amusing', 'entertaining', 'enjoyable'. I hope that the stories listed in this section have created in you some, if not all of those emotions. We are all on a search for fun, amusement, pleasure. There's a good chance that if we're having fun, then others will be having fun too, even if at times, it's at our expense.

I've discovered that life can be fun when we set out to give others a fun time. I loved Christmas when I was a child. Nothing could compare to the thrill of unwrapping presents on Christmas morning, or so I thought. When I became a parent and my children were old enough to enjoy Christmas, it was equally, if not more thrilling, to feel their excitement, and sense of fun as they opened their presents. Now as a grandparent, I'm going through that all again. Yes, it can be great fun creating enjoyment for other people.

I once heard a radio interview that really impacted upon my thinking and illustrates this point about fun and the need to make the most of our lives. A Baptist Minister from America told the story of how he had become bored with his work in the church and had gone off and joined a travelling circus, as a trapeze artiste. Within a few years of travelling and entertaining thousands of people, he had well and truly got the bug, and the money, to be able to buy his own circus. It was a truly remarkable story and his closing comment was, "Life is one big trip; all you need to do is learn to keep your bags packed".

I love that, because it conveys a picture of adventure and of a person who is ready at all times, to take control of his life and do something positive and enjoyable with it. He took a bold decision to get out of his personal rut. It was a brave step; I believe many need to be equally courageous with their lives today. We were not created to live humdrum, boring lives, drifting aimlessly towards a pension (if we're lucky) and then on to death. Of course I realise there's a down side to this, in that it can lead to instability. But in essence it speaks to me about the heart of a person and of being a pioneer and not a settler, about waking up each morning with a zest for life.

Sometimes we have to decide to have fun. We have to break out of the routine of life and start to do the fun stuff. I never used to think that way but since I invited Jesus to come and live in my heart, fun has become an integral part of my life. Not surprising really, because the Bible says of God that in his presence, there is fullness of joy and at his right hand are pleasures for ever more. Of Jesus, it says that he has been anointed with the oil of gladness above every other person.

Some more of the fun stuff that I have done, or become involved with…

Blackpool

I remember walking home one October night. I knew that Sylvia would have our three daughters, all under five years of age in their pyjamas and ready for bed. The thought came into my head. "Wouldn't it be great to drive off to Blackpool now and let the kids see the illuminations!"

I was still mulling over these outlandish thoughts when I entered the house, to be greeted with hugs and kisses from the children with the usual pleas: "Daddy, can we have a story before we go to bed?" Oh yes, they were all in their night attire.

"Sure," I said, "but just a few moments while I talk to mummy".

Sylvia was in the kitchen, so as the girls went back to playing their make-believe games I went in to speak to her. Sylvia was putting the dirty clothes into her new washing machine (I'll tell you about that next) and I blurted out, "Do you fancy taking the kids to Blackpool to see the illuminations?"

Sylvia turned towards me and said, "When, on Saturday?"

"No, now" I replied.

"You must be crazy", came the reply from a somewhat incredulous Sylvia.

With that I disappeared into the living room. I wanted to be with the kids. Perhaps my wild musings about Blackpool had to subside.

A few minutes later, Sylvia emerged and asked me, out of earshot of the children, whether I was really serious about going to Blackpool there and then. She knew I was, of course, and as soon as I said so, to my utter surprise she said, let's do it then.

With that I turned to the kids. "Come on girls, we're going on an adventure". That was it, I had their attention and we left their pyjamas on, just putting trousers, socks, anoraks etc over the top so that they would be nice and warm. They were so excited and wanted to know where we were going. I said I would tell them in the car.

Soon, we were out of the house, cruising along in our recently acquired blue Ford Escort (I'll tell you about that shortly too). It was about 6.30pm as we headed off towards Spaghetti Junction to take the M6 north bound. Soon into the journey and with three excited little girls in the back of the car, I proceeded to tell them a story of someone's great night out to see the pretty lights in a place called Blackpool. I then let the cat out of the bag, to indicate that that was where we were going on our adventure. None of us will ever forget the events of that night. It was truly magical.

We arrived in Blackpool around nine. We stayed for two or three hours, going the full length of the Golden Mile as well as visiting the famous Pleasure Beach for a whole host of rides. We eventually set off home with three tired, but very happy children in the back. Sylvia did a great job with the driving and thankfully, it was only me who had to be up early in the morning.

New house

Houses and cars have formed an amazing part of our life as a family, and much of it will be revealed in this book, but for now I will restrict the saga so as to illustrate the fun aspect.

At the age of twenty five, I'd never actually lived in a house with a garden and I longed for that. I would imagine sitting out in the summer, listening to the cricket on my radio and it sounded idyllic, but would it ever happen to me I wondered? We were living in an upstairs, three bedroom council maisonette at the time, where indeed all of our three girls had been born. Someone told us that a three bedroom house had become empty, just around the corner in Lakes Road. Sylvia and I couldn't resist going to have a look at the house, peering in through the front windows at the long living room and even lifting the letterbox to look into the hall and up the stairs! It looked good to us, ideal for our growing family and wonder of wonders, it even had a small back garden.

I became very proactive at this point, and immediately went home and telephoned the Council Housing office and requested an interview, which I was able to obtain for the following day. I duly arrived at the office in good time for the interview and was seen by a most understanding lady, who listened sympathetically as I explained our housing need; indicating along the way just how perfect the particular house in Lakes Road would be.

The housing officer asked appropriate questions. She told me that I had put forward a very convincing case but warned there was very stiff competition for such a property. I would hear something within the week. I left feeling quietly confident.

In the days that followed we prayed a lot about that house, and we had one of those block calendars where you have a poem, prayer or Bible verse for each day. On the morning in question, Sylvia looked on the calendar and it read "Joy comes in the morning". You could have added to that phrase the word 'post', because when the postman arrived he did bring joy in the form of a letter from the Birmingham Housing Department, stating that we were being offered the very house we had requested in Lakes road. This sure felt like fun, and within a few days, we were moving in to my very first house with a garden. Oh, the joy that filled my soul! That went for the rest of the family too, I'm sure!

After we'd been in for a week or two, Sylvia and I felt that we'd like a house-warming party with a difference. We felt so profoundly grateful to God for blessing us with this gift, we planned a night of thanksgiving to God, plus one of Sylvia's exceptional buffet-type meals – I am persuaded, in the words of the song, "nobody does it better".

We sent out invitations to friends far and wide, explaining why we wanted them to join us in this celebration. About thirty people gathered in our living room on that momentous night, for an evening of singing praise to God, prayers of thanksgiving and to dedicate the house to God's service. One or two people brought presents, even though we'd stipulated that no presents were to be bought for us. But the biggest surprises were saved for later in the night, when all the people had gone home. Bearing in mind that we'd specified NO presents, we began to tidy up and we started to find money scattered around; hidden behind cushions, at the back of the clock on the mantelpiece, on the stereo, in the kitchen and so on. There were £5, £10 and £20 notes and even a cheque for £50. Later, when we went up to bed we even found money in the bed! Later in the week we discovered money in the biscuit tin. It was truly an amazing evening and whoever it was who came up with the idea of everyone leaving us all that money certainly made it a whole lot of fun for us. I don't love money, but I did love the fun that lay behind this wonderful gesture.

Washing machine

During the course of the housewarming evening, Sylvia had an unusual conversation with a friend of ours in the kitchen. The friend in question, Jenny, was keen to know how Sylvia managed without an automatic washing machine. At the time we just had an old fashioned electric boiler which was supplied by the Council and already installed, when we moved into the house. This was in the days before disposable nappies, so with the twins still being only a few months old there was washing to be done.

Jenny, thinking of Sylvia and wanting to see some of her time freed up, said "Why don't you pray and ask God for an automatic washing machine?"

I think Sylvia was stunned by such a question. It hadn't entered her mind to even imagine such a thing would be possible. After that we did discuss the idea, and though we certainly couldn't afford such a luxury, I do believe that the seed had been sewn in Sylvia's heart and from time to time, she did mention the matter to God in prayer, obviously not seriously expecting much, in light of what was to happen next.

Sylvia was home with the children one morning, when the doorbell rang. When she got to the door a deliveryman thrust a piece of paper at her and said "Can you sign for this please, madam?"

Sylvia inquisitively asked, "What is it I'm signing for?" as she noticed a huge box being wheeled down the path by another man.

"I don't know madam, I'm just paid to deliver the goods" said the first man.

"But I haven't bought anything" insisted Sylvia.

By now the deliveryman was getting a bit frustrated and said "That's not my problem. Can I wheel this inside and get on my way?"

The big box safely inside, the two men left for next delivery. When I arrived home an hour or two later, Sylvia was still mystified and had been wondering whether I'd ordered something without telling her. Or was this delivered to us, by mistake?

I was keen to open our mystery box. I eventually persuaded my dear wife that it would be good to open it, if only to see what it was. With eager anticipation we tore off the metal fasteners and began to slit the tape that was around the lid of this massive cardboard box. Once inside we lifted out the packing to gradually discover a frontloading automatic washing machine. There was a short note attached to the top of the machine, which read "A Gift From the Lord – Fully Paid – Psalm 34 Verse 10. Which I now know says, "The young lions lack and go hungry, but those who trust in the Lord lack no good thing".

Sylvia's reaction was to burst into tears. "I can't believe it".

About a week later, we received a phone call from a Jenny, the same Jenny who told Sylvia to pray for a washing machine. She asked Sylvia if anything interesting had happened. At first Sylvia couldn't resist teasing her. "No, nothing at all". After a moment or two she couldn't keep it up any longer. "Yes! As a matter of fact, it has. We've had this huge package and we don't know where it's come from".

"Oh that's good" said a relieved sounding Jenny. "It's not from us. But the people who it's from, want to remain anonymous and for you to give the glory to God, for it was he who put it on their hearts".

"But I haven't got a clue what to do with it!" admitted Sylvia.

"You mustn't worry about that" affirmed Jenny. "A plumber friend of ours will be over in the next few days, to plumb it in and set it all up for you".

Not that it mattered, but we found out who it was who'd bought that washing machine, many years later and then only quite by accident. The machine achieved what it was sent for, in that it was a great blessing to Sylvia, lasting for many years and freeing up a considerable amount of precious time for her. We don't want to be materialistic, but we thank God for that which became a real gift to us.

Ford Escort

When we lived in our first floor maisonette, after the unexpected arrival of twins, it meant initially that we had three children all under a year old. I was out, working all day at the Inland Revenue and life became very difficult for Sylvia, in the day. Getting three little children ready to go out was a big job in itself, let alone getting them down four flights of stairs in a twin pushchair (no lift) and then back up again on their return. It was almost impossible for Sylvia to get out and about, though my mum, who lived nearby, was always willing to lend a hand wherever possible.

Needless to say I felt some responsibility for the predicament my wife was in, and as I became more and more aware of the physical demands being made on her, I found myself searching my own heart as to what could be done to relieve some of the burden. I was already well into my practice of getting up early in the morning, to pray before going to work and on this one particular morning I felt a heavy burden to pray for Sylvia. I remember throwing myself on to my knees, burying my head in the armchair and crying to God in desperation for help. I felt deeply concerned for my lovely wife. I needed God to hear my cry, on her behalf.

As I poured my heart out to him I had this very strong impression come into my heart, almost as a phrase, "Sylvia needs to learn to drive". I couldn't get this thought out of my mind, and so I gave up trying to pray and went off to work feeling a little disconsolate.

Next morning, exactly the same pattern emerged and the morning after that and so on. Eventually I began to suspect that this wacky thought might just be from God! Not quite on the building an ark in the desert proportions, but not far off in my view. We could hardly make ends meet financially, so how could we afford driving lessons, let alone buy and run a car!

By this time I was just beginning to discover that God is a God of fun and of doing the seemingly impossible, but I was still very much a novice in these areas. However, God had convinced me. Now we had to convince Sylvia.

I needed to broach the subject carefully and choose my moment with great care, but even then I knew it wouldn't be easy. When I seized my opportunity my worst fears were realised.

"My love, I think God is saying that you should take driving lessons" I said nervously.

Sylvia gave a derisory laugh and said "Oh yes, in my spare time! That's just about the craziest idea you've ever come out with".

"Yes I know. But I'm convinced it's God's idea and he will provide", I replied, much more confidently this time.

Sylvia could see I was serious and to her eternal credit she agreed that if it really was God's idea, then she would at least give it a go. We knew someone through church who was a driving instructor, and after speaking with him, he agreed to give Sylvia driving lessons at half the regular price. Another sign I thought, that God was in this.

For the first few driving lessons, Sylvia would come home shaking with fear. Denis, her instructor was heard to say, "She'll be a hard nut to crack, but we'll get there". In the end, Sylvia took her driving test on a very foggy day, except that where the test was held, it was as clear as a bell. She passed first time. She rang to tell me the news and I was so happy and proud of her.

Sylvia was still in the process of taking driving lessons when something remarkable happened one Saturday. It had nothing to do with Aston Villa either! It was fairly early in the morning and we were just sitting down for breakfast when there was a knock on the door. I went to answer it and was greeted by a cheerful sounding man with more than a hint of a London accent.

"Hi John, it's Chris Thacker here, from Croydon – you remember you visited our church a few months back?"

Chris and his wife Janet were youth leaders at Woodside Baptist Church, in that particular part of London and I'd been there to speak only a short while before. Now, he was on my doorstep with his wife saying that they had just stopped off for breakfast, en route to their holidays in the Peak District.

What seemed strange was that Chris and Janet were in no hurry to get away afterwards. In fact, they stayed for dinner through to tea. We chatted about lots of things, mainly family and church issues, and although it was very enjoyable it was only towards the end of their visit that I was to discover the whole purpose of their arrival. After tea Chris got his car keys out of his pocket and I thought that this was the indication that they were about to leave and indeed they were - but not before Chris had lobbed the keys across the room and landed them right into Sylvia's lap.

"What are these?" asked my startled wife.

"They're the keys to your car" said Chris calmly.

"But I don't have a car" said Sylvia. Janet and me looking on intently.

"You do now" Chris responded, "The Lord has told us that we are to give you Janet's Escort. Would you like to take a look at it?"

This was a truly awesome moment for us. Our children were soundly asleep in their cots as their mum became the new owner of a beautiful Ford Escort, which was only eighteen months old with low mileage. Chris and Janet took a totally bewildered Sylvia for a little test drive before leaving in their other car, to commence their holiday in the knowledge that they had been obedient to what God had asked them to do.

I know that they had fun in giving their car away. Even more so when they arrived home from holiday to find that their house sale had gone through, and the house they wanted to buy had been dropped in price by several thousand pounds, during the week they were away. Although they didn't do it to gain reward, I believe that God acknowledged them for their generosity and obedience to his voice.

We had some great fun in that car, not just with spontaneous trips like the one to Blackpool but also in the day to day help it afforded Sylvia, in simply getting out and about to the shops, local parks and to visit family and friends. God had heard my desperate cry and answered in spectacular fashion.

Night Out with the boys

I've always tried to have fun with my children, right from when they were babies, through to their adult life. Hopefully, they still regard me as fun to be around. As they've got older it's obviously been easier for me to do things with Ian, such as attending football and cricket matches together. On Ian's 20th birthday we even went to Wembley Stadium together, not for a football match, but to see The Bee gees in their 30th anniversary concert. We both really love their music and it was magical spending the day together.

Ian enjoys a good night out on the town with his mates. By way of a wind-up I once threatened to accompany them, just to see what they got up to. To my surprise, Ian called my bluff. He repeatedly teased me about it, saying that I was all talk and no action.

There was only one thing for it. This was a matter of honour! We arranged a date for our own night on the town.

The day came and Ian asked me how much money I was taking with me. I said I could afford a 'tenner'. He just laughed. "You won't get far on that". I quietly began to realise that it would be an expensive evening for me.

I set off with Ian into Solihull and made for a local wine bar. We were joined by one of Ian's closest friends, a Muslim by the name of Javed, who didn't drink alcohol but pints of Coke, instead. Javed said that he just liked being with Ian and seeing him get drunk. I had a couple of beers before the three of us set off by taxi into Birmingham. We stopped off at an Irish pub, The Dubliner, which was packed, and there was a really good sounding Irish band playing at the time; it was already a case of standing room only. I was really beginning to enjoy myself. Ian pushed his way through to the bar and bought a double round of drinks, to avoid going through the crush again for a while; there was a great atmosphere with lots of singing along to the Irish tunes. Many had been made famous by Van Morrison, a man with plenty of religious concerns of his own, over the years.

A few quid lighter and a lot more happier, we made our way out of the pub, around midnight. "Okay dad, it's your shout. So where do we go now? We can either go on to a nightclub, or go and have a curry somewhere."

I was feeling rather peckish. Once again a taxi was called and we were on our way to one of Birmingham's celebrated balti restaurants in Sparkhill, which has become known as "The Balti Belt".

We duly took our places at the table and browsed the menu - Chicken and mushroom balti was my choice, I seem to recall. None of us got to receive our meals because Ian noticed that I'd suddenly gone a funny colour. I suddenly felt really ill and thought I was going to be violently sick. The three of us dashed out into the early morning air and I took some deep breaths. Fortunately, another taxi pulled up at that very moment and the driver asked if we wanted to go anywhere. He was requested to take us home to Solihull, dropping Javed off on the way. I did actually start to feel a whole lot better before we arrived home, and was really sorry that I'd now deprived us of our balti experience that night. For all that, it had been a good evening and even though it was a few years ago now, it's nevertheless one we talk about from time to time with much affection. It was a lot of fun. Ian often says, "It must've looked strange, a young English bloke walking into an Irish pub with a blind middle-aged Englishman on his arm, and a very tall, well built, coke-drinking Pakistani guy, by his side!"

Marriage fun

Whilst not always succeeding of course, I've made it a practice to try and inject barrel loads of fun into my marriage with Sylvia. We've passed through many trials and dark valleys during our thirty six years together. However, we've managed to laugh our way through many of them and come out the other side, much stronger individually and with a deeper love for each other.

Having an affair can seem a pretty attractive proposition. People have obviously become bored with their existing relationship and found that an extra-marital affair has breathed some much needed excitement into their lives. There's no doubt about it, having an affair must offer...something. Otherwise, why would men and women the world over continue to go down that road? It's a dangerous road, of course. Maybe therein lies its appeal.

As a married man, I believe that it can all exist within my existing relationship. I am committed to having a wild, passionate affair with my wife. Someone once said that any man can go from woman to woman having sex, but it takes a really great lover to keep one woman fulfilled and happy for a lifetime. With the inspiration of God, my Creator living in me, I want to be the very best lover I can be and that means satisfying the very deepest needs of my wife in all areas, not just the bedroom. This is what I aspire to, but you'd have to ask Sylvia to find out how I'm really doing!

Here are some of the things that I try to do, in order to keep the fun, fire, passion and excitement in our marriage.

Be up early in the morning to pray, especially for my wife and so set the atmosphere for the day. She is my lover and after God, she takes first place in my life.

Make a point of telling her that I love her at least once a day; often more than that.

Show affection every day with a hug, or a touch and a little of what you might call flirting. We did it before we were married; it felt good; so why stop now?

Regularly show appreciation for the work she does in keeping a nice home, doing the washing, the cooking and a myriad of other things.

Remember birthdays, Mother's Day and most of all, our Wedding Anniversary.

These are all wonderful opportunities to make my wife feel really extra special.

Buy her presents of flowers, chocolates and so on. I remember going into Marks & Spencer once, to get Sylvia a nightdress and I have to confess I was looking for something a little bit sexy for my benefit too. I walked into the shop, managed to locate an assistant and when I told her what I wanted she bellowed to a colleague, "Betty! Take this young man to find a nice nightie, will you". Of course I felt embarrassed, but it was all worth it, seeing Sylvia open this attractive little number and even better on the evening of course! When she wore it!

Whilst on this, one of my favourite topics, I believe it's important to be very creative in lovemaking and I know that Sylvia loves it when I talk to her while we are being intimate and I make up all kinds of stories with us as the lovers at the centre of them. If you're not inspired when you're making love then you never will be. In the Bible is a most wonderful erotic book, 'The Song Of Solomon' or 'Songs Of Songs'. Below is the first two chapters of this beautiful poetic book of love, taken from the *Message* Bible, which is a very modern paraphrase.

Song of Solomon 1

1 The Song-best of all songs-Solomon's song!

The Woman
2 kiss me-full on the mouth!
   Yes! For your love is better than wine,
3 headier than your aromatic oils.
   The syllables of your name murmur like a meadow brook.
   No wonder everyone loves to say your name!
4 Take me away with you! Let's run off together!
   An elopement with my King-Lover!
   We'll celebrate, we'll sing,

we'll make great music.
Yes! For your love is better than vintage wine.
Everyone loves you-of course! And why not?
5 I am weathered but still elegant,
  oh, dear sisters in Jerusalem,
  Weather-darkened like Kedar desert tents,
  time-softened like Solomon's Temple hangings.
6 Don't look down on me because I'm dark
  darkened by the sun's harsh rays.
  My brothers ridiculed me and sent me to work in the fields.
  They made me care for the face of the earth,
  but I had no time to care for my own face.
7 Tell me where you're working
  I love you so much-Tell me where you're tending your flocks,
  where you let them rest at noontime.
  Why should I be the one left out,
  outside the orbit of your tender care?

The Man
8 If you can't find me, loveliest of all women,
  it's all right. Stay with your flocks.
  Lead your lambs to good pasture.
  Stay with your shepherd neighbours.
9 You remind me of Pharaoh's
  well-groomed and satiny mares.
10 Pendant earrings line the elegance of your cheeks;
  strands of jewels illumine the curve of your throat.
11 I'm making jewellery for you, gold and silver jewellery
  that will mark and accent your beauty.

The Woman
12 When my King-Lover lay down beside me,
  my fragrance filled the room.
13 His head resting between my breasts-the head of my lover
  was a sachet of sweet myrrh.
14 My beloved is a bouquet of wildflowers
  picked just for me from the fields of Engedi.

The Man
15 Oh, my dear friend! You're so beautiful!
And your eyes so beautiful-like doves!

The Woman

16 And you, my dear lover-you're so handsome!
  And the bed we share is like a forest glen.

17 We enjoy a canopy of cedars
  enclosed by cypresses, fragrant and green.

Song of Solomon 2

1 I'm just a wildflower picked from the plains of Sharon,
  a lotus blossom from the valley pools.

The Man

2 A lotus blossoming in a swamp of weeds-that's
  my dear friend among the girls in the village.

The Woman

3 As an apricot tree stands out in the forest,
  my lover stands above the young men in town.
  All I want is to sit in his shade,
  to taste and savour his delicious love.

4 He took me home with him for a festive meal,
  but his eyes feasted on me!

5 Oh! Give me something refreshing to eat-and quickly!
  Apricots, raisins-anything. I'm about to faint with love!

6 His left hand cradles my head,
  and his right arm encircles my waist!

7 Oh, let me warn you, sisters in Jerusalem,
  by the gazelles, yes, by all the wild deer:
  Don't excite love, don't stir it up,
  until the time is ripe-and you're ready.

8 Look! Listen! There's my lover!
  Do you see him coming?
  Vaulting the mountains,
  leaping the hills.

9 My lover is like a gazelle, graceful;
  like a young stag, virile.
  Look at him there, on tiptoe at the gate,
  all ears, all eyes-ready!

10 My lover has arrived
  and he's speaking to me!
  Get up, my dear friend,
  fair and beautiful lover-come to me!

The Man

11 Look around you: Winter is over;
   the winter rains are over, gone!
12 Spring flowers are in blossom all over.
   The whole world's a choir-and singing!
   Spring warblers are filling the forest
   with sweet arpeggios.
13 Lilacs are exuberantly purple and perfumed,
   and cherry trees fragrant with blossoms.
   Oh, get up, dear friend,
   my fair and beautiful lover-come to me!
14 Come, my shy and modest dove-leave your seclusion, come out in the
   open.
   Let me see your face,
   let me hear your voice.
   For your voice is soothing
   and your face is ravishing.

The Woman

15 Then you must protect me from the foxes,
   foxes on the prowl,
   Foxes who would like nothing better
   than to get into our flowering garden.
16 My lover is mine, and I am his.
   Nightly he strolls in our garden,
   Delighting in the flowers
17 until dawn breathes its light and night slips away.
   Turn to me, dear lover.
   Come like a gazelle.
   Leap like a wild stag
   on delectable mountains!

Now, isn't that just beautiful. It gets even better as the story develops. From God's perspective dating, courtship and love-making should always be fun and full of creativity and emotion.

In a busy life, plan days or nights together. Block everything else out of your diary for that day or night and say, "That time is for my wife". Then take a drive into the country and/or have an evening in, to watch a movie and share cheese and wine together. Keep the telephone switched off and if the doorbell rings - unless it's an emergency - explain politely that you are enjoying a much needed evening alone with your spouse!

Do something spontaneous occasionally, like book a few days away at a hotel, get tickets for a show or a dream holiday. Remember this is my princess I am talking about so I will lavish my love upon her. She is worth it.

When she does upset, hurt or offend me, which she will because she's human and a woman with feelings and emotions, I try to forgive her quickly and determine to do an act of kindness to bless her. I have found that that's the best way to prevent anger and bitterness setting in, though it's often far from easy to do, and my well meaning intention is not always reciprocated immediately, in the way that I would like. In the long run, however, if I behave in that way, then my wife will appreciate it and grow in respect for me.

When I can, I go with Sylvia to do the weekly shopping. I sometimes wonder why I'm there, because I don't actually do anything other than push the trolley! I did make that point to Sylvia once, stating that I may as well stay at home, because I don't actually do anything. Her reply was that she just liked me being with her. That was good enough for me; the time to be concerned is when she says she doesn't want me around!

One of the advantages of me being blind is that over the years, Sylvia has read a lot of books to me, and in that way we have shared a lot more together than most couples would. Many married people do their own thing, reading their own books. A book takes you into another world, and when Sylvia reads a book to me, we share that world together and are able to discuss it. It brings us together. Nowadays I suggest to couples that they should try this, and where they are both sighted and enjoy reading, they could read a chapter to each other. They could just find it fun.

Obviously I have related everything in this section from a man's perspective. But it applies equally to men or women. In essence, whilst fun can be spontaneous, quite often, especially in marriage, it does require some hard work, planning, imagination and a little will-power. If we apply ourselves to do some of these things, then the rewards can be tremendous.

Have a passionate affair with your spouse and keep that going, year after year. Keep on rekindling loves fiery passions. This little acrostic based on the word 'Affair' will show you the ingredients necessary, to any ongoing passionate relationship.

A	**Appreciation**
F	**Fun**
F	**Forgiveness**
A	**Affection**
I	**Intimacy**
R	**Romance**

Go for it guys! As the old soldiers used to sing, "Keep the home fires burning…"

Fear, Fun and Faith
SECTION THREE - FAITH

The dictionary tells me that faith means assurance, confidence, conviction, reliance and trust. It certainly embodies all of those things and much more besides. I have come to regard 'faith' as one of my most favourite words, vying for supremacy alongside such greats as 'love' and 'forgiveness'. There are many kinds of faith, of course. Every time we walk into a room and sit on a chair, we exercise faith in that particular piece of furniture to take our weight don't we? That is unless you are in the habit of testing out the chair beforehand, of course. I have never met anyone who does that. We put our faith in people very often, and then get extremely hurt or disappointed, when they fail to live up to our expectations. We put our faith in machines to do the things they were made to do and so we could go on. The faith I want to tell you about, however, is the faith that totally transformed my life and turned me from being a person who was full of fear and timidity to one who is now able to live a life free from fear, and over many years now, has been able to undertake exploits of faith.

The Great Exchange

It was the beginning of May 1968. I was in the audio typing classroom at Pembridge Place along with three other students, Ian, Barbara and Chris. We were just building up to our RSA Audio Typing (Elementary and Intermediate Level) exams. Towards the end of the lesson our teacher, Mrs Craig, said, "I think you all know that my husband and I attend church each week and we were wondering if you would like to come along with us some time?"

There was an embarrassed silence for a moment or two. Mrs Craig broke the silence by saying, "You're a Christian, aren't you John?"

I felt awkward at this question being directed at me, and muttered back hesitantly, "Yes, I think I am".

"You don't sound too sure about it" came our teacher's reply, "maybe we can talk about it sometime".

Later on that evening, as I lay on my bed after tea, Mrs Craig's question was still bothering me. Was I a Christian, or not and did it really matter? My thoughts were interrupted as Graham, one of the three lads I shared a room with, came in to talk about cricket, before I set off back to the classroom because we always had work set for us in the evening by our diligent, hardworking teacher. I was not prepared however for the long night that lay ahead as I tossed and turned in my bed, bombarded by questions in my mind, all triggered off by Mrs Craig's question as to whether I was a Christian or not.

I know that my turning back and forth on my squeaky mattress disturbed my roommates, but I couldn't help it! I was going through mental and emotional turmoil. One question after another kept rising up and assailing my mind. Thoughts like, am I a Christian?, Does it really matter? Is there a Heaven and is there a Hell? Where will I go when I die? I was in turmoil that night. Over the next few days I continued to think about those questions quite a lot, but never coming up with any suitable answers.

Then came the evening of 29th May. A crowd of us gathered in the lounge at Pembridge. It was the European Cup Final at Wembley Stadium, between Manchester United - featuring all the greats: Best, Charlton, Law - and Portuguese champions Benfica, whose side included the great Eusebio. The occasion was being televised live. It went on to indeed be a great final, which Manchester United won in impressive style, but it was actually during half-time that led to a watershed moment in my life.

Most of the lads nipped off to the kitchen for refreshments, but I stayed behind to listen to the interval summary. That night our teacher Mrs Craig, was on staff duty and she just happened to wonder into the lounge during half-time. She drew alongside me and said quietly,

"Did you think any more about my question, John?"

Knowing full well what she meant, I asked, "Which question was that?"

"The one about whether or not you are a Christian" Mrs Craig ventured.

It was then that I told Mrs Craig about my troubled night, on the evening that she had asked the question. I explained that I had always thought I was a Christian, regularly saying the Lord's Prayer before going to sleep at night. She concluded by saying that she felt that God was speaking to me and that we should talk further, at another time. Thankfully, she was sensitive and left the room in good time for what turned out to be a very exciting conclusion to the big match. But I often wonder if things would have turned out differently, if the question hadn't been raised again.

Over the course of the next few weeks I did think about religion a lot, turning all kinds of questions around in my mind. Mrs Craig did talk briefly with me on one further occasion, but she felt that it would really benefit me if I could meet with a couple of friends of hers, who had previously been at Pembridge and were now attending Westminster Chapel.

The mystery couple were Tony and Margaret Abbot, and as it turned out they rang and invited me to join them for tea at their flat in Acton. I agreed and duly made my way there, by tube. It turned out to be a very pleasant, introductory type of an evening where religion was just one of many topics we covered in conversation.

Both Tony, a softly spoken, rugby loving Welshman and Margaret, a cheerful Irish lass, were registered blind. Tony, an architect by profession, had been blinded as the result of a motorcycle accident, whereas Margaret had lost her sight due to the effects of diabetes. Whilst I very much enjoyed my night with my new friends, there was nevertheless something about them that made me a little bit nervous.

I was to meet them again on a few occasions briefly, over the course of the next few months, but it was into September of that year before I was to spend a life-changing weekend with them. By that time I had finished my typing course at Pembridge, having gained distinctions in my audio typing exams (thank you for being so strict Mrs Craig!) and was in the process of applying for the previously mentioned job at the Ministry of Overseas Development, in Clerkenwell. Tony had rung my parents home in Birmingham, and issued an invitation for me to go and spend a weekend with them in Acton, in west London.

Tony and Margaret were waiting at Victoria Coach Station to meet me, and in no time at all, we were back at their little ground floor flat in Acton. It was about 9.30 on a Friday evening, and we enjoyed a pleasant buffet supper together, with the obligatory, refreshing cup of tea. After some general conversation and a bit more of a getting-to-know-you session, we retired to bed, ready for the more important matters that were to follow on Saturday and Sunday.

Next morning after breakfast, Margaret went off shopping leaving Tony and me to chat. Having said that, it was mainly Tony who did the talking explaining how it was that he had become involved with Christianity. I have to say that I cannot remember anything of what he talked about even though it was interesting at the time. Margaret returned from the shops and once she had put her stuff away, she came in and joined with the conversation. Tony filled his wife in with what we had been talking about, and then it was her turn to explain to me how she had become a Christian and of the difference it had made to her life.

In turn, I explained that I had been christened as a baby and I was rather of the opinion that that 'made me' a Christian. Tony pointed out that you wouldn't find that in the Bible. He told me that Jesus had said to one very devout religious man called Nicodemus, "You must be born again", when he had been asked the question, "What must I do to have eternal life?"

We discussed matters well into the afternoon and early evening. Only pausing at around 5 o'clock to listen to Sports Report on BBC radio, so that we could catch up on all of the football results. As we sat down for our evening meal, a very tasty mixed grill incidentally, there was a very unusual record playing in the background. I quickly recognised the voice; Cliff Richard, 'mainstream' at the time for his music and films. Remember my earlier comments about *The Young Ones*, which was followed by *Summer Holiday*? On this record, however, Cliff was singing traditional hymns such as *What A Friend We Have In Jesus* and *When I Survey The Wondrous Cross* along with Gospel favourites such as *It's No Secret What God Can Do* and *Take My Hand Precious Lord*. It was certainly very nice to listen to, and Margaret explained that it was Cliff's first Gospel album as he had only become a Christian about a year before.

Before going off to bed that night my charming hosts asked if I would like to go to church with them the following morning, or evening. I said I would give it some thought, but that I would probably sit it out. I think I slept well that night, despite all the things going round my brain; I was probably exhausted with it all.

Next morning, following a breakfast of cereals, boiled egg and toast, Tony and Margaret got themselves ready for church, and I kept to my word and stayed at home. I was left with a wide choice of music to play whilst they were away, along with my ever present pocket radio. In that quiet couple of hours, I had plenty of time to reflect and wondered why it was that I had been so uptight about going to church. "I may have found some answers" I mused to myself, and I considered whether I should go with Tony and Margaret to the 6.30 evening service - that would really thrill them, I thought.

By the time they arrived home, the roast lamb smelt delicious in the oven. That was a special treat for me, as Margaret had asked me what my favourite roast dinner was! I remember the whole dinner was lovely; I'd realised, by this time, that Margaret's lack of sight did not impair her ability in the kitchen in the slightest way for she was an excellent cook. Tony told me about the morning service and in turn I said that I'd enjoyed playing some of their records, particularly Cliff's Gospel album, *Good News*. I then broke the news that they were eagerly awaiting by saying that I would go to church with them, on the night. They tried hard to contain their excitement, but I know they were delighted!

It seemed no time at all, before we were on the tube heading up to Westminster Chapel. I was extremely nervous as we approached the church. We stepped inside and I remember being surprised at how big the building seemed and how many people were attending. It also sounded from the voices that there were a lot of younger people there, which again was a bit of a shock to me, because I was under the impression that it was mainly old people who went to church. I've heard it said that you never get a second chance to make a first impression, and in this case my impression was of a warm, friendly group of people of all ages and it didn't feel religious in the way that I had expected.

We found our way to a pew, shook hands with a few people and then it was time for the start of the service. I cannot remember what we sang, but I do remember that it was wholehearted and pretty uplifting. Surprisingly, however, I do remember the sermon. That was the part I thought I would fall asleep at, but in truth it was very interesting and challenging, very well delivered by the preacher. He spoke from the book of Ruth, in the Old Testament, a book which I didn't know existed before then. It's a short book, but a beautiful love story between Ruth and a man called Boaz. I've always been a sucker for a good love story and this one had me well and truly hooked. The preacher spoke a lot about God's love and drew examples from the life of Boaz. He also introduced the subject of sin and every time he mentioned that word, although I felt uncomfortable, I thought he was talking about other people in the congregation. Perhaps there were some real sinners present, like bank robbers. I certainly didn't regard myself as a sinner. In fact, I was in the process of justifying myself by thinking of all the kind acts I had done or would do, if the circumstances were right, when the preacher metaphorically hit me right between the eyes. He quoted a verse from the Bible saying, "All your good deeds are like filthy rags to a holy God". I immediately felt incensed, thinking, "What a cheek! Who does he think he is, to talk about people like that?"

At the end of the service I felt I still had many unresolved questions. I knew that Tony and Margaret wanted to stay behind for an hour or so for coffee and a chat, but part of me wanted to make a quick getaway. While I was still making up my mind, however, I was introduced to a young man called Mark, who helped lead a young people's Bible Study and Fellowship group at the church, called Antioch. I later discovered, that that is the name of the place where, according to the Bible, people were first called Christians.

Mark shook my hand firmly and asked how I had found the service. I said I'd enjoyed it very much and that there were lots of questions still buzzing around in my head. "Such as what?" he enquired.

I thought for a moment and said "Can you prove to me that Jesus was actually raised from the dead and that he is alive today?"

Mark then gave me what was one of the most disappointing answers of all Time, followed quickly by a pearl of wisdom. He said, "I cannot prove it, nor can anyone else, but then neither can I prove to you that I love my wife. If, however, you were to come and live in our house for a month, I would hope that you would then come to the conclusion that I do love my wife. In other words you would have experienced the love that is present in our home. In the same way, if by faith you believe that Jesus died for your sins upon the Cross and you then invite him to come and live in your heart as your Lord and Saviour, in about a month's time you will know that he is alive, because you will have experienced him and felt him moving in your life".

What a brilliant answer that was. It seemed to dispel the vast majority of my questions. I was still struggling however with the questions of me being a sinner and why did Jesus have to die? By now, we were in a side room with what sounded like forty people and a friend of Tony's had already brought me a cup of coffee and a biscuit. I sat there quietly, by myself, for several minutes and in that time it was almost as if I had pulled a one-arm bandit, and the lemons came down one by one and lined themselves up and things seemed to fall into place as far as my questions about eternity were concerned. Almost instantly, I knew that I was a sinner and that Jesus had come from heaven to pay the price for my sins in his own body upon the Cross. Because he is God, he rose from the dead and after forty days on Earth during which he appeared to many groups of people, he ascended into heaven from where he now has all rule and authority. In that sovereign moment, I received Jesus as my Lord and Saviour.

As I came to the end of my cup of coffee, I was heard to say "I've got it!"

The person sitting next to me said "Did you say something?"

"Oh yes" I replied, "I've seen it, I believe in Jesus".

In no time at all I was surrounded by Tony and Margaret, together with Mark and several other people, hugging me and shaking hands, reassuring me that this would be the greatest decision I could ever make. In fact, just to make sure I was truly as they say "Born Again", Mark insisted on saying a little prayer with me that I repeated line by line after him, which went along these lines:

"Dear God, I want to thank you for loving me so much that you allowed your only son Jesus Christ to come and die for me. Thank you that my sins are forgiven. I now receive Jesus as my Lord and Saviour. I thank you that I am now forgiven and that I have the free gift of everlasting life. Amen."

Everybody was so happy for me, but I didn't feel any different. Obviously Tony and Margaret were overjoyed, as would Mrs. Craig be, when they told her. I left for home that weekend, with the encouragement ringing in my ears to talk to Jesus every day, find a good church and to read the Bible verses that had been brailed out for me, by Tony.

In the ensuing weeks I told many people about my "born again" experience. Almost without exception I was laughed to scorn. My mum and dad were very upset, because they had taken the decision to have me christened as a baby and now as an adult it seemed as if I was pouring cold water (sorry!) on that practice. I did feel inwardly that something wonderful had happened to me at Westminster Chapel; but bombarded with all this negativity and ridicule, caused me to have many doubts, leading up to that point on the London to Birmingham coach, when I cried out to God for a girlfriend and he answered me spectacularly.

This was it then, the great exchange had taken place. I had swapped all of my fears for the faith that God gives. I had begun my walk of faith, but little did I realise what a rollercoaster of a ride it would prove to be.

I've discovered that faith is like a muscle (not a cockle) and the more you exercise it, the more it grows and the stronger it gets. At the time of writing I've now had nearly forty years of learning to live and walk by faith so I would hope to have at the very least, a few helpful things to pass on. I trust you will stay with me for the journey.

In the beginning

The term "born again", when it comes to describing a new Christian, is most apt because, as I discovered, you are starting a brand new life. You are like a newly-born baby, in that you don't quite know where to start when it comes to prayer, reading the Bible and finding the right church. I had my few Bible verses brailed out, that were given to me by Tony and I read them over and over again. That was probably very good for me, because it ensured I remembered the truths they contained and also that I didn't get 'spiritual indigestion' from trying to take in too much. These are the Bible verses I was given:

> "For God so loved the world that he gave his only begotten Son so that whoever believes in him will not perish but have everlasting life" (John 3:16)

> "If we confess our sins God is faithful and just to forgive us our sins and to cleanse us from all unrighteousness." (1 John 1:9)

> "He who has the Son of God has life and he who does not have the Son does not have life." (1 John 5:)

> "I write these things in order that you may know that you have eternal life." (1 John 5:13)

> "I can do all things through Christ who gives me strength." (Philippians 4:13)

I now know that God's word, The Bible, is likened to milk for a new born baby. It gives and sustains life.

Prayer was another matter. I had learned the Lord's prayer at school but apart from that I did not know what or how to pray. However, having been encouraged by the prayer on the coach ("Oh Lord, please bless me with a girlfriend") I deduced that God must like that kind of heartfelt prayer.

After Sylvia and I were married, we used to pray silently. For instance when we got into bed at night, we would turn our backs on each other, pray our silent prayers and then as a sign that we had finished praying we would turn back to face each other. It was a couple of years before we developed the confidence to be able to pray out loud, firstly in front of each other and then in the company of others.

Finding the right church posed quite a challenge in itself. Totally naïve in such matters, we knew we were born Church of England, so we quite logically started to attend the local church where we were to be married. This was at St. Margaret's, located at Somerset Road in the Erdington area of Birmingham. The Vicar there, Reverend Power, was very friendly and as indicated earlier, an Aston Villa supporter too, so that counted in his favour! However, nice though the Vicar was, I have to say the services themselves were disappointing to me. I was looking for something of the atmosphere I'd felt at Westminster Chapel, a few months earlier. But St. Margaret's, with its congregation of about twenty, mainly elderly people, it was singularly lacking in atmosphere. The singing was a bit of a dirge and the ten-minute sermon did nothing to set the pulses racing.

After a few weeks, we decided to give up on St. Margaret's and look elsewhere. But where?

I then had a brainwave. I said to Sylvia, "Maybe the biggest church is the best". At that stage I had no idea of the other Christian denominational churches, such as the Methodist, Baptist, United Reformed, Pentecostal churches and so the good old C. of E. was our only option. Like any good Brummie kid, I knew of St. Martin's in the Bull Ring and so decided to go there.

Sylvia, at this stage, had not had a conversion experience like me, but it wasn't far off. We started to attend the 11 o'clock morning service and also the evening one, at 6.30pm. Both services were very well attended, with over five hundred people at each service. The great organ sounded majestic, as it pumped out the hymn tunes and I was surprised just how many hymns I knew from schooldays. It was really good to stand beside my girlfriend and hear her singing heartily. Sylvia has a good, tuneful voice and so I know where our kids get it from! The Rector at St. Martin's was Canon Bryan Green, a well known and sometimes controversial speaker throughout the '50s and '60s. When he came into the pulpit, he would always begin with the same prayer: "Lord, uphold me that I may uplift thee". Canon Green was always interesting and challenging to listen to, but never more so than one night after he had returned from preaching in the United States.

On arriving at St. Martin's that Sunday evening in January 1970, there were actually song sheets in the pews, along with the traditional hymn books. Sylvia read down the song sheet to find such gems as *Were You There When They Crucified My Lord, Go Tell It On The Mountain* and *Give Me Oil In My Lamp.* Definitely not the usual type of songs we would sing at St. Martins. From the moment Bryan Green stood in the pulpit that night, you could tell he was fired up. At one point he got us to sing *Amazing Grace* and part way through, he stopped the congregation and said, "If you don't sing it with more conviction and fervour, you may as well go home". Whether anybody did, I don't know - but I loved it. I still do, whenever a preacher brings his congregation up with a jolt and lifts them out of their comfort zone; somehow it brings a fresh touch of reality to what is going on. On this occasion Bryan Green certainly did and we proceeded to sing *Amazing Grace* with the desired passion, instead of going through the religious motions. That night the Rector was to introduce a new hymn that was to become one of my favourites. He'd heard it on his American trip, and brought it back for us to enjoy and in fact his sermon that night was based upon it. The hymn is *I'm Not Ashamed to Own My Lord* and has the rousing chorus, "At the Cross/at the Cross/where I first saw the light and the burden of my heart rolled away/It was there by faith I received my sight and now I am happy all the day". These are fantastic words; the truth behind them is awesome.

Bryan Green had another surprise in store that night. At the end of his preaching he made a Billy Graham-style appeal, inviting people to the front who wanted to commit their lives to Jesus. At the time, we'd been attending that Church for a good eight or nine months, and nothing like that had ever happened before – surprising what a trip to America can do for a weary Vicar! As the congregation sang *When I Survey the Wondrous Cross*, Bryan Green continued to invite people to go forward and quietly Sylvia said to me, "I'm going forward" and in a flash she was gone. As we sang the last two lines of the hymn, "Love so amazing, so divine/demands my soul, my life, my all" the tears streamed down my face because I knew that Sylvia was taking the most important step that any human being can take this side of the grave.

When Sylvia returned to join me in the pew, she told me that she had received prayer from one of the clergy, Chris Mayfield. Years later, Chris became a Bishop.

So now we were both, 'born again', and it sure felt good to be together in Spirit as well as body and soul.

New Job, New Friends, New Life!

In March 1969 I began work as an audio typist for the Inland Revenue. I was based at King Edward House in New Street, in Birmingham's busy city centre. It was an area I knew well, the third floor office being situated just a few metres away from the Odeon where I'd gone to see *The Young Ones* and queued for several James Bond movies, a few years earlier. I worked in that office as part of a team of four typists for nearly five years and had a wonderful time. Two of my favourite characters, out of many in fact, because I find all people fascinating to some degree, were Gillian and Kay. Gillian was a kind soul, who performed in a local operatic society and would often tackle her frustrations when it came to listening to inaudible dictation, by bursting into song. I found it very amusing. Kay on the other hand, was a different kettle of fish. She was in her late twenties, Welsh and with a fiery temper. Her way of dealing with the poor dictation was to slowly simmer until she got to boiling point, and then she would ring the Tax Inspector and demand they came and listened for themselves. I'll never forget the day she summoned Bill Thomson to the typing room. Bill, or Mr. Thomson as it was in those more austere days, was an amiable man with a very broad Scottish accent. He did himself, and the typists, no favours by mumbling into his microphone, thus making him very difficult to listen to. He dutifully arrived in the typing office, cheerful as usual, to listen to his own 'dulcet' tones. He listened several times to the incoherent text and having not been able to make sense of it himself, then made up something that Kay could type in. As Mr. Thomson walked away he muttered something in jest about Welsh women, which totally enraged Kay and she pulled off one of her shoes and threw it at the startled Inspector, who just about managed to get out of the door before the flying missile thudded into the wall, narrowly missing his head. There was stunned silence in the room for a moment; which was then broken as Kay erupted into fits of laughter, her pent up frustration now fully released. Within a few moments she got up from her seat and went off to offer her apologies to Bill, who thankfully, not for the only time, took it all in good heart.

It was Kay who got me into crosswords. In those days, unlike today, we actually had a scheduled fifteen minute tea break, morning and afternoon. Kay or one of the other girls in the office would, at 9.30am ring down to the Hasty Tasty snack bar on the ground floor, just next door to King Edward House to order the toast. My job was to nip down at 9.45 to pick up and pay for the toast. When I arrived back, a couple of minutes later, the tea would be ready and the Sun newspaper opened so that we could, as a team, attempt the coffee time crossword. That was fun. I really enjoyed that.

It was whilst working in the office, that I was to meet someone who was to become one of a group of really good friends and mentors to me, as a young Christian. As I have said, in those days everything was much more formal. Rank counted for a lot, and senior people were always addressed by the title of Mr, Mrs. or Miss. One of the tax inspectors I used to work for, was a Mr. Pullinger. One morning he brought me a tape for typing and he stood by my desk for an introductory chat. He said his name was Bryan Pullinger, and we spent two or three minutes chatting about this and that, but nothing particular that I can recall, or though football probably came into the conversation somewhere along the line. After he had left the room I just happened to say to Mrs. Doig, one of the more senior typists in terms of age, "He seems like a really friendly bloke".

"Yes, he is" came Mrs Doig's reply. "But just be careful, because he's quite religious".

I didn't say anything at that point ,but a little excitement rose on the inside of me. I thought to myself, "Oh good, another one, maybe he's a Christian like me!" This was the time when I was getting a lot of flack from my family and friends for being a Christian and I was becoming desperate for some encouragement.

At lunchtime, when the part time staff had gone home and the other two typists had gone for their break, I decided to give this Mr. Pullinger a ring on his office extension.

"Hello, Mr. Pullinger" I said nervously, "..this is John here, from the typing office". I think he thought I was calling about his tape.

"Hello, John" he said in a warm, friendly manner, "...what can I do for you?"

"One of the ladies here, says you're religious, so does that mean you're a Christian?" .

He said that he was and I quickly told him a little of my story from Westminster Chapel; but since coming back to Birmingham, I had worried my family and received criticism from friends. With that, Mr. Pullinger spoke some reassuring words and said that on the following day he was going to a lunchtime service at St. Philip's Cathedral, in Birmingham. It was a special service for half-an-hour, geared towards business people working in the city centre. Mr. Pullinger offered to meet at my office at 1 o'clock and get me back afterwards, for 2 o'clock. I readily agreed and there began a longstanding friendship. Bryan (no longer Mr. Pullinger to me!) spent a lot of time over the next few years helping me to understand more about the Christian life I had committed myself to. It was through Bryan, and the weekly lunchtime thirty minute service at St. Philip's Cathedral, that I met a group of mature Christian men who were to have a profound effect upon my life. They really helped me to establish some firm foundations of faith in my heart. Let me tell you about three such men in particular.

Reverend David MacInnes was, at the time, on the staff of the Cathedral (Chief Diocesan Missioner, I think) and he undertook most of the Tuesday talks at the Cathedral. After a hymn and a prayer, David would teach on a theme for just over twenty minutes, as part of a four or five week series. I found him to be a riveting speaker, with plenty of valuable spiritual insights and no end of interesting and amusing anecdotes. After a final prayer, there was time for a cup of tea and a decent sandwich at a very reasonable price. During this period, I was able to chat with a few people, before heading back with Bryan to the office. I grew to deeply love and appreciate the man and the ministry, that is David MacInnes.

It was through those times at the Cathedral that I subsequently met two further people who were to play a significant part in the development of my faith. John Tupper was employed at the then Midland Bank, in New Street. We had some good chats together and at his suggestion, we would meet one lunchtime a week every week for coffee and sandwiches. We would walk and talk about a variety of things. Quite often on a lovely, sunny day we would sit in the Cathedral grounds and John would read a book to me. Usually, it was a biography of a great missionary of the past and I found myself being inspired by their exploits of faith. John lived in Sutton Coldfield, with his wife Thelma and their three children. Once a month they held a prayer meeting in their home, in support of an organisation called Operation Mobilisation. Sylvia and I started to attend these prayer meetings at John's invitation. We'd go to their house, straight from work and join them for their evening meal. The prayer meetings would start at 7.30pm. We learned a lot about Operation Mobilisation and its work around the world to spread the Christian message. We were particularly inspired by George Verwer, the founder of the movement and of the story of the two ships they had purchased, to carry Bibles and other Christian literature to remote parts of the globe. One of the ships was called Logos. When it was anchored in London, Sylvia and I travelled by coach with John to have a look around the ship and to meet some of its crew, who were there as missionaries from various parts of the world.

Later, at the prayer meetings, Sylvia and I became a little uncomfortable with everybody else praying out loud, audibly. We just prayed quietly under our breath. We both wanted to pray out loud, but couldn't summon up the courage. We chatted with John and Thelma about our concerns and they encouraged us just to pray out something very simple, like "Lord Jesus, thank you for coming into my heart and for bringing me here tonight". They stressed that we didn't have to pray long prayers. It was a really hard thing, to pray out in public like that for the first time and it probably took us about seven or eight weeks to be able to do so. Once we had, however, it was such a relief and we found that we were more able to contribute to the prayer meetings after that.

The other person to became a big influence on my life, was a real gentleman by the name of Maxwell Doig (no relation to the typist by the name of Mrs. Doig mentioned earlier). Maxwell was a Senior Tax Inspector. He was the District Inspector of Birmingham 10 Tax District, in City Centre House, Birmingham. On Wednesday lunchtimes he would hold a Bible study group in his office, from 1.10 until 1.55pm. Around a dozen people would gather each week, with different faces taking it in turns to lead. Again, this proved to be another area of growth for me and gave me an opportunity to meet other Christian colleagues from the Inland Revenue who were practising Christians. It was here that I first got to know a lovely lady by the name of Celia, who became a good friend to Sylvia and I, especially when the children were little. She even came on holiday with us once, spending a week in a caravan with us at the Caple Bible Week in Surrey, during the very hot summer of 1976.

Going back to Bryan for a moment, his wife Jenny was the same lady who'd suggested to Sylvia that she pray about an automatic washing machine. Bryan later gave up work as a Tax Inspector to work full time as a Pastor, with Solihull Christian Fellowship.

As a young Christian, recently married, these were heady days and over the years there's not been much of a let up. Ronan Keating's song Life Is A Rollercoaster hadn't been written then, but it aptly sums up my life then and now. Certainly not boring!

During the early '70s there were a number of life-changing events for me, Including, of course, the arrival of our children. On a spiritual level, however, there were two that stand out. I will take them in the order in which they happened, though to me they are of equal significance.

I was admitted to Birmingham General Hospital for an exploratory operation on my left ear. My hearing on that side has always been seriously impaired, and it was hoped that a quick look around would reveal the reason, but unfortunately at that time it didn't. I was, however, lying in bed following the operation, listening to the hospital radio. My one good ear pricked up when I heard the announcer say that he would shortly be talking with an eccentric hippie American preacher, who would be carrying a twelve foot cross into Birmingham's Bull Ring for an evangelistic rally. As I recall the interview took place over the telephone line, but it was still absolutely riveting. The preacher in question was someone called Arthur Blessitt, and he told his story of how he had reached thousands of hippies, prostitutes and drug addicts in the United States with his Jesus message. He had also bought a nightclub on Sunset Strip and turned it into a Christian nightclub, without alcohol and drugs. It was a place where people could meet for a good time, without all that other baggage. Arthur told compellingly of how Jesus had spoken to him to carry this wooden cross around the world, and as he walked the roads he would meet people and tell them about Jesus. He would then very often lead people in a prayer, enabling them to give their lives to Christ.

Arthur spoke a lot about fun and became renowned for his extravagant use of 'Jesus Stickers'. They were various sizes but always orange and round, with messages on them such as 'Smile, God Loves You' and 'New Life In Jesus'. He told of the innovative (and sometimes corny) ways in which he used the stickers; one being that he would go into a toilet cubicle and unwind the toilet roll, putting his stickers on to the perforations, so that when anyone went to the toilet they would get the message "Smile Jesus Loves You". He would also go into bookshops and while browsing he would place gospel tracts inside the books and magazines. Arthur oozed love for Jesus and everywhere he went he just had to be a witness to that fact.

The interview concluded with the information that Arthur would be arriving at Birmingham's Bull Ring the following night along with his wife, four young children and of course, the cross. There would also be a Gospel band playing by the name of...11.59.

When Sylvia came to the hospital to visit me later in the day, I was full of it. I think she wondered what I had been on. In fact one of Arthur's quips on the interview was that the only pill he takes is the 'Gospill'. He also said that when people call him a nut he just says, "Yes, I am a nut, but at least I'm screwed to the right bolt".

But this was now the middle of Sylvia's visit. "I've got to get out, by tomorrow", I said, "I want to go to the Bull Ring to hear this amazing preacher".

It was November. It was very cold. The last thing you want to be doing after an ear operation, is standing around late at night. Sylvia knew I was determined. So she went out the following morning and bought me a Parka - even though the original Mod movement was over, they were all the fashion then. I managed to get myself discharged from hospital and duly took my place alongside Sylvia in the Bull Ring. Several thousand people were present. The atmosphere was joyful and there was an excitement in the air, as we gathered around this large stage which had been erected. At around 7.30pm the band came on stage and sang about half-a-dozen songs They were really good, getting us clapping and singing along. They were to make quite an impression on me, as a year or two later I invited them to do a gig for me at a coffee bar outreach I was running with Sylvia. I was full of enthusiasm, and at first I didn't give any thought at all as to how much they would cost, or where they would sleep for the night!

Soon, the time came for Arthur to step up to the microphone and from the very first syllable he uttered, I was hooked. I loved this guy and everything about him. He was like a modern day St. Paul. He was radical. Arthur introduced his wife and children, saying that they nearly always travelled with him and that the kids got their education along the way. Arthur's message about Jesus was plain and simple, but so full of fun. I was smitten with Arthur's approach to the Christian faith. Through this long-haired American preacher, I fell in love with Jesus in a whole new way.

Arthur stayed in the news quite a lot over the next couple of years, but I eventually lost track of him. Recently, however, thanks to the Internet I have made fresh contact with him. Via email I have reminded Arthur of that night in the Bull Ring and he remembers it well. Arthur has now walked with his cross to every nation on the planet and his achievements are now recorded in the Guinness Book of Records, as the human being who has done the longest walk in history. Arthurblessitt.com is one of my favourite websites, which I visit at least once a week. Truly one of the greatest men of faith in ours, or any other generation.

Only a few months later, I was to have another truly amazing experience, which was to stay with me to this very day. I know it may sound strange to some, but I have to tell it like it is and that is that I had an encounter with God the Holy Spirit. The Bible calls it 'Baptism in the Holy Spirit' and speaking in tongues – in other words, a language that is not your own. You can read about this in the Bible, in Acts of the Apostles, Chapter 2. Summarising what it says, in my own words it is like this:

Following his resurrection Jesus had spoken to his followers that he was going to go away again into Heaven, but that he would send his Holy spirit into the world to be their strength and comforter. Although this concept was hard to understand for the disciples, nevertheless Jesus instructed them to go into Jerusalem and wait there until the Holy Spirit came and filled them with power. Jesus accordingly went back to Heaven (riding on a cloud) and his followers gathered in an upper room in Jerusalem just as Jesus had directed them to. Eventually, on the day of Pentecost (what we used to call Whit Sunday) the Holy Spirit came like tongues of fire and filled the place where the people were gathered. Immediately they were filled with power and given the ability instantly to speak other languages. From that moment on these people were transformed from being frightened individuals, grieving the loss of their charismatic leader, into bold men and women who went everywhere speaking about Jesus and his resurrection. On that day the Christian Church was born with around 3,000 people surrendering their lives to Jesus Christ.

Getting back to my experience then, Sylvia and I had gone on a week's holiday to Sidmouth in north Devon; a beautiful place with some gorgeous scenery. This was what we used to call a Christian 'house party holiday', which I know sounds a little boring side nowadays. It was far from that, however. The idea was that you met with other Christians from around the country and enjoy what we call 'fellowship'. We contented ourselves with some delicious food, good chats and in the mornings, we would have a short time of singing to God and then have a 'Thought for the Day', given by a guest speaker. In the evenings, we would have another longer meeting when another guest speaker would teach from the

Bible. It was good fun; being totally different to any holiday we had experienced before.

One of the speakers turned out to be from Birmingham. He was also blind. The man's name – Peter Jackson. We were destined to become very good friends, though he frightened me at first because he was so sold-out to God and very challenging. Peter had (and still has) a wonderful sense of humour. Apart from regularly telling jokes he's also very quick-witted and a master of the one-liner. Typically, Peter would say "I love throwing people in at the deep end, because it makes them dependable". On numerous occasions later, I was to discover that to be true, personally. Peter has made a large number of piano recordings in a variety of styles; firstly for Word Records and now on a smaller, independent label.

During that week I actually spoke in public for the first time. One of the Evenings, I stood up very nervously to explain to people how I had come to know Jesus. At the end of a great week, Sylvia and I travelled back to Birmingham on the train and guess who was with us? That's right, Peter Jackson. For part of the journey, Peter was busy brailling letters on his Perkins Brailler, but during one of our conversations when I was telling Peter about Arthur Blessitt in the Bull Ring, and how I would love to have that much confidence, he said to me "What you need is the Baptism of the Holy Spirit". Peter didn't say any more however and I didn't follow it up, because I hadn't a clue what he was talking about!

A few weeks elapsed before Peter called me on the phone. "Hi John", Peter exclaimed in his usual, cheerful manner. "I'm preaching at a church near you next Sunday. Why don't you and Sylvie come along?"

"Where is it?" I asked with genuine interest.

"Kingstanding Elim Pentecostal Church, Warren Road".

"That's where my brother and sister go," I mentioned, "...they say it's really lively."

So we arranged to meet Peter there. But not before he had put me under a little pressure by asking me to sit at the front with him, for support. I agreed, knowing that Sylvia would sit in the congregation with my brother Paul and sister Susan. It was also a good opportunity to meet Margaret, Peter's wife, who brought him by car from their home in Acocks Green.

We met Peter and Margaret as arranged in the foyer of the church, a pleasant, modern building accommodating about three hundred people. Folk were very friendly as they greeted us with warm handshakes and we entered the auditorium to some very relaxing music, played softly in the background. Peter and I were shown to the Pastor's office at the back of the church, where we had a short chat and prayed together. I was introduced to Pastor Morrison, a warmhearted Ulsterman, about sixty years of age, with a rasping Belfast accent. He said he'd lead the service and then hand over to Peter at an appropriate point. Out in the main church, could now be heard the joyful sound of Gospel choruses being sung with great vigour.

We duly took our seats and about twenty minutes in, Peter dropped his bombshell.

"It would be really good if you could, just in a few sentences, tell the people how you came to know Jesus and just what he means to you".

My heart seemed to sink into my boots. I began to sweat profusely. I protested to Peter that I felt very nervous, but he just said that that was natural and that I would be fine. Peter was then taken to sit at the piano and he began to speak.

"Good evening, everyone! It's great to be back with you at Warren Road.

Before I play a piece for you, I want to introduce you to a young man by the name of John Flanner, who is going to share with you about how he became a Christian." I stood up and Pastor Morrison came across and led me to the microphone. I was incredibly nervous, but felt I did okay in talking for two minutes, before so many people. At least, they gave me a clap when I had finished. It was then back to Peter, who came out with that priceless line about throwing people in at the deep end.

Later, Pastor Morrison brought the service to a close, but not before he had given a plug for the church prayer meeting to be held the following Thursday. He said that it would be a special meeting, to pray for people to be 'Baptised in the Holy Spirit'. Peter nudged me and said, "Be there, that's for you – remember our chat on the train".

It was to be a fateful night. Sylvia and I walked to the church with my brother and sister and a few of their young friends. In fact that was quite a characteristic of the church at that time, with so many young people attending.

Arriving, we were told that the prayer meeting was in the room at the back of the church and once there, we took our seats near the back. In all I suppose about forty people gathered on that night for the prayer meeting. After a couple of hymns and other songs Pastor Morrison read some verses from the Bible and then explained what 'Baptism in the Holy spirit' was all about. He told us about Jesus' disciples being very afraid after his death, fearing that they too may be crucified. Once the Holy Spirit had filled them, however, there was no fear any more and each person discovered they had been given a gift of being able to speak in other languages. Whatever, it is recorded that on that day, the 'Day of Pentecost', some three thousand people gave their lives to Jesus and many were healed of their diseases. On the day the church was born, those disciples went from strength to strength, boldly proclaiming the message, not fearing for their own lives. Many were tortured and imprisoned for their faith in Jesus, whilst others were martyred. Peter, who had previously denied knowing Jesus on three occasions, was eventually crucified upside down for refusing to deny his faith in him and the reality of the resurrection.

Pastor Morrison further explained that the same power was still available

Today, to anyone who was hungry and thirsty for it. He asked people who were timid about admitting they were followers of Jesus to come forward for prayer. Sylvia and I went forward and stood at the front along with about a dozen others. We were encouraged by Pastor Morrison to just begin to praise the Lord. I didn't know what he meant, but as I listened to others saying audibly "Praise the Lord", "Hallelujah", "I love you, Jesus" and the like, I soon got the idea. I began very quietly saying "I love you, Jesus" until one of the other church leaders came to me and gently encouraged me to be a little bolder and not so quiet. Over and over again, I began saying 'Hallelujah' until I was struggling to get the word out. It was as if my tongue had been tied up, the word just wouldn't come. Then all of a sudden, my tongue was loosed and out of my mouth came a language I had never heard before. It flowed like a river from deep within me. It was exhilarating. There was so much joy flooding my being, I felt ecstatic. I was a bit surprised, therefore, when somebody came to me and asked me to be quiet for a moment and sit down. He said into my ear, "I have asked you to do that, because this is a gift that God has given you and with all gifts, you can use it whenever you wish."

It was explained to me that this was a good gift. I had control over it and not it over me. When something evil comes into our lives, it seeks to control us, but with God he does not take away our free will.

Well, I went home that night on the proverbial cloud nine, and in all honesty, I don't think I've ever really come down since! That same Holy Spirit is still with me, and even in the darkest and most testing of times, I know that joy is still on the inside.

Sylvia didn't get 'the same' as me that night, but a few weeks later at another church, she went through a similar, if not identical experience. That's an important point to make: we're all individuals - God knows exactly the right way to meet with us. All that he requires is that we are hungry and thirsty for him.

In essence, that is the night I believe I really began to step out of fear and into faith, leaving behind the negative experiences and the hold they had over me, for all those years. The new John Flanner was about to emerge from the shadows. Did I say The Shadows?

Talking of music, which I do frequently, one artist who had quite an impact on my life, particularly in those formative years of my Christian faith is the late great Johnny Cash. Three of his works caused me to exercise my faith in most unexpected ways.

Firstly, Johnny himself financed the making of a film, *The Gospel Road* which tells the story of Jesus with Johnny himself narrating words straight from the Bible. Johnny's wife June played the part of Mary Magdalene in the movie, which contained some great songs, but sadly as far as I am aware, has never been shown on the big screen or on television in the UK. When it was first made available on video in this country, I managed to hire a copy for a month and together with a few friends we took it on the road to show it in churches, schools, a prison and even to a couple of Country & Western clubs, which were held in pubs. One of the latter venues was at The Roebuck pub in Erdington, Birmingham where the 'Silver Saddle Country & Western Club' used to meet. At the end of the film, a man came up to me to say how much he'd enjoyed it and told me that it had brought tears to his eyes. He said that it reminded him of the time when he'd given his life to Jesus, many years before, in Sunday School in Truro. This man's name was Tony Buzza; he was an avid fan of Roy Rogers and was dressed in cowboy gear including the gun safely tucked away in the holster! It was a memorable month, in which many lives were touched. At the end of it however, I ended up in hospital suffering from viral meningitis. I remember my head hurting badly and all I could hear were the words of Johnny Cash: "So come along with me and I'll take you in the footsteps of Jesus, as we travel along the gospel road....."

Secondly, I remember being challenged by the words of one of Johnny's songs, contained on an album I had just purchased. The song, if it's right to call it that (because it was more of a monologue) was I think called *Dear Mrs.* It told the story of a guy in prison, who, each morning looked out from his cell as the letters were delivered, only to be disappointed day after day and year after year, because of no letter. Every time I listened to it I felt a 'stirring' inside, as if I should do something.

I knew someone through attending the lunchtime services at St. Philip's Cathedral - Don Bissell was a senior Probation Officer in Birmingham, and so I contacted him with my thoughts and asked him if he could give me any advice. It turned out that he ran volunteer courses from his office in Birmingham, for people who wanted to get involved in prison visiting or writing to prisoners. I then attended the six one-hour meetings at Don's office and eventually was assigned a prisoner to write to, which I did until his release and integration back into the community. Unfortunately, he did make a bit of a nuisance of himself at the time, and so with having a young family I never actually kept it up, but you never know what the future may hold in this regard...

Finally, Sylvia read a book to me, entitled *The New Johnny Cash*. A biographical account of Johnny's life and particularly, how he'd rediscovered his Christian faith through the love of his wife, June Carter. I loved that book and it touched me so deeply. I wanted everyone to enjoy it. That's part of the new John Flanner by the way, I just love passing on good news stories!

On what was then BBC Radio Birmingham, was a country music show, Sounds Country, presented by the exotically-named Ken Dudeney. I was a regular listener and wrote to Ken, telling him about the book with my usual enthusiasm and recommending that he review it on his show one week. Well, to my surprise Ken rang me at home one night and suggested that it would be far better if I went into the studio to review the book myself, on the programme.

I was very excited, but still a little on the nervous side (even though I had the Holy Spirit!) as I made my way on two buses across the city, to the Pebble Mill studios. Ken met me at reception and was gob-smacked to discover that I couldn't see. I hadn't thought to mention it in my letter. I later discovered that Ken was wondering how I would read my script! I reassured him that I'd be okay and would just ad-lib. Well, my little spot was recorded and to be truthful it was a good job it was, because I made a right mess of it! I think I was so keen to talk about Jesus, that I actually forgot to review the book.

Over a coffee afterwards, I talked to Ken about my love of country gospel music, and a few weeks later he asked me if I would play six of my favourite tracks and talk about what they meant to me. He thought it would be a great, and slightly unusual show, for Easter week. This to me was like Heaven coming early. To have the opportunity to indulge myself by playing some of my favourite songs on the radio, and then talking about the spiritual significance of them, was such an incredible privilege. The programme went down well with the audience.

I played a song called *I Know* by Wanda Jackson which created a lot of interest, with people calling in to know where they could get hold of the album it appeared on. Also an elderly, housebound lady wrote in and sent a small amount of money earmarked for the young man who played the music, to give to his favourite charity. From that moment on, I had a regular monthly spot on the show, to play Country Gospel.

A few years later the station underwent some major policy changes, including changing its name to Radio WM. The specialist music programmes, such as country, folk and jazz were dropped in favour of more general and mainly, speech-based programmes. I was retained however, and given the opportunity to assist Michael Blood on his Sunday morning religious programme, then called *A Word In Advance*. I was able to go in, again on a monthly basis, to review the latest Christian record releases. I did that for about twelve years, until music was dropped almost entirely from the schedules. Michael and I got on well together, and listeners used to appreciate our little chats about this, that and the other. Basically, I would just respond to Michael's questions by telling stories of what God was doing in my life. I really love radio, on both sides of the microphone. I've never been paid for any of it. The trouble is, that I've said I love it so much I would do it for nothing and people have taken me at my word.

When eventually I get to heaven and I hear those immortal words, "Hello, I'm Johnny Cash", I'll respond by thanking him for his life and music, which God has used to open up some exciting doors for me.

Turn Your Radio On

I'm always turning my radio on. Sylvia has said that if I die before her, she intends to place radios in the coffin with me, so that I'll feel most at home! Seriously though, there's been many an occasion when I believe God has spoken to me through the radio and prompted me to take action, in some way.

One morning, whilst listening to the local news my attention was grabbed by the news of a car accident quite local to where I was living. I heard that a young lady had to be cut from her car, and was taken to Solihull Hospital where, after surgery, she had lost part of her left hand. Her name was Karen and I was immediately moved with compassion to pray for her. Birmingham Evening Mail that day, reported on the crash and actually named the road where Karen lived with her parents. I wrote a letter to Karen, letting her know that I was praying for her and that Jesus really loved her so much; then having obtained the address from the telephone directory, we posted it off to her. It was several weeks later that I heard from Karen's dad, saying how much she had appreciated the letter and what encouragement it had given her.

Not long after that, another news item grabbed my attention when I heard that a young man named Simon had broken his neck when a rugby scrum had collapsed on him, whilst playing for Solihull School. Simon was a brilliant student and was a very promising rugby player. Again, I was moved with compassion to write and on hearing that Simon had been switched to the Royal Orthopaedic Hospital in Oswestry. I felt I should go and visit him, in order to encourage and pray for him. Incredibly, in the same period, we heard that a colleague of a friend of ours had been involved in a serious accident at work and broken his back. He had been taken to the same hospital in Oswestry, as Simon. So it was, that I found myself visiting the hospital with two people to encourage and pray for. I really felt as though I was being led by God's Holy Spirit. It didn't even stop there, because a few months later a young lad near to where I live was knocked off his bicycle, into the path of an oncoming bus. Philip suffered serious head and spinal injuries leading to him being in a wheelchair. I visited Philip on a number of occasions, and met with his parents - I'm happy to say that the last I heard, Philip was married and doing very well in a successful career. It could be argued that I didn't achieve very much, but I'm happy in the knowledge that I obeyed those inner promptings and was at least able to let these people know that Jesus loves them.

My most dramatic night of radio listening was the 29th May 1985. Liverpool Football Club were in the European Cup Final, against Italian champions Juventus, at the Heysel Stadium in Brussels. I listened to the build up to the game with the fondly remembered commentary team of Peter Jones, Mike Ingham and summariser Emlyn Hughes. Suddenly a horrific picture began to unfold. Marauding Liverpool supporters had caused a wall to collapse, leading to the deaths of thirty-nine people in the mayhem which ensued. The commentators struggled to hold back the tears as they described what they were seeing, an hour or so before the match was due to begin. It eventually got under way, but with the stench of death in the air it was all a massive anti-climax and though Juventus won the game, nobody really cared. The 'beautiful game' lost many friends that night, and the United Kingdom, with its reputation for football hooliganism, made many more enemies around the world. That night I lay prostrate on the lounge carpet, shedding many tears for those who had lost their lives and for the low state that our country had now sunk to. I felt so ashamed. At that moment I felt I would never attend another football match again. I wanted to disassociate myself from the thugs who were invading our great game and destroying the reputation of our country.

In the days that followed, my heartfelt prayer was "God, what can we do?" When Sunday came, I was at church, lost in worshipping God when suddenly I felt what I can only describe as a surging from my stomach. Emotion was rising within me, and a phrase came to my mind very strongly and it was, "Let your voice be heard above that of the heathen". I knew that it related to football in some way. The cry came from deep within me to God, to let His voice be heard above all the other political and religious voices who were trotting out the same old platitudes such as "Bring back the birch" and "Lock 'em up and throw away the key". Along with many others I'm sure, I desperately wanted God to act. However, it was almost as if God turned the statement back on me and said "I live in you, by the power of my Holy Spirit, so now let your voice be heard above that of the heathen".

I decided to go for it - and go along with the old maxim that nobody can change the whole world, but each of us can change *somebody's* world. I am a devoted follower of Aston Villa. Even at my beloved Villa Park, the atmosphere had been becoming increasingly ugly, with the aggression and the hate-filled and obscene chanting. I therefore put together a little strategy to improve things and put my suggestions in a letter to the then Commercial Manager, Tony Stevens.

A few days later, Tony called me to say that he'd like to meet me at his office to discuss my ideas further. It wasn't long before I was at Villa Park and sitting in Tony's office. Tea was served in china cups as I outlined my proposals. From my perspective I wanted the club to give me permission to start up an Aston Villa Christian Supporters Association. We would meet before every home game, in a local church to pray about the atmosphere on the terraces. We would pray for peace, harmony and fun at the ground and for it to be a safe place for families to come along. We would also pray for a positive atmosphere to be present in the ground as well as for new levels of sportsmanship between the players. In addition, if our credibility was sustained we would also pray for people within the club who were going through difficult times, especially players with career-threatening injuries. Among a number of other suggestions I made, was that when the two teams come out on to the field, they should actually come out together side by side, as they had always done in the FA Cup final. Even be seen talking and joking together. In that way, the players would emerge from the tunnel to a chorus of cheers, instead of cheering for one side and booing for the other; thereby starting off proceedings with a positive atmosphere.

Would you believe it, but when the fixtures came out for the new season, Aston Villa's first home game was against Liverpool of all people. The club agreed to my request and the teams did indeed come out side by side. Now it's done like that, at all home games. I can't say for definite, but I think that that was the first time it had been done in a normal league game and now it's accepted practice, around the country.

The club and in particular, Chairman Doug Ellis were extremely supportive of our venture and the then-manager, Graham Turner was always available to chat and help out when ever he could. In fact Graham's wife, Anne would often attend our prayer meetings with her two young sons. The numbers attending those prayer meetings were not great by any means, but they were effective and powerful and in that first season Aston Villa won an award for having the most sporting and well behaved supporters.

Our venture attracted quite a bit of media interest, and it transpired that a number of other prayer groups formed around the country, to get behind their clubs too. The Aston Villa prayer group continued for about four seasons and eventually folded after I'd moved out of the area and my successor, John Gosnall (who did a wonderful job) collapsed and died very suddenly. We had to trust that, in ways we couldn't understand, all of this was ultimately in God's hands.

Next time you turn on your radio or television, listen for the heart of God and be open to what he would have you do or say. He'll probably take you out of your comfort zone, but it'll be an adventure.

Living by Faith

In the Bible, there is an account of Jesus having a meeting with a man by the name of Nicodemus, one night. Nicodemus was a very religious man, a devout Jew, but he came to Jesus enquiring about what he must do to obtain eternal life. In this conversation, Jesus says "You must be born again", something which has become an in-phrase in our generation. Jesus, however, was talking about spiritual rebirth. In the narrative (and this is something I love) Jesus says that the person who is born of the Spirit, is like the wind in that no one knows where it comes from and no one knows where it is going to. That speaks to me, of a glorious freedom and of an incredible unpredictability that should be the hallmark of every Christian. Christians, I believe, should be on the biggest high and get the greatest buzz from life. No need to take artificial stimuli such as alcohol or drugs, when you have the Son of God living on the inside of you.

So it was, that after that experience of being filled with the Holy Spirit and speaking in tongues, I set off with an expectation of God being with me and that I was on planet Earth to represent (or more accurately, represent) Jesus. I truly believe that I am God's gift to women and to men and to boys and girls, but then, if you're a Christian, so are you. Created in the image of God, full of exciting potential.

On the subject of boys and girls, we were sitting down for tea one night when a friend from church called to see us. John Place, saddened by a recent divorce had become a regular visitor to our home. He enjoyed our company (and Sylvia's cooking) and he was great with the kids.

John said, somewhat tongue in cheek, "There's a crowd of young children playing outside your house, maybe you could start a Christian club for them".

Though it was said in such a light-hearted way, it actually turned out to be God's will for our lives at that time. We'd just finished reading a book called *Take My Home* and it was all about different people who had seen their home as a gift from God and had dedicated it to God's service. We'd done that with our home already (remember that housewarming we'd had, when all that money was left lying around?), but we didn't know what we could do. Now just maybe, we had heard the voice of God through our friend.

After praying about this with a few people and giving the matter careful consideration, we decided to launch a club called 'One Way Special', Jesus being the one way to Heaven according to his own words, "I am the way, the truth and the life; no one can come to the Father except through me". We adopted a little song called *One Way Jesus Christ* as our theme tune, which was taken from an album by a local Christian band, Dave Pope & the Alethians. We set a date for it to start on Mondays, from 6-7.00pm. We'd have singing, a Bible quiz, memory verses and stories with a gospel message, either by me or by a visiting speaker. We'd also run a shop where the kids could trade in tokens, which they'd receive for attendance, or for bringing their Bibles, inviting friends, answers to questions in the quiz, good behaviour and so on. 'One Way Special' would be aimed at children between the ages of seven to eleven, and I wrote letters to all the parents explaining who we were and saying that it was basically a Christian Sunday school, but on a Monday night in our home.

We started with a dozen kids and very quickly we were averaging around thirty each week. After a few months, numbers continued to increase dramatically, week by week, so we had to move out from our house and hire a local community centre. We reached our peak one week, when we had 180 children, by which time we had built up a good team of helpers from various local churches to assist with the music, teaching, register and maintaining discipline. These were amazing, heady times and though it was tiring it was also extremely rewarding to be sowing this good seed into these young lives.

The financial cost of doing this was fairly substantial - what with the hire of the hall, materials and paying speakers. God wonderfully provided.

Sylvia and I were baptised together, by total immersion at Kingstanding Elim Church in Birmingham on Sunday 13th February 1972, along with six others.

As part of the service, all of those being baptised were required to explain to the congregation why it was they were taking that step to make their faith public, in such a way. We were all very nervous, myself included. During my testimony, I had said something to the effect that Sylvia and I loved Jesus and we were using our home in order to make Jesus known to children and teenagers. We were already providing our house every Friday evening for several of my brother's teenage friends, to come in and have supper and discuss matters of faith. At the end of the service a businessman came up to me, and said that he had never been to such a service before and that he had found it deeply moving. He also said that he was a Christian and he had just set up a Charity in which he would give money and provide materials for any work that was involved in sharing God's love with children and young people. He said that if there was anything we needed, then or in the future, then I had only to ask. A few weeks later this kind man, Bob Perry, arranged for a piano to be delivered to our house so that we could have music at our meetings and he set up an open account for me to go into a Christian bookshop in Birmingham, to purchase anything I wanted for the young people and later for the children who came to 'One Way Special'. Bob became good friends with us for many years, and though we haven't seen each other in a long time now, I know that he's living happily in Tiverton, Devon with his wife Janet.

This Divine Appointment with Bob, now set the tone for our walk with God, as we had seen Him act in providing in such an unexpected way. In books we were reading about how God provided for those who are prepared to step out on a limb and trust him, so we determined to try and live in that way ourselves.

Our home was open to children on a Monday night, teenagers on a Friday night, and we regularly saw them giving their lives to Jesus, just as we had done. They were thrilling days, but hard ones too, with a young family ourselves to contend with.

I referred to this earlier, but even though Sylvia and I were the driving force behind this work on the housing estate, God raised up a wonderful team of people to support and be there for us. I'll always be appreciative to each of them for that. On occasions, when things got too much for Sylvia and I, a number of these people were there for us with words of encouragement and arms-around-the-shoulder where necessary. On one occasion we were at our wits' end, knowing how we could pay our electric bill when one of the helpers, Christine, rang up from work to ask if we had a need. Sylvia and I were, at that very moment discussing (arguing would be more precise) as to how we were going to pay the bill. Never one to hide things for very long, I said to Christine,

"That's amazing, how did you know?"

"Know what?", she replied. "God just…put you on my heart and so I've rung you."

I told Christine that Sylvia and I had just been having a 'slight disagreement' over how we could pay the electric bill, as we didn't have the money. Christine asked me how much it was. She then said she'd drop the cash round after work. It was very humbling to have to learn to receive in that way, but at the time we were extremely grateful to God for putting it into Christine's mind to ring. Appreciative too, that she was obedient to God.

It was around this time, that I started to feel very pressured in terms of time. I had a wife and three young children plus a job, where I was working forty hours a week. In addition, we were seeking to be faithful in attending the meetings of our local church and running two meetings in our home, together with the follow up work which was involved. For instance, some of the children would like to come around after school and talk about issues going on in their lives.

I began to pray earnestly, about this feeling that we would have to give up the work with the children and the teenagers. Increasingly, however, I began to sense that God was saying that it would be my job at the Inland Revenue that would have to go. My first thought, was that it was crazy to think like that! Finances were tight as it was without giving up my job to work for God with no regular income. However the thought persisted and even grew stronger. Verses in the Bible kept hitting me in the face (metaphorically, of course) about living by faith, trusting in God and whenever we went to church meetings it seemed like that was the subject. Also we'd just read a book called God's Smuggler, the story of a Dutch man called Brother Andrew, who'd spent much of his adult life smuggling Bibles into countries where they were banned. As Andrew's story unfolded it was thrilling to read the way in which God provided for all of his needs, often over and above what he could have imagined. All of this served to unsettle me at work. It took six months of God 'being on my case', before I was eventually able to type out my notice of resignation. I rang Sylvia to tell her that I'd at last done it, and we were both so relieved, full of joy and at peace once again. At that stage, I have to say that our biggest concern was how we would pay the rent on our Council house. Mum and dad lived just down the road, so if we ran out of food we could always go knocking on their door, but paying the rent and other bills that was something else. We needn't have worried however because God had gone ahead of us and answered our prayers in a way that we couldn't have imagined.

The day after finishing my job as an audio typist with the Inland Revenue, Sylvia and I, together with our three small children - all under the age of two - set off with some friends from church for a week's holiday at Pontins Holiday Camp in Blackpool. It wasn't the usual sort of Pontins holiday; instead a week-long conference of the Elim Pentecostal Church, and it involved meetings for all ages through the day and night. We had a great time that week, with our friends Brian and Janet with their four young children. We got to visit Blackpool's Golden Mile and the world famous funfair though it was at the meetings where we really had an opportunity for our faith to be encouraged. The praise and worship times were incredible, as we filled out the various auditoriums and nearly lifted the roof off with some rousing traditional hymns and modern Christian songs, or choruses as they were then called. The teaching sessions too, were very uplifting and inspiring. I particularly enjoyed visiting the late night coffee bar where I came to know and love the music of Len Magee. Len was a Folk singer-songwriter who had had an amazing conversion to Christianity, following his desperate cry for help when he was hooked on hard drugs. God heard his cry, restored him, led him to Bible College and eventually brought him into the ministry and to Pastor a church. Len recorded several best selling albums during the seventies and eighties. I understand he is currently a Pastor in Australia.

Once the holiday was over we all returned to Birmingham. Brian went back to the welding business he was running with his brother-in-law, whilst I was about to take up my new full-time role of caring for people on the Wyrley Birch Housing Estate, and trusting God to unfold each day, according to his perfect will.

Arriving home from Blackpool, we saw God's handiwork straightaway and it concerned the rent which we'd been so concerned about. A letter from the Birmingham Housing Department explained that they were sending us a cheque for just over £200, in respect of unclaimed rent rebate stretching back over the previous year, and in addition, for the next six months, our rent would be 48p per week, which they would require us to pay fortnightly. I can't tell you the great sense of joy and relief that we felt, at that point! It was incredible news, and Sylvia and I agreed that though our faith was small, it did run to trusting God for less-than fifty pence a week in order to cover the rent.

Over the course of the next few years we saw God provide for our needs in some remarkable ways. We were continuing to have the children coming along for 'One Way Special' on a Monday night; the teenagers (up to forty of them) also in our house every Friday night, for Bible study and a little supper. We had the occasional coffee mornings for the elderly and I started to deliver a Christian newspaper called *Challenge* to about two hundred homes on the

Estate. My mind went back to when I was thirteen years of age, when I used to have a newspaper round on that very estate. I loved delivering the news to people's homes, then - but now I was delivering the good news about Jesus and I loved that even more. I think a number of people were more than a little shocked to find a blind person undertaking this kind of work. I didn't mind, however, because there's something about me now that quite likes to surprise people. I've continued to do that through the years and why not? Although in myself I'm very ordinary, living on the inside of me I have an extraordinarily amazing God.

I remember one Monday night when I was feeling really tired. I just didn't feel like leading 'One Way Special'. Even with our wonderful team of helpers, it took a lot of exuberant energy to participate with the children in some of the lively songs, quizzes and Bible stories which often had to be dramatised in order to get the attention of the kids. After 'One Way Special' had finished I was then driven by my friend, John Place, to Cannon Street Baptist Church in Handsworth, where I was to give a half-hour talk to a ladies' group about the work we were doing on the Estate. I couldn't have felt less like it and I had to pray and ask the Holy Spirit to flow through me in order to inspire my audience, which consisted of about twenty, mainly elderly ladies. Well, God did help me enormously and his presence filled the small room in which we were gathered. At the end of the meeting people came up and shook my hand and most said that God had spoken to them and they wanted to give me money. Coins and notes were being stuffed into my jacket pockets by all and sundry to the point where I was quite bewildered by it all. John was quite amused by the proceedings, and as he drove me home to Sylvia, he was chuckling to himself most of the way. When we arrived home, we told Sylvia what had happened as we counted the money. There was just over £40, on a night where maybe I expected no more than £5. It was a lot of money back in the mid-1970s, and ensured that we wouldn't have to go cap in hand to mum and dad for a week or two, at least.

This phase of my life was very different to anything I had known before. No regular income, no set pattern to my day and nobody telling me what to do. Sylvia enjoyed having me around to help a little with the children, which suited me fine. However, God had called me to work for him and I learned to build discipline into my life and create a whole new framework for myself. Having said that, I was becoming very concerned about an ugly side to my character that had started to manifest itself.

Temper! Temper!

Throughout my life I'd never really displayed much of a temper, even when kicked on the football field! When the children would wake up at night however, and not go back to sleep, I found it very annoying. Particularly when the twins were babies, it was as if they had night and day mixed up. They would sleep in the day and then lie awake, crying throughout the night. Given that we were in a first floor maisonette at the time, it was increasingly difficult for us as there were neighbours either side and underneath. It became a pressure-cooker situation, trying to keep them quiet so that the neighbours would not be disturbed, whilst at the same time desperately needing rest ourselves. It was then that I discovered I had a threshold beyond which lay a very nasty temper.

Once, Sylvia and I were in Torquay with our three children and were having a heated exchange of views. I felt myself getting more and more tense, until Sylvia said something which I didn't like and I lashed out with my hand and slapped her around the face. Immediately blood began to pour out of her nose and the children were horrified at what I'd done and so was I of course. Ironically within seconds a photographer came up to us and asked if we would like him to take a 'happy' family photograph. You can guess what Sylvia's reply was, I'm sure!

If that wasn't bad enough, a short while later, back home in Birmingham, it was around teatime one night. The kids were all ready for bed, having been in the bath and dressed in their pyjamas. I was getting ready to go out and give my Christian testimony at a remand home for girls, a few miles away. A friend of ours, Denis Guest, was picking me up in his car. Denis would preach at the event, I would give my testimony of how I came to know Jesus and two sisters, Sue and Carol would sing two or three songs. Unfortunately, a few minutes before Denis was due to arrive, something triggered off another argument between Sylvia and me. It was horrible. Again, it led to me lashing out and this time, Sylvia fell back on to the floor as she tried to avoid my blow. If she'd banged her head she could have been killed. The whole scene was horrendous as the doorbell rang.

Sylvia, understandably shouted, "Go off to your religious meeting and don't bother to come back."

I went to the door. As we were already running late, Denis was back at the car. I got in and we dove away. We hadn't gone more than a few hundred yards when I began to cry. I told Denis what had gone on. He pulled over to the side of the road, stopped the car and prayed there and then for Sylvia and me. Denis encouraged me to believe that God had something good in store that night, and even though I felt totally unworthy to be out representing a God of love, Denis reminded me that we are all sinners saved by God's amazing grace. He said that I should give it my best shot and then, when we arrived home later in the evening, he would come in and talk with Sylvia and me.

We duly arrived at the remand home and it turned out to be a great night. Twelve of the teenage girls giving their lives to Jesus.

Later, Denis was as good as his word and came in to pray with us, but Sylvia had actually gone off to bed, so in the end he and I prayed about the situation before he headed off home.

A short while later, we went away for a week's holiday to a cottage on a farm near Port Isaac in Cornwall. We were with our friends, Brian and Janet Davis and their four kids and overall we had a very good time. Sylvia however, was still emotionally raw from recent events and she would take herself off to bed at about 8 o'clock each night. I felt embarrassed and awkward about this, for I knew that our friends would be wondering what the problem was. One evening, after Sylvia had gone to bed and while Brian and Janet were busy in the kitchen, I was reading part of my Braille Bible. I read a verse which said, "Confess your faults to one another and you shall be healed". As I read those words I knew that I needed to go and confess to my friends what I had done to Sylvia. I went into the kitchen where they were preparing food for the next day.

"Hi John" said Brian, "…how's Sylvie?"

"That's what I want to talk to you about" I said. Before breaking down in floods of tears.

Brian, a big man in every sense of the word, immediately left the sink and came over to me.

I blurted out, "Brian, I think I'm demon-possessed, Because I keep on hitting Sylvia."

Brian held me tight in a bear hug for several minutes as we sobbed deeply in each other's arms. When words eventually came, Brian didn't condemn me or ask any questions. But simply prayed a blessing over me, following which I felt totally clean.

In the days that followed, Janet was able to chat with Sylvia and release some of that pent up anger and confusion. As for me that verse in the Bible, "Confess your faults one to another and you shall be healed", must be true because I have never lashed out at Sylvia again, since then.

If you're reading this and have a problem with your temper, let me encourage you to be open about sharing it with someone you love and trust; if it's perceived to be a serious problem, then go and get professional help. Don't be too proud. As I see it, it's every bit as much a disability as being blind.

Early to Rise

In those days I developed the habit of getting up early in the morning, 6am, to spend time in prayer and reading from my Braille Bible. When you have no money coming in from a regular salary, it's amazing how it motivates you to focus on God and his Word. As well as placing our needs as a family before God every morning, I would also look to him to guide me each day with regard to what I should be doing. Sometimes, it was visiting the elderly in their homes. Sometimes delivering the *Challenge* newspaper and sometimes preparing for the children's or the teenagers' meetings. On other occasions, it might mean meeting with other Christians in the locality, or going to speak at a meeting somewhere or other. It was all very thrilling to see the way in which God mapped out the days and created the openings for me.

Through delivering *Challenge* around the housing estate I got to know many people, but among the most interesting were Bobby and Sylvia Evans. They were Christians and a very unusual and cheerful pair. Our three little daughters loved them, because they were so jovial. Bobby was a dwarf (no more than 3-foot tall) whilst Sylvia, his wife, was about 6-foot so you can imagine what they looked like! Great fun they were, with no hint of self pity. It was a wonderful sight to behold, when Bobby would jump into the shopping trolley and Sylvia would wheel him along the road.

It was teatime in the Flanner household one magical night just before Christmas, when there was a knock at the door. I went to answer, only to find Sylvia and Bobby there, but before I could welcome them in Bobby had nipped around me and was into the lounge playfully teasing the children with talk of Father Christmas coming soon. He wasn't far wrong, in that Sylvia (not mine, but Bobby's girl – that was a great song by Susan Vaughan wasn't it?) wheeled the aforementioned shopping trolley minus Bobby on this occasion, into the kitchen, where she found my Sylvia slaving over a hot stove. This could get confusing, but Sylvia said to Sylvia, "God has been talking to Bobby and me, about your needs this Christmas, so we have done something about it".

With that, Bobby's Sylvia proceeded to unzip the top of the trolley to reveal a bag jammed full of all kinds of foodstuff. Everything you could imagine for a week's family shopping was included in there, plus a few little surprises for the kids. There was an abundant supply of tights for my Sylvia and the thing we remember to this day, there were eight hundred tea bags. My reputation had obviously gone before me. There was even a Christmas pudding and a small box of Christmas crackers.

Needless to say, we'd been praying about various needs which we had at that festive season and it was typical that God should respond in such an extravagant manner. Bobby and Sylvia always said that it was well worth the expense, to see the look of incredulity and wonder upon our faces. Beverley, Sara and Allison, young as they were, fully entered into the excitement of the occasion too.

During these years, I have to say that we really looked forward to seeing the postman; always wondering if he was carrying another miracle or two in his bag for us. From the time the postman delivered the letter from the Council Housing Department, telling us we had been offered the very house we had requested, right up to the present day we have fond memories of God doing some amazing things and using the postman as his delivering angel.

I was then working as a self employed person, purchasing my own National Insurance stamp. I had to keep records of income and expenditure for the Inland Revenue. With regard to the income I split that into two categories, fees and gifts. The fees are what I earned for speaking engagements, which wasn't much. The gifts were the amazing amount of donations that were either handed to us at Church or what came in the post and many of these gifts were anonymous. Financial gifts ranging from £1 up to £500 came our way, from many different people, all of whom had one thing in common: they were directed by God to do so, and from our point of view, we were extremely thankful they were obedient. True, we went through times of lack and we also went through times of abundance, and it was a difficult balancing act knowing when to spend and when to save, when to give out to others and when to withhold. If anything we tended to err on the carefree (as opposed to careless) side of things.

One particularly difficult time when money was scarce, I remember praying really hard about needing to pay a gas bill. I was also aware that we needed a holiday. It was our family GP, the same Dr. Griffiths who'd been almost 'in' on the birth of our twins, who'd spoken to me and sensitively brought the conversation around to make me aware that Sylvia needed a break. As I prayed earnestly about these matters, a strange thing began to happen. Every time I prayed about these issues, in my mind's eye I could see my collection of pop singles. This was my pride and joy. There were around seven hundred of them. It took me a while to realise what was going on. But could it be that God was requiring of me to sell my beloved record collection? The thought was too painful to contemplate. I tried to push it out of my mind. Day after day however, the thought wouldn't go away. Then my brother Paul came to our home to look for a particular record, which he wanted to borrow. Quite spontaneously, as he was looking and admiring he asked, "I don't suppose you would consider selling any of these, would you?"

"No way," came my immediate response.

After Paul had gone, having found what he wanted, I couldn't get his question out of my mind. It troubled me for days. I came to the conclusion that it was probably God's way of answering part of my prayer. The upshot was, that Paul purchased half of my record collection and it more-than paid for the gas bill. It almost broke my heart. Worse was to follow. As I prayed about the holiday matter, I felt again that God was saying I should get rid of the rest of the records. Eventually I decided I had better co-operate with my Lord and went to a local dealer and sold them, raising enough money to book a week's holiday for the family. I got rid of all the albums as well thinking, "If God wants all of me, then all of me he can have".

I've since learned of course, that this is what God wants. He gave himself, totally for me and he wants nothing less in return. I've also discovered that you can never outgive God. I've become aware that if God asks you to give something up for him, it's only because he wants to replace it with something far better. Later, through my friend Peter Jackson, then a recording artiste with Word records, I had the opportunity of presenting 'Discovery' evenings. What this was, in effect was an opportunity to promote Word Records by going to homes and churches and before an invited group of people, play tracks from the latest Christian record releases. I would take along a selection of discs that people could purchase at the end of the evening, if they so wished. I was then allowed 30% commission on all I sold, to plough back into the work on the housing estate. So here again we saw God's wonderful provision.

It led to me having quite an extensive knowledge of the Christian music scene and stood me in good stead for the time when I would get an invitation to play this kind of music on BBC Radio Birmingham, and then later Radio WM, with Ken Dudeney and Michael Blood. The old hymn writer got it right when he penned those words, "God moves in a mysterious way, his wonders to perform".

I have also featured on local radio stations in Leicester, Devon and Cornwall over the years. I also had an exciting opportunity to share something of my life story and faith in God, on a Christian radio station, Heaven 97, in the Cayman Islands; it led to me receiving an invitation to preach at a church in Grand Cayman, called Faith Deliverance Centre. That was a wonderful experience, with Sylvia and I being the only white people in a congregation of over a hundred. The place was rocking with the sound of praises to God, as people from a Jamaican background gave vent to their joy at being 'saved'. At the end of the service, the Pastor encouraged his congregation to come up to me and show their appreciation. I can honestly say that I have never been hugged and kissed by so many people in a such a short space of time! I felt well and truly loved. What were we doing in the Cayman Island? I'll tell you later, but let's just say it was another of God's little surprises.

It's not just on radio that I've been able to talk about my faith. The God of surprises I've come to know and love, had another one in store for me when I received a phone call from a Bernard Cartwright at Central Television. Bernard worked as a researcher on religious programming for Central TV and a friend of his, Jill, had told him about my work for a local church. She suffered from multiple sclerosis and I used to visit her at home and pray with her, and from time to time Sylvia and I would go there in the evenings when Jill's charming French husband was home from work, and he would treat us to red wine and French brie cheese.

Apparently Jill had told Bernard about me and sufficiently intrigued, was now, in true researcher style, proceeding to ask penetrating questions about my life, attitude and beliefs. He said he would talk with his boss and get back to me, to let me know if they were going to make a programme.

A couple of days slipped by, and Bernard was back on the phone saying that it was looking promising and that he needed to come to my house for a chat. An idea was put to me, that I would take part in a 15-minute interview for a programme called *Come Close* which would go out across the Midlands on Central

TV, late on a Monday night - after the darts coverage. I would be interviewed by Stuart White about my faith and how, as a blind person, I could believe in a God of love. Although the programme was to be recorded, it had to be done in one take because they were on a tight budget and they couldn't afford any more studio time. I had to sign a contract, agreeing to abide by certain criteria and for which I would receive the princely sum of £25.

It was exciting going up to the studios in Birmingham and being made up with face powder, to look as if I had a wonderful tan. Stuart White himself was a lovely guy, really gentle and genuine as a person. I'd heard him on radio as a disc jockey on Radio Derby and BRMB in Birmingham. Stuart went on to do a lot of football reporting for the BBC and regularly appeared on Five Live's *Sports Report*.

Although very nervous, it all went pretty well as I talked about my life and adjusting to being a blind person. I demonstrated how to use the white stick, and some of the equipment I have for writing Braille, writing cheques and playing games like scrabble and dominoes.

The interview must have been well received. A month or two later and another phone call from Central TV. This time it was from Michael Hart, brother of the famous television artist, Tony Hart. Michael, who I believe was the senior producer in religious broadcasting at the time for Central, said that following the success of *Come Close* they were now considering me as a subject for one of their *Encounter* documentaries. *Encounter* was a 30-minute piece which went out at 2 o'clock on Sunday afternoons, just before the weekend's football highlights. Encounter was networked across the country, through the ITV regions.

We actually had a film crew come and spend a week with us, filming around the house as I went about my daily chores. They filmed me making tea and waking up the kids early in the morning for school, even though we filmed it in the middle of the afternoon. The kids just wore their pyjamas on top of their day clothes. I think I was the worst actor in the family. I was filmed at my typewriter; going out to get the bus into Solihull; attending an Aston Villa match; working on an afternoon radio show at Pebble Mill; speaking in a local school; taking part in a church house group meeting and also visiting a sick person in their home and praying with them. The team were great to work with, and it gave us an insight into the amount of painstaking work, that goes into making a film. Even the tea-making sequence took two hours to film! I can't begin to tell you how many times that tea went back into the pot, as they took shots from so many different angles.

When the programme was shown, it was again well received and we heard that some schools in the south of England took the video recording of it and used it as part of their religious education syllabus. Once more we had to sign a contract, regarding exclusive rights to the programme and this time we got a bit more than £25. In fact we received £240, and with it we were able to buy school uniforms for each of our children, who were about to start at their new Comprehensive School. So you see, God again found a most unexpected way of providing for our needs. Doing so, in such an enjoyable way.

Over the years I have come to love Psalm 34. So many of the verses have become real and personal in my life. Remember the washing machine story and the verse in the box, "The lions may grow weak and hungry, but those who seek the LORD lack no good thing."? Then there was the grapefruit story and the verse, "Taste and see that the LORD is good...". To those I would like to add "My soul will make her boast in the LORD; let the afflicted hear and rejoice." More than anything else in life, I love to boast in the Lord confidently, expecting that needy people will hear my enthusiastic heart of joy and themselves be made glad. Whilst I may be physically blind, my vision is to see the spiritual eyes of people opened to the glorious reality of God's love, as revealed through his dear son the Lord Jesus Christ.

Whilst talking about the relevance that Psalm 34 has played in my life, another story comes to mind. I was preaching one night in a Pentecostal Church in Birmingham, on the verse in Psalm 34: "I sought the LORD and he answered me; he delivered me from all of my fears". As usual I was speaking fervently and with conviction, believing every word to be true. As I preached, however, God began to speak to me. This is an amazing thing in that while you are doing something else, the Lord can still engage with your spirit. It was happening to me, on this occasion. The only thing was, it was somewhat uncomfortable for me. I was preaching truth of course, but God was saying to me, "Hypocrite". I continued to preach with nobody, I'm sure, having a clue as to what was going on inside me. I knew however, that God was on my case again and that he wouldn't let me go. Some time later, I began to 'enquire of the Lord' what he was talking to me about, when he called me a hypocrite. Immediately God reminded me that, although I was convinced that I'd been delivered from all of my fears, there were in fact two things that he still wanted me to get victory over – water and the dentist.

I had pushed the two areas to the back of my mind and didn't think they were important. God, however, desired for me to have no fear and he wanted me to live in victory over these two areas.

A new club had been formed. 'Solihull Seals' were basically a group of people who were giving their time freely, to take and teach disabled people to swim. I felt that God was providing an ideal opportunity for me. I went along to the Tudor Grange swimming baths for several weeks on Monday nights, and was introduced to a Dr. McKenzie, then a local G.P. I felt confident with him in a way which I never had with the teachers at school. I trusted that he wouldn't let me drown, and within a few weeks he had me swimming and the 5-metres badge on my shorts, for many years, was one of my proudest possessions! Yet another fear was met head on and overcome.

My fear of the dentist again went back to childhood, and the full horror of my trip to the school dental clinic is told in the 'Fear' section of this book.

As a result of those childhood experiences, many people have ignored their teeth and refrained from visiting a Dentist for the rest of their lives. I may well have come into that category, had God not got hold of my life. In effect what God, through the Holy Spirit, was saying to me was, "How can you expect your children to look after their teeth, and go to the dentist every six months, if you as their dad doesn't set an example?" I understood the rationale and agreed with it totally. I had to do something about this area of inconsistency in my life. So I went ahead and booked an appointment.

Mr. Fraser didn't have horns and wear red clothes. In fact, he didn't look like the Devil at all. He was rather kind, a gentleman who listened to my childhood experience of the school dentist with plenty of compassion, saying that he had heard the same story so many times, from different people of my generation. On the first visit I was booked-in to have a tooth out, a couple of fillings and a general clean-up. I felt relaxed and confident. The sophisticated equipment and gentle nature of the dentist seemed light years away from the nightmare on Sheep Street. Since then, I've gone every six months to see the dentist and never even had to have another tooth out, just the very occasional filling. I've been able to set a good example to Sylvia and the children and once again, God has been glorified. I again say with confidence, and this time hopefully with no interruptions from the good Lord, "I sought the Lord and he heard me and he delivered me from all my fears".

If I do find myself getting scared or facing a really nerve-racking situation, I find it helpful to think of Jesus suffering upon the Cross, from the most incredible pain. Yet he endured it and overcame, without the need for painkillers. As a Christian I believe that I am born again, and that Jesus now lives in me, through his Holy Spirit. If that's true, and that same Jesus who endured the pain upon the cross lives in me, then I too can endure anything, if I allow him to live through me. A risky thought, to pursue!

Those were the days when God was certainly on my case. He'd allowed me a few years, to get established in the faith and to grow in my knowledge of him. There were, however, certain anomalies in my life which he wanted me to get to grips with - and so God the Holy Spirit started to get to work on me. Having already sorted me out with regard to my record collection (and then the dentist) it was now time to turn his attentions to another big god in my life, namely Aston Villa.

My good friend Peter Jackson was working full time with Torch Trust for the Blind. Torch used to hold fellowship meetings in Birmingham on Saturday afternoons at 3pm, for about two hours. Of course, for any self-respecting football fan (in those pre-Sky Television days, at least) 3 o'clock on a Saturday afternoon was sacrosanct, being the time that most games kicked off. I hadn't missed an Aston Villa home game for years and had no intention of doing so. Consequently, whenever Peter invited me to attend Torch meetings, which was frequently, I would first of all consult the fixture list to see if Aston Villa were playing at home. If they were at home on the day of a Torch meeting, then I would make an excuse to the effect that I already had a prior engagement. Even when Villa were playing away, on the Saturday of the Torch meeting I would still take my transistor radio and have a sneaky listen to the score from time to time, throughout the meeting. I must confess to feeling somewhat awkward about this clash of loyalties.

One night while sitting at home I received a phone call.

"Hello John, my name is David McCulloch and I'm Pastor of the Church of the Nazarene in Small Heath, Birmingham".

David spoke in a soft, but clear Scottish accent and was inviting me to speak at a coffee bar that his church was running in their locality. He wanted me to tell my story; how I came to faith in Christ and the difference he'd made to my life. They usually attracted about thirty young people to the coffee bar.

"Yes, of course David, I'd be thrilled to come along", was my enthusiastic reply, "…when do you meet!"

I was shocked and disappointed. The coffee bar was held each Saturday afternoon, from 3 o'clock.

"Just a moment", I said as I sent Sylvia scurrying for the diary and the fixture list.

David gave me a date. It coincided with Villa being at home. I asked for another date and eventually, I managed to agree to when Villa were playing away, but I was still upset. Saturday had always been my day for sport. By now, of course, I was sensing that God was pinning me down on the issue and I was starting to feel uncomfortable. Jesus was definitely my personal Saviour, but I couldn't say with absolute conviction that he was my Lord, also.

On the original date that I was offered for the coffee bar, Villa were at home to Bristol City and I naturally went to the game, but can't say that I enjoyed it. I don't remember the game or anything about it. What I can remember is the terrible feeling of guilt. I should've been at the coffee bar, serving my God and though I had deceived the Pastor, the God who sees and knows all, knew what was in my heart. There were split loyalties. That day I made up my mind, that when the season finished a few weeks later, that that was it for me and football. In those days I had a privileged seat at Villa Park in the press box, where I was able to listen to a commentary on the headphones, which was being broadcast to local hospitals and the commentators were really surprised when I told them that I wouldn't be going back.

With God's help, I kept to my word and for the next four season I never went to Villa Park, though I still maintained a very close interest in the scores and performances, via my radio. I felt relieved and happy that I could again say with conviction "Jesus, is Lord of my life".

I refused a number of invitations to go to Villa Park and some were even questioning if I was inferring that going to football matches was a sin. I said that it'd become a sin for me, because it was rivalling God for the most important place in my life. There came a time however, when a friend, Brian Davis, rang me up to say that he had a spare ticket for a Villa - West Ham game. Was I interested in going with him? Initially I politely turned down the offer, but Sylvia had words with me.

"I feel that you should go to that game, with Brian. The time together, would be good for you both".

"But what if I get hooked again?" I protested.

Sylvia said, "I don't think you will. Because God has done a work in your heart".

Somewhat nervously it has to be said, I got back to Brian and accepted his offer. We went to the game, had a great time together and Villa won 4-0, which made my day. What was even better, was that when the next match came around, I didn't go and didn't have any great desire to go, either. I've since discovered that I can go to games, or not, as the case may be. I still love Aston Villa and follow them passionately. That's the way I am, but I rarely go to the games these days.

There were several years when I possessed a season ticket, along with my son Ian. I started to take him to Villa Park when he was seven years old and we've shared some magical times together, as father and son. One little tradition that we developed, was that on the way to the game we'd stop off at a favourite fish and chip shop near to the ground, in Manor road; the same fish and chip shop where I used to go before, as a teenager with my friends Ronnie and Brian. Ian and I would have a 'Matchday Special', which consisted of fish, chips, a jumbo sausage and optional curry sauce or mushy peas. Ian always had the curry, but I declined because I didn't fancy the idea of fingers smelling of curry for the rest of the afternoon! In all weathers, we've stood outside that fish and chip shop, enjoying our pre-match meal. We often joked, saying that even if the match turned out to be lousy you could always rely on the 'Matchday Special' to be brilliant - and excellent value, too, at £1.60 which it remained for many years!

I've learned from this, that if anything has a hold over my life and takes the place of Jesus Christ as number one, then it has to go. Some people, like drug addicts or alcoholics for instance, find it better to cut the object of their addictions out of their life completely; I fully understand that, especially in those cases. There are other things however, like football in my case that can dominate our lives to the point where God is relegated to second or third place. God doesn't want to rob us of the enjoyment of such things, but simply to help us to put everything in its rightful order. The Bible teaches that one of the evident fruits of the Holy Spirit ruling in our lives, is that we'll have self control. We'll know when to say "yes" and when to say "no". Hopefully I've learned that lesson, though as life goes on, my experience is that there are always new challenges to face, when it comes to walking by faith and listening to the Holy Spirit as he seeks to lead me in the will of God the Father.

I'll keep coming back to this again, but possibly the most exciting thing about being a Christian, is having the Holy Spirit, God himself, living on the inside. That's what happens when a person becomes a Christian. The Bible calls it, "Being born again of incorruptible seed". It's truly amazing, and I only wish, I along with millions of other believers, were quiet and still often enough to hear the voice of God. Though he is so mighty, awesome and powerful, yet more often than not he speaks in a still small voice, as gentle as a dove.

One such time, was when I sensed that God was speaking to me about the need for some kind of pedestrian crossings outside Lode Heath School, in Solihull. A few children had been knocked down and seriously injured over the years. It seemed like only a matter of time before somebody would be killed. On two occasions at least, I felt a stirring on the inside that I should start a campaign to get some crossings, but I chose to ignore the thought until one eventful day.

It was around 3.15 in the afternoon and I was just about to leave home to meet a friend in Solihull town centre, when the phone rang. The call was of no great importance and only lasted a couple of minutes, but it was sufficient for me to miss my bus. My choice now, was to wait thirty minutes for the next one and arrive late for my meeting, or walk a little further to catch a bus on a different route. I chose the latter option and it was a good job I did - thank you Jesus, for the phone call. Whilst I was striding out in the general direction of Lode heath School, I was met by the anguished voice of a girl running breathlessly home from school.

"Mr Flanner" she shrieked, "...one of the twins has been involved in an Accident. She is lying on the road in Lode Lane".

The distraught girl was not able to give me any more clear information and so I hurried along the winding road as fast as my legs would carry me, occasionally breaking out into a trot and flailing my white stick around in front of me. Other children came along and confirmed that it was Allison who had been hit by a car and that an ambulance had just arrived.

Getting to the scene, I discovered that Allison had just been placed in the back of the ambulance and was going to be taken to Birmingham's Heartlands hospital. She was conscious, and though in a lot of pain she was able to give me a hug and between the tears talk to me a little. Outside of the main school gates is a dual carriageway and though there were traffic

lights about a hundred yards up the road, most of the children who lived on the Damsonwood estate tended to come straight out of school, cross halfway and then wait on the small embankment in the middle of the road. Often a crowd of children jostle on the embankment, as was the case on this particular day. Allison then eleven years old, was pushed slightly in the back, causing her to slip into the road into the path of an oncoming car. The car caught the handle of Allison's school bag and dragged her along the road for a short distance at speed. The impact caused Allison to suffer a broken ankle and a collapsed lung. I was so thankful that God had changed my schedule and arranged for me to be there, to comfort Allison, to pray for her in the ambulance and to accompany her to hospital.

Ironically, Sylvia was stuck in a traffic jam at the end of Lode Lane, which had been caused by this accident. Sylvia was returning from visiting someone in the very hospital where her daughter was now being taken to. In the traffic jam which ensued, Sylvia wound her car window down and enquired of a passer-by, "What's happened?"

"A child has been involved in an accident while coming out of school" came the reply.

Sylvia immediately began to pray using the gift of speaking in tongues, which I spoke about earlier in the book, not knowing at that stage that it was one of her own children. As she got nearer home however, she did ascertain that it was Allison who had been involved in the accident. On arriving home, Sylvia picked up Beverley and Sara and then set off for the hospital to meet up with Allison and me.

Thankfully, after a few months Allison had made a full physical recovery from her injuries, though in truth it probably took a lot longer to overcome the emotional scars of what had happened. On that particular day, Allison was in a hurry to get home as we were taking delivery of a pet bird – a cute little yellow budgerigar who we named Chico. Yes, the very bird who later learned to bite the dots off my Braille Bible!

The accident to our own daughter prompted me into action. I started a campaign to get crossings installed. I invited people to sign a petition, getting over two hundred signatures and I also secured a very convincing letter from Mr Evans, the Head Teacher from Lode Heath School at the time. I eventually submitted the application to the Solihull Council and was overjoyed when the news came through that permission had been granted for some pelican crossings to be installed, right outside the school gates near to where Allison had sustained her injuries. In my eyes now, these are the 'Allison Crossings' and it got even better some years later, when across the road from the school right by the crossings, planning permission was granted for a church to be built on the site of an old coach factory. Now the 'Allison Crossings' not only guide children safely to and from school, but they also guide people safely to the Renewal Christian Centre, which has a congregation of around 2,000 people and is one of the fastest growing churches in the United Kingdom!

I'm glad that I heard and obeyed the promptings of the Holy Spirit, and I only wish I'd done it earlier - it may have saved Allison, her mum and a lot of other people a great deal of heartache.

I've heard it said that Christianity is not a religion, but more a relationship. A Father with his children. I go along with that, entirely. It really is about intimacy. Many of us were taught the Lord's Prayer as children, which features some amazing words. Of course, these are words directly attributed to Jesus and he begins by saying, "When you pray, say Our Father...." The word used for father is "Abba" which means "daddy". God therefore, as well as being creator of all things is also my daddy and that's amazing! When we are born again, God our Father speaks right into our hearts, often in a gentle whisper. In our busy, noisy world it's no wonder we miss out on his will and blessings for our lives on so many occasions.

I recall one occasion when it was pointed out to me that one of our leading daily tabloid newspapers was carrying a full page advert to do with witchcraft and black magic. They were offering free books to anyone who was interested in knowing more. This was the time when we had 'One Way Special' running for the children, and a youth meeting in our home, also. That week I felt that God wanted me to say some things by way of warning to the children and young people, about the dangers of such occult practices and how much God hates them. I was surprised then, when one of the children said that her Dad had sent for some of those books that were being advertised in the newspaper, and other older children told us how common it was, for kids in secondary school to be messing around with tarot cards and ouija boards. Shocked at the level of interest being shown in these practices, I had a concern to protect the children and also make known to their parents just how dangerous these kinds of things were.

Of course we prayed with the kids about such matters. But there was something stirring in my heart that would not leave me alone. A few months before, Sylvia had read to me a book called From Witchcraft To Christ. It was the truly incredible story of Doreen Irvine, a working-class girl from the south of England, who had gone from the world of prostitution, where she had made a good living, into witchcraft and to eventually become queen of the black witches. It went into great detail about her life and of her initiation into witchcraft and the powers that she possessed. Thrillingly, she had an amazing conversion to Jesus Christ and was delivered from evil, to the point where she was now serving God. My thought, which hopefully was inspired by God, was to bring Doreen to Birmingham; to tell her story in schools, churches and anywhere else I could get her, in order to warn people off from this rising interest in the occult and point them towards Jesus Christ, the Light of the World.

I checked this crazy idea out with a few close friends, and they encouraged me to go for it, and so I found out an address where I could contact Doreen and I wrote to her home in Bristol. Sadly, I heard nothing. Then, rumours began to circulate that Doreen had gone back into witchcraft. I have to say that some of those rumours were coming from some fairly senior Christian leaders in Birmingham and further afield. Something in my heart, however, didn't want to believe this and I kept on hoping that I would hear some good news about Doreen.

One day, right out of the blue, I received a letter from America. It was from Doreen Irvine herself. She wrote that my letter had taken a long while to reach her and that she was living in America. She went on to explain that rumours had arisen, suggesting that she had returned to witchcraft. They were most definitely not true. She knew how the rumours had come about, but she was definitely still serving the Lord. Doreen was so hurt that the Christian community were all too ready to believe the lies, rather than taking the time to check out the facts for themselves.

Doreen promised to get in touch when she got back to the UK, and would try to fix something up. She kept to her word and a few months later, I received a phone call from Bristol. A couple of friends and I went down to visit Doreen, and her husband at their home there. We arrived at a simple terraced house, sparsely furnished, as Doreen was praying with two drug addicts who had just given their lives to Jesus.

Later, after a lunch of tomato soup and cheese sandwiches which Doreen kindly prepared for us, we sat down and discussed what we had in mind. Doreen appeared to be a very genuine lady who loved Jesus passionately, and having seen the error of her ways, wanted to warn people of all ages about the dangers of prostitution and witchcraft. This was clearly a costly ministry for Doreen and her husband, because of the possible reprisals from her former 'colleagues'.

Doreen would later travel up to us, for a ten-day visit. Stayed with our friends Phil and Angie, she was a most charming guest. We had arranged for her to tell her story in many different places, including churches and schools. The most memorable moment, however, was the night she was invited as a guest of Brian Savin, then a presenter on BRMB radio in Birmingham. He presented the late night show and Doreen was to be interviewed between 11pm and midnight. Brian had read Doreen's book, so he was well informed. As she told her story with no little humour, but a great deal of honesty, the telephone lines became jammed with interested callers. Due to the level of interest, Brian extended the feature by an hour up to 1am, before closing with these memorable words, "Well, this has been truly amazing. When I knew I would be interviewing a witch, I wondered if you would be coming on a broomstick. However, having met you, I have to say that you are a lovely lady and as your book says, you are a living miracle and I want to thank you for coming in to the studio tonight. We've never had a telephone response on the like this".

When we left the building in Aston, at around 1.15am there were about twenty people outside, some of whom had driven miles to meet Doreen; to shake her hand and to have a brief chat.

It was a truly memorable time, when many people were helped. I'm so glad that I listened to, and obeyed, the voice of my Heavenly Father. It led to much blessing and to ten days that we'll never forget.

On the Move

Having resolved the issue of who was really Lord of my life (Jesus Christ or Aston Villa), Saturday afternoons were freed up and I was able to attend the meeting of the Birmingham Torch Fellowship. Held monthly at 3 o'clock on a Saturday afternoon in a purpose-built Social Services' centre in the Edgbaston area of Birmingham, about a hundred people would gather to sing traditional hymns, modern choruses, hear Bible readings, maybe listen to a soloist and hear a short presentation, usually from a visiting speaker. The meeting lasted around ninety minutes, followed by a tea of sandwiches, cakes, jelly, trifle, with tea or coffee. These fellowship meetings depended greatly on volunteers from local churches, picking up the blind or partially sighted person by car from their home, taking them to the meeting and then taking them home afterwards. Some volunteers would stay for the meeting, whilst others would go home or do shopping and then come back, at the end of the meeting. From a personal point of view I found the meetings to be somewhat old fashioned. I cannot deny that they were meeting a great need. Many of the folk who came along were not just blind, but often had other disabilities as well. They were usually lonely people, who wouldn't go near a traditional church for a variety of reasons, so in that respect Torch Fellowship groups were meeting a very clear need, both socially and spiritually.

The driving force behind such fellowship groups, of which there were over a hundred across the United Kingdom in the 1970s, was my good friend and inspiration, Peter Jackson. At one of the Birmingham Fellowship meetings Peter began to talk to me about his conviction of a need for a Torch Fellowship group to be established in Sutton Coldfield. Having sewn the seed in my mind, Peter was never slow to remind me of his desire for a Sutton Coldfield Torch Fellowship, whenever we met or spoke on the phone. I was still working with Sylvia and others on the Wyrley Birch housing estate and had developed links with six or seven local churches. In those churches, I knew of folk who did voluntary work for Torch and I decided to call a meeting of those workers, and anyone else, who may be interested in seeing a Torch Fellowship group in Sutton Coldfield. I invited Peter along to share his vision and arising from that, about eight of us began to meet together for prayer meetings and to seek God for his guidance. Eventually, we put together a committee to get the project off the ground. We did some deputation meetings in churches around Sutton Coldfield to share the vision of what Torch and the fellowship groups were all about. We stressed our need for further volunteers. After a lot of ground work, the Sutton Coldfield Torch Fellowship group was launched and it ran for many years with attendances usually hovering around the hundred mark. A tremendous sense of fellowship was created and many new and lasting friendships were forged. It was a real thrill, too, of course to know that a considerable number of blind and partially sighted people came to know Jesus in those days and though they have now long since died, it's heartening to know that they are safe and present with the Lord. It cannot be stressed enough, the value of being a part of so many local churches from different doctrinal persuasions, working together for the one cause.

A wonderful group of people worked with me at the Torch Fellowship Group. I don't mention any of them by name, in case I miss somebody out. All involved in the work at Sutton Coldfield, and also in supporting Sylvia and me on the housing Estate, will have their rewards directly from the Lord Jesus Christ one day.

The Torch Trust for the Blind was growing rapidly at this stage, not just in the fellowship groups around the country but also at the very heart of the work, which was mainly concerned with producing Christian literature in a form accessible to blind, partially sighted and deaf-blind people of all ages.

The full and amazing story of the Torch Family can be read in an autobiography by the founders, Ron and Stella Heath.

When I became involved in the early 1970s, the headquarters of the ministry was based at Torch House at Hurstpierpoint, Sussex. Space was at a premium and bigger facilities were required to house the growing number of books and tapes, as well as live-in staff; many of whom themselves were visually impaired. After much prayer and miraculous financial provision, the Torch Trust purchased the beautiful Hallaton Hall, situated in the quaint village of Hallaton, near Market Harborough in Leicestershire. An elegant large property, it was once the home of the former cricketer and missionary, C.T. Stud in the early 20th century. Now it became the new Torch House, with printing presses for the Braille books, a library, office space, a chapel, large lounge and much more besides. It became known as 'Big Torch', whilst at Hurstpierpoint the other property was kept on, and used for conferences and gained the moniker, 'Little torch'.

I became aware that Peter was looking for someone to assist him on the outreach side of the work. With the move to the much larger facility, allied to the desire of the founders Ron and Stella to increase the production of Christian books and magazines to visually impaired people, the need became clear for more folk with the necessary communication skills to go around the country to make known what it was that Torch had to offer. When I became aware of this need I did wonder, whether this was the kind of thing I should be looking at, as a next step in ministry. It interested me, but I wasn't sure if I was mature enough, or if I had the necessary ability, to carry it off. I was then contacted by Peter, who asked me if I'd prayerfully consider becoming his assistant, which would mainly mean me travelling to some of the fellowship groups around the UK, to speak at their meetings and to meet with, and encourage, the workers on the local committees. In addition I would be expected to undertake some deputation meetings in local churches, to talk about the work, set forth the vision and stress that there was always a need for more volunteers. Torch needed people who would agree to put themselves forward to be voice tested, as there was (and still is) a great need for people to read books onto tape.

I was starting to feel that, with regard to the work on the housing estate, Sylvia and I had given so much of ourselves over a five year period that, in a way, we and the kids needed something fresh. For several months Sylvia and I were very hesitant about what we should do. After these years of not having a regular income, at least working for Torch offered us that. So it was appealing in that regard. A big downside for us, was leaving our beloved council house that had come to mean so much to us.

I cannot remember what eventually clinched it for us. We came to a point where we were able to say to Peter, that I was willing to come on board as a member of staff and work alongside him in the outreach work across the country. The work on the housing estate was handed over to the church which we were members of, at the time.

Sylvia drove us to Torch House at Hallaton Hall, appreciating and taking in the lovely Leicestershire countryside as we travelled. Our three daughters, Beverley, Sara and Allison came along too and revelled in the vastness of Torch House, and in its superbly manicured lawns and gardens. I met with Ron, Stella and the other Committee members. A job description was drawn up, a salary agreed and a few encouraging prayers were said over me, including one that, as a family, we would find somewhere to live in the Market Harborough locality very quickly. Peter and his wife Margaret had already made the move from Birmingham, and were buying a nice house on a new housing development called Farndon Fields, in Market Harborough itself.

I quickly discovered that I would need to have a diary with me at all times when attending Torch House. There were always piles of letters from churches and social service groups, requesting visits from Torch in order to explain about the work. So it was that ministry and deputation tours were put together on a monthly basis. Indeed, it was on my very first trip I undertook without Peter being there to support me, that led to something truly astonishing taking place.

There were three of us on the Torch outreach team, that weekend in Sussex. We helped out with leading the Eastbourne Torch Fellowship group on the Saturday afternoon, and then did a deputation meeting on the Saturday night, in a small Gospel hall. On the Sunday morning we were still in Eastbourne, attending a Baptist church at which I was the guest preacher. Little did I know at the time, but my words were to have quite an impact on a particular lady sitting in the congregation that morning.

On returning home from Eastbourne, Sylvia and I began to make plans for our family holiday. We'd booked a caravan for ourselves and our three daughters, together with a family friend, Celia (who I mentioned earlier, as she was part of the lunchtime fellowship meeting at the Inland Revenue). We were attending a Christian event, the Caple Bible Week, which was situated in a beautiful part of Surrey. 3,000 people were expected on site for the event. This was a holiday we were greatly looking forward to.

It was the high summer of 1976. Celia, a single lady, had helped us in our work on the estate, and given us tremendous prayer support. We wanted to bless her with a holiday, include her as part of our family and allow her to serve us with baby-sitting duties, on one or two nights so that Sylvia and I could get to some of the meetings together! There were always specialist meetings in huge marquees for children and young people. For adults there were meetings in the big top morning, afternoon and evening, each one lasting around two hours. Some of our favourite speakers were present. With great music, great speakers, great weather and a babysitter we were guaranteed a wonderful week. What we were certainly not guaranteed were the unfolding events of Wednesday afternoon.

Sylvia and I had already decided that we were going to take a day off from the Bible Week, and whisk the children off to the beach in Brighton, about an hour's drive away. We were able to have some quality time together. Arriving back at our caravan at tea-time, Sylvia was about to insert her key into the caravan door when she saw a note pinned to the door itself. It simply requested that we telephone a number in Godstone. We were puzzled. We didn't know where Godstone was. Nor did Celia. We were obviously intrigued, but half-dreaded ringing the number in case our lovely week was about to be brought to a halt by some bad news.

Sylvia stayed behind at the caravan, to start getting the tea ready. I went off to the pay phones with Celia. I hesitantly dialled the number, as Celia read it out to me.

A well spoken lady answered the phone. There was a warm, "Hello Mrs. Watts speaking".

I didn't recognise the name. "My name is John Flanner. I'm attending the Caple Bible Week and I have a message to ring your number".

With that, Mrs. Watts relaxed. "Oh yes, I drove up to the site this afternoon, but you'd obviously gone out for the day. So I pinned the note on your caravan door." Mrs. Watts continued enthusiastically, "John, I was in Eastbourne on holiday last week, and I attended the church where you were preaching on the Sunday. I'm a prayer and financial partner with the Torch Trust and I felt that

God spoke to me about your need of a house".

I was riveted to her every word by now. She continued, "I have been up to Market Harborough this week, and across the road from Peter and Margaret Jackson is a brand new, Georgian-style, three-bedroom house, which is still empty. I hope you don't mind John, but I actually put down a deposit on it and reserved it for you…"

This was turning into one of my more-interesting telephone calls. I was thinking, "Does this lady know I can't afford to buy a house?" It soon transpired that this wasn't in Mrs. Watts' thinking, at all. "I recently came into some money, John, and I want to buy the house for you, so that you can move from Birmingham and be more fully involved in the work of Torch. So is that okay?"

I was stunned. Of course it was. "Yes, that's amazing".

Realising that I was a bit gob-smacked, Mrs. Watts picked up the conversation again, informing me that there was a very tight time-limit on this, as the houses were in great demand, so…could we go over to Market Harborough the following week to have a look at the house? She needed to know as a matter of priority, whether we wanted it or not, as she needed to make arrangements for the money to be released.

Celia had been listening to my end of the conversation. She'd gathered that something unusual was happening. She heard me thank Mrs. Watts many times, before I closed the conversation with a series of "thank you's". I just did not know what else to say. I did discover from my conversation, that Godstone was only a few miles down the road from where we were camped and that Mrs. Watts' son, Phil, with whom we were to become good friends, also worked at Torch and was resident with other staff at Hallaton.

I got back to the caravan and relayed the story to Sylvia. It sent her, quite understandably, into a bit of a spin. We were excited as we talked this over, and having already visited Peter and Margaret in their new home, Sylvia already knew that Watson Avenue was a really lovely road and that the house in question, was probably very nice indeed. road with Margaret In fact, on our visit to the Jacksons, Sylvia had gone across the road and looked through the windows, with Margaret saying, "Wouldn't it be great if you could afford to buy that?"

The Bible Week over and having had a feast of spiritual food, we arrived home looking forward to our trip to Market Harborough, to visit what looked as if it was going to be our new home. Time and time again, we marvelled at the fact that anyone should be generous enough to want to buy us our own house. We concluded that it was just a small sample of God's immeasurable love to us, in that he freely gave us his only Son to die upon a cross for us.

Over we went to Market Harborough to look at the house, and as we inspected it, it was hard to imagine that this was going to become home for us. As the Agent showed us around, Sylvia was busily working out in her mind where all the furniture would go, whilst I took the opportunity to go across the road to the

Jacksons' house, to ring Mrs Watts to confirm our acceptance of her kind offer.

"Wonderful" she said. "I'll immediately set the wheels in motion and get the relevant paperwork to you, as quickly as possible".

Back in Birmingham we began to make plans for our first ever move from the city of our birth. It was still hard to comprehend that through somebody else's incredible generosity, we were shortly going to be the owners of our own house and mortgage-free too, which was even more amazing. Those thoughts, however, turned out to be a bit premature though as the days turned into weeks while we waited in vain for the promised paperwork to arrive. Finally, our curiosity at the seemingly long delay got the better of us and I decided that I would have to ring Mrs. Watts, to find out if everything was still okay.

As she answered the phone I said, "Please forgive my impatience, but we're very excited and wondered what the latest position is."

Mrs. Watts, who we now knew as Vivian, was clearly embarrassed as she Explained, "I'm really sorry John, but there's been a serious hiccup in proceedings. There has been a legal problem in regard to some money I have been bequeathed and as a result I cannot buy the house for you. I'm so terribly sorry."

I gulped with disbelief and disappointment. Vivian continued to explain.

"I can buy the house in my name, and then invite you to move in and just be responsible for paying the Rates".

We were left to make a decision, and though it was a far cry from owning our own house, eventually, we did come to the conclusion that it was still an answer to prayer. We'd been praying for accommodation in Market Harborough and God was providing us with a beautiful home, in an ideal location. Sure we were disappointed, but we had to overcome that and move forward, in good faith that God was in it. It was still a tremendous act of generosity.

Things began to move quickly now. Having sorted out any embarrassment with Vivian, who was clearly even more upset by events, we were soon safely ensconced in our new home. It was so good to have our friends Peter and Margaret across the road and we got together regularly for meals, shopping trips and games of scrabble!

Our three little girls all attended Farndon Fields school, where they settled in really well. We had quite a few visitors from Birmingham coming to see us and Sylvia loved to take them out to visit the nearby Foxton Locks, for a gentle walk along the canal towpath. It was so tranquil living close to the countryside, far removed from the hustle and bustle of the big city.

With work I was beginning to develop a schedule of trips across the country, to undertake a mixture of deputation and preaching engagements. I enjoyed the travelling, meeting new people and especially having so many wonderful opportunities to share my faith. Paradoxically, however, it was a classic case of relishing the travel but hating being away from home. I missed Sylvia and the children so much.

One of my first trips was a ten-day tour of the west country, taking in churches in Somerset, Devon and Cornwall. Two events stick in my mind from that trip. They didn't help me feel as if I was an integral part of the 'Torch family'.

When going out on tour like this, we usually went in teams of three or four. Others occasionally joined us for certain events, en route. Journeying from Leicestershire down to Somerset, our driver and fellow team member said, "You're a Pentecostal, aren't you John?"

I'd been a Christian for about eight years then. In that time I'd been part of the Church of England, Brethren and Pentecostal Churches, and so actually, I was 'a bit of each' one; all of which had contributed something significant and good to my life. I simply and naively just agreed with my colleague's question. I was then, however, totally taken aback and hurt by his next statement.

"I need to say, therefore, that if you ever stand up and start preaching about speaking in tongues in a public meeting, I will have to stand up and denounce you".

My driver's terse comments shook my confidence and started me thinking, "What am I doing here?"

I'd always taken the view that I'll say whatever God puts on my heart and tells me to say. Now what this guy had said to me had put me in some kind of a predicament. I no longer felt 'free' around him. This was something I had to deal with, but it didn't help in my settling in period with Torch, such was the venom and well, judgement in his manner.

A few days later at Upton Vale Baptist Church in Torquay, on a Saturday afternoon for their Torch Fellowship meeting, we entered the traditional church building as the person acting as my guide read the Scripture verse that was over the entrance. It read "Dear friends, let us love one another, for love comes from God. Everyone who loves has been born of God and knows God. Whoever does not love does not know God, because God is love." (1 John 4, 7-8) Those words became fixed in my mind.

I was still mulling over them over when the chairman opened the meeting by relating some sad news. He said that he'd received that morning, a prayer request by telephone regarding one of the leaders of the Torch Fellowship group in Belfast. Apparently, his business had been the target of an IRA bomb attack and his shop had been almost totally destroyed. There was a gasp of shock around the room. We were in the company of around sixty blind, partially sighted and fully sighted people - plus a few guide dogs, of course. After a short prayer for the man in Belfast, and for the restoration of his business, the meeting proceeded as normal. I could not, however, get the words out of my mind: "Dear friends, let us love one another...", along with some other words from the same book in the Bible. "If you see your brother in need and do not help him the love of God is not in you. If you do not love your brother who you have seen how can you say that you love God who you have not seen?"

I was still feeling uncomfortable about things when Sandy, a member of our team and from Northern Ireland stood up and sang "He touched me, he touched me and oh the joy that filled my soul. Something happened and now I know he touched me and made me whole". At that point the presence of God was so heavy on me, the tears of compassion ran down my face. I felt compassion for my Christian brother in Belfast whom I'd never met. When Sandy stopped singing, I sprang to my feet with an unusual boldness and went to the front of the meeting and said, "Beloved, let us love one another for love is of God and the one who does not love does not know God for God is love". I said that those words were on the entrance to the Church and having just heard what we had about our friend in Belfast, how could we sit there and do nothing? I proposed that we passed around a basket and put in whatever money God 'put on our hearts' to give. We would then, from Torch House, send that money out as an encouragement to this man and his family, to let them know that we were not only thinking about them and praying for them, but we were actually doing something to help them rebuild their business. It may not have been much, but just like the boy in the story gave his loaves and fishes to Jesus, resulting in thousands of people being fed, so we were doing what we could do, and in the hands of God, he was well able to multiply whatever we raised by way of generosity and love.

The amount raised that afternoon was in a sense, irrelevant. It was about being obedient to what God was saying. Later in the day, as we were joined by other senior members of the Torch family, regarding my spontaneous love offering I was told in no uncertain terms, "That's not the way we do things at Torch. So it would be appreciated if you would check such things out, in future"

I felt hurt and deeply despondent. After all, somebody was about to be greatly blessed and encouraged by our act of love and fellowship. Would they have preferred it if I'd just 'passed by on the other side'? I'd just uprooted my family fifty miles or so, to a brand new location away from relatives and friends. What I needed most was encouragement. On my first ministry trip I'd upset two leading members of Torch. I started to feel very ill-at-ease, as doubts as to whether I had done the right thing, began to flood my mind.

In the following months I enjoyed ministry trips across the country, visiting Torch Fellowship groups throughout the British Isles. I worked hard at being friendly and getting on with people at all times. But there was still a suspicion that if I said the slightest thing wrong, I'd be pulled in line. My favourite times were when I was travelling with Peter Jackson. We got on so well. He was a wonderful encouragement to me. I gained so much from seeing him in action, talking with people. Whether with Social Services or people in church, Peter was always courteous, respectful and never afraid to call on his sharp wit to lighten an atmosphere, or defuse a potentially difficult situation.

Back home, the kids had settled well into school. Sylvia was relishing some good times with Margaret, discovering the new shopping opportunities in Market Harborough, Leicester and Kettering. As well as driving into Torch House and helping out there, from time to time, with a variety of odd jobs!

As the months went by, a few situations began to concern me. Although we were making some good friends at Torch, and the ministry they have is a wonderful one, somehow I never felt as though I truly belonged to the 'family', in the way that many others did. One of the regular meetings at Torch House was the Diary Meeting, when we prayed over invitations that were coming in, for deputation and preaching work. Tours and itineraries were prayed about and planned. On the one hand, I felt quite good about seeing my diary getting booked up, two years in advance; it was nice to be wanted. What I wasn't happy with, was the amount of time I was going to be spending away from Sylvia and the children, especially at weekends. Sylvia was lonely. It was extremely hard work having three young children around, with dad away so often.

As I travelled around the country and stayed in the homes of many Christians, it was very interesting the way people opened up their hearts to me, in a way they maybe wouldn't have done, to their local Minister. I became seriously concerned about the number of Christian marriages which were on the rocks. One night, I felt God say to me, "Yours will go the same way, unless you give attention to it".

I tried to negotiate a reduction in the amount of time I was spending away from home. Even offering to go and do some work in the office, using my audio-typing skills. I was told that I was called to the work of an evangelist, and that being away from home, was one of the prices that an evangelist had to pay. I just said, "Well I'm not prepared to pay it" and shortly afterwards, I wrote out my letter of resignation, which was accepted without a fuss. My slightly rocky years as a full-time worker with Torch came to an end.

There was the matter of the house, of course, on which we were only paying rates, but only as long as we worked for Torch. Vivian was very gracious and didn't put any pressure on us to move. In fairness, Torch were very good; even though my leaving must have been a disappointment to them, they agreed to keep paying me a nominal sum, until we'd found the way forward for our lives. It was one of the most difficult times of my life. In everything, I'd sought to do what was right and be obedient to God. I was now overwhelmed with a sense of failure. I felt I was a big disappointment to Torch, to Peter and Margaret after so much support from them, and in particular, to Sylvia and the children after making the decision to move from Birmingham. We were now in a strange town, with no job and no local church affiliation. So where do we go from here?

One of our priorities, was to find a church where we could worship as a family. There were some really nice Christian people in Market Harborough, but they all came from fairly traditional and quite staid backgrounds. With the experiences gained from visiting many churches of various doctrinal persuasions around the country, and also through reading magazines, not to mention the Caple Bible Week, I become aware of a new style of church which was being raised up by God across the country. Indeed across the world. Places where the praise and worship was lively, spontaneous and containing many new songs, mixed in with the traditional hymns. In the newer churches was a strong emphasis on loving one another, helping each other in practical ways and sharing God's love into the community. This fresh approach was appealing to us and very Biblical.

Leicester Christian Fellowship was about fifteen miles away. There was a cliché at the time, 'A Church alive is worth the drive'. A departure from the norm with regard to Leicester Christian Fellowship, was that they met for worship at 3 o'clock on a Sunday afternoon and we'd certainly not known that before! After a few weeks of attending we were enjoying being there, without really feeling totally at home. One Saturday, Leicester Christian Fellowship were holding a leaders' day, and it was open to other church leaders from their particular group of churches, from around the Midlands area. I was pleasantly surprised when one of the Elders of the Fellowship invited me to attend the day and he even arranged transport for me. I was even more shocked on arriving for the first session, to find that two of my friends from Solihull Christian Fellowship were there; Steve Wood (who was actually doing the teaching for the day) and my old friend and former boss, Bryan Pullinger.

I enjoyed the day enormously and it was a great opportunity to be refreshed in a spiritual sense. During the break times, especially over lunch, I was able to talk with Bryan about how I'd come to leave Torch and how I needed to find work. Most important of all, at this time, was to rediscover God's will for us as a family. Bryan agreed to go back and to get the folk at Solihull Christian Fellowship to pray for us.

A week or two later Sylvia received a phone call from Bryan's wife, Jenny, who said that if we were available she and Bryan wanted to drive over to see us. They duly arrived suitably loaded up with bags of groceries and a gift of £50, which all came with love from the church. It was much needed and a great relief.

Later, after a gentle stroll around the wooded lanes we arrived back at our house in Watson Avenue, ready for Bryan and Jenny's departure back to Solihull. I'll never forget Jenny's parting words, "Lovely house, but don't stay here if God is not in it".

"But where can we go?" queried Sylvia.

"Why not Solihull?" Jenny said, "after all, God is able to provide".

He truly is able to provide and the way in which God got us out of Market Harborough is every bit as remarkable, if not more so, than how he got us there in the first place.

I'd signed-on at the Job Centre in Market Harborough and began looking for work. I've always known that God had called me to work for him ever since he said "Launch out into the deep", in relation to working on the housing estate back in Birmingham. I sensed that that was a once-and-for-all call, and that my life would be characterised by me becoming a man of faith, who would be continually launching out into the deep. At this particular point in my life, it was time to turn to the only employable skill I had. Nothing had materialised when out of the blue, came yet another telephone call. It was again, my friend and former work colleague, Bryan Pullinger.

"John" he said, "…the Inland Revenue are going to be opening up a new office in Solihull in a few months' time. I do know that they will be recruiting audio-typists, so if you're interested I'll have an application form sent to you".

I said yes to Bryan, but without a great deal of enthusiasm. We hadn't been in Market Harborough a year and the thought of moving again wasn't a realistic prospect. I didn't want to put Sylvia and the children through that ordeal, especially as the kids had settled into a nice country school. The other thing was that it would've seemed like admitting failure. My pride didn't like that.

I continued looking for work in Market Harborough, without any semblance of success. Then a most surprising letter came in the post. It was from the Inland Revenue and stated that I was being offered a job as an audio-typist at the new Special Office, which was being opened at Chadwick House in Solihull in the autumn of 1977. On the strength of my previous service I would be taken on without having to go through an interview procedure, although I would have to complete the application form. This was a pretty interesting development and in terms of seeking God's will for the next stage of our lives, one not to be discarded lightly.

I telephoned the personnel officer whose name was on the letter. We chatted about the job and I explained my situation in terms of where I was living, and that I would have to find somewhere to live, in the vicinity of the new office. The lady was understanding and even agreed to hold the job open for a month or two, to enable us to move to the area.

Sylvia and I chatted further with Bryan and Jenny on the phone. Bryan agreed to check out the situation with regard to Council housing in Solihull and also write to a number of Housing Associations for us. They invited us over to Solihull to have lunch with them on Sunday and visit their church.

The decade of the 1970s proved to be an interesting and exciting one in the life of the Christian Church in the UK and indeed, around the world. A song we used to sing at that time sums up the feel of what was going on:

"All over the world the Spirit is moving
all over the world as the prophets said it would be
All over the world there's a mighty revelation
Of the glory of the Lord as the waters cover the sea".

Christian people of all ages seemed to be coming into the experience that I had had a few years earlier, in that they were being 'baptised', 'drenched' or 'soaked' with the Holy Spirit and speaking in new tongues; or as I came to understand later, a love language to Jesus.

When something like that happens to you, it isn't easy to keep quiet about it. You're so excited that you just want to tell people, just as you would if you'd passed your driving test, gained a place at your favoured university, or were expecting your first baby. Unfortunately the experience I have described didn't sit too well with certain people's theology and in order to go on experiencing the new found freedom in the Holy Spirit, thousands felt they had to leave the established traditional churches. Some Church of England Vicars such as David Watson and Colin Urquhart, experienced this work of the Holy Spirit for themselves, and managed to adapt their set Anglican services in ways to accommodate people who wanted to move into new and freer expressions of worship. The majority of people however, were either forced out, or voluntarily left their churches and together with other like-minds, formed new ones. Many of these new groups began to meet in homes for prayer and fellowship and this gave rise to the phrase 'House Church Movement'. These new house churches grew numerically and there came the need to move out of homes; schools, community centres and even old cinema buildings became alternative places of worship.

The Solihull Christian Fellowship came into being in this way. At the time we visited, there were about fifty people, mainly young and middle aged, meeting in a room at (what was then) the Solihull Civic Hall. What struck us was the warmth and friendliness of the welcome; I have never been hugged so tightly, by so many people, in such a short time in all my life! The music and singing were really joyful, exuberant and demonstrative, with hands raised and plenty of dancing going on. It was great fun and we really enjoyed it; so too did the children, which was very important to us in view of the changes taking place in their lives too.

After dinner with the Pullingers we headed off back to Market Harborough, with Sylvia commenting, "I really felt at home in that church".

I did, too - but I think my confidence had taken a battering, because I still couldn't see how we would get to move to Solihull, or anywhere near it.

We decided to continue going to Solihull each Sunday for the morning service, all the time praying and hoping that something would turn up from an accommodation perspective. Bryan had worked tirelessly for several weeks contacting Solihull Housing Department and also writing to numerous Housing Associations, all to no avail. I was grateful that the Inland Revenue were still keeping an audio-typing job open for me, but for how long I wondered.

One Sunday whilst attending the Fellowship, it was announced that the following week after the morning service the whole of the Fellowship and any others who wanted to join them would be meeting for a simple lunch in Dorridge

Park, just a few miles outside Solihull town centre. The idea was that each family brought something simple to eat, such as soup and a few bread rolls and that the money that was saved from not having the traditional Sunday roast would be given to the charity TEAR Fund, for use amongst the hungry in the third world. It sounded a great idea and it gave us the opportunity to get to know a few more people and so we agreed to get involved, having no idea that God had yet another of his surprises in store for us. They don't come much bigger than this one.

The following Sunday, one by one, car loads left the centre of Solihull, making for Dorridge Park. We were happy to follow another family as Sylvia was not too sure where we were going. It was a lovely late-summer's afternoon, ideal for a picnic and games of cricket and rounders. We sat around on the grass in family groups in a very pleasant scene. There were lots of children and Beverley, Sara and Allison had some great fun with their newly-found friends. By about 3 o'clock, the clear blue skies had given way to cloud and a few spots of rain and along with a few other families, we decided it was time to pack up and make our way down the M6 in the direction of home. We were almost back at the car when we became aware that we were being called by a couple who were running after us. Somewhat out of breath, they eventually arrived at our car and I think, by way of making initial conversation asked if we were going home at that moment. We said that it had got a bit chilly and as we had a fairly lengthy drive ahead of us, thought we would make tracks.

"Before you go…" the gentleman said [although he has always preferred to remain modest about this, his name is Alan Cameron, married to Heather], "there's something we need to tell you. For some time now, we've been aware of your need for somewhere to live and we've been praying about it."

My mind was already going back to Mrs. Watts. A feeling of *deja-vu* swept over me.

The lady picked up the story. "We've seen your commitment in coming all this way, week after week, and as we've recently come into some money we thought we'd like to help you buy a house,. We'd like you to receive this cheque as a gift, with our love. There's a modern housing estate in Solihull, called Damsonwood, and there are some nice family homes up there, near to schools and shops. So if you're not in too much of a hurry, why don't we take you for a look around?"

At this point Sylvia shed a few tears. I was trying hard not to shake with emotion. Our three little girls sat in the car, probably wondering what mummy and daddy were up to.

Having recovered our composure only slightly, we got in the car to follow this benevolent couple with me still clutching the envelope with the mysterious cheque still hidden from view. I opened the envelope and showed Sylvia the cheque. She gasped loudly when she saw the amount, and had we not been following someone, she would have pulled over in order to have a good cry. She could hardly get her words out as she said, "It's for thirteen thousand pounds..."

This time we all gasped, including the children as I put them in the picture as to what was happening to us on this amazing Sunday afternoon. Even though they were only five years of age, they dissolved into squeals of delight. Even though it's a lot of money today, it was a mini-fortune back then!

Soon we were pulling into the estate in question with loads of modern looking flats, maisonettes and a variety of different styled houses. We drove around following our benefactors and they slowed right down, each time we saw a "For Sale" board outside a house. We got out and looked in through the windows of some of them. Our friends (who we later discovered, were the same people who bought that washing machine for us, four years earlier) knew the Damsonwood estate very well, as they had other friends living there; knew exactly what kind of house they were looking for and which would suit us down to the ground. We pulled up outside one and it certainly had a feel-good factor about it for us. The following day we fixed up a time for viewing. This was the house from where the 'wallpaper story' emanated from, and as you know, we went ahead and purchased the property.

We said our goodbyes to Market Harborough and to our great friends, Peter and Margaret Jackson, and departed for Solihull just fifteen months after leaving Birmingham in the first place. We left Watson Avenue on the Friday and I commenced my new job as an audio-typist with Inland Revenue Special Office, on the following Monday.

This was the beginning of a very settled and happy period in our lives. Church life was great, work was extremely interesting and the children were a joy to us as they grew up in this most pleasing of environments. Outside our three bedroom, end-town house we had a nice garden with a cherry tree in the middle of it where our daughters would often sit and play with their friends. Beyond our garden was a lovely green area, with trees where again the many little children living around the green could play in safety.

I suppose you know the old saying "New house, new baby"? Well, it was true in our case. Settled into our new home, church and work we discovered that Sylvia was pregnant. After a reasonably trouble-free pregnancy (you can tell it's a man writing can't you!) Sylvia gave birth to our one and only son. Ian Paul was born on 5th September 1978, in Solihull Hospital.

A single lady from church made herself available for baby-sitting, whenever I wanted to go hospital visiting to see Sylvia and my new son. Joy was a wonderful provision from God for us, during those years. Every time the children needed new shoes, she made herself available to buy them for us. Which was no small expense, even then.

Since getting married, wherever we lived and went to church, God saw to it that we had some truly wonderful, faithful friends. Our lives were enriched because of them. Now it was about to happen again. Gordon and Julia Coleman really were, and still are, quite a remarkable couple. Their capacity to love people seems to know no bounds.

Julia invited us to their house for Boxing Day celebrations, on our first Christmas in Solihull. They met and married in London. Julia was a nurse and Gordon had trained as a Doctor in general practice. They moved to Solihull not long before us, and like us, had settled into life at the Solihull Christian Fellowship. It was on that Boxing Day that Gordon did a pregnancy test on Sylvia and was able to confirm that she was, in fact, expecting.

When we first met they had two small children, Jonathan and Mark and two others soon followed, in Timothy and Ruth. We got on famously as two families, and as the children were growing up we had some wonderful holidays together, with many laughs along the way. Gordon and I had this terrific banter going between us, and we would bounce-off each other, in a jocular kind of way.

You never saw Gordon without a shirt and tie, as befits a man of stature like a Doctor. We used to wonder if he even slept in his shirt and tie. Being the man he is, he would often play up to this role and on holiday once, we were on a beach near Towyn in Wales and Gordon was getting changed into his swimwear, under a huge beach towel. Suddenly Gordon began to make the sound of a trumpet fanfare and emerged in just his swimming trunks - and his tie around his neck. He then took off, dragging me with him, running along the beach with his tie trailing in the wind, to the great amusement of our wives and children, with plenty of bemused holidaymakers looking on.

Gordon was actually born in Iran, one of four sons to medical missionaries John and Audrey Coleman. This could explain why Gordon hardly ever buys anything without bartering for it first! The family were forced into the international spotlight in 1981 when Gordon's parents were taken hostage in Iran, on suspicion of spying. They were captive for six months until the Archbishop of Canterbury's Special Envoy, Terry Waite, flew into Iran and negotiated their release. It turned out to be a wonderful story because John and Audrey, who had warm affection for the Iranian people, gained the respect of their captors and became good friends with a number of them, almost seeing them as their own sons. It was such a privilege to be close to the family in those days, to witness the dignity with which they handled the whole episode. Truly this was Christian love and character being lived out before our very eyes. Terry Waite describes how impressed he was by John and Audrey, when relaying the story of their release in his bestselling autobiography, Taken On Trust.

The couple have only fairly recently passed-on, and they are two of my heroes who demonstrated to one and all, the rich values to which we should all aspire. They were exemplary parents and true Christian leaders who walked in humility and integrity at all times.

Before leaving the Colemans behind there's story that has always stuck in my mind. This was during one of our family holidays and we were on the beach at Paignton in Devon. We were going to take the children to a show and the comedian, Jimmy Crickett, was appearing in his summer show. Gordon left us on the beach and went back to his car for a short nap, something he had to have every day. A power nap of five to ten minutes did him so much good. On this occasion, however, it was about an hour before he returned to us. He began to confess what he'd been up to. He'd been to the theatre box office and bought tickets for the Jimmy Crickett show that night. He told us that he'd negotiated for the best seats in the house at a discounted rate, on the grounds that they had with them a blind man, who was partially deaf. He also inferred that I was a bit simple, too! We got the best seats and enjoyed a magnificent show. We laughed so much. I remember Jimmy Crickett's opening line, "Sorry I'm late. I couldn't find the M6 , so I went down the M3 twice".

I later wrote to Jimmy to congratulate him. I had a really lovely letter back from him, which I have kept to this day.

These were relatively contented years for us, what with me having a settled job which I enjoyed and with us being happy members of Solihull Christian Fellowship. I still had a passion for sharing the good news about Jesus and I managed to persuade our church Elders to agree to a mission in our local pub, The Golden Acres. I'd heard that my good friend from Torch, Peter Jackson, was in town. I'd an idea to use him in our local pub. I had chatted with the pub landlord, saying that I had a blind friend who was a professional pianist. Could I invite him along as a guest to the pub, to play a medley of old favourites and incorporate into that, some Gospel tunes? The manager thought it an excellent idea, as did the Elders of our church. The evenings went well, with more than the usual number of people turning up on a Monday and Tuesday night, to hear Peter playing and sharing about the love of God between each medley. A couple of months later we had an American drama group visiting the local churches, and I was able to get them into the pub as well, to present the Christian message through their well-performed drama sketches.

I set up a meeting in our local Damsonwood School, for the ex-Leeds United footballer and Birmingham City manager Willie Bell, to come and share his Christian faith.

A group of us from the Fellowship leafleted the area about the event. We had a disappointing response. Apart from church people, only two others attended. However, a man by the name of Ed Ryder, with whom I became good friends, prayed with Willie Bell after the meeting and gave his life to Jesus. Both Ed and his wife Mavis, later became members of another local church in Solihull. Our event and all our hard work was by no means in vain. I am reminded of what the Bible says, in that all Heaven rejoices when one sinner turns back to God.

Willie Bell's name always takes me back to our days at Market Harborough.

I was having a nice, relaxing bath one Friday night. I'd taken my radio into the bathroom with me, to listen to a football phone-in programme. The programme was coming from BRMB radio in Birmingham, and in order to get any kind of decent reception, I had to dangle the aerial on an angle outside the bathroom Window. Before you ask, yes it was a bit breezy! On this phone-in, Willie Bell, then manager of Birmingham City was under fire from highly animated and often insulting fans, who were aggrieved over their team's recent performances. I couldn't help but admire the gracious and gentlemanly way in which Willie dealt with all of the callers. I was moved to write to him, saying that he'd shown me a glorious example of how to behave in the face of hostile criticism. For an Aston Villa fan like me, to write to the 'opposition' in such a way, shows how impressed I was! I went on to say that I'd be praying for him and his family, in all the tests and trials that they were going through. I explained to Willie in my letter, just how I'd become a Christian and the massive difference that knowing Jesus Christ personally, had made to my life.

On the day that my letter was due to have arrived on Willie's desk, Birmingham City were at home to the mighty Liverpool. The Merseysiders won by four goals to nil. Willie Bell was sacked. I found myself in the unusual position of being concerned for the plight of City and their manager. "So much for my letter and my prayers. What must Willie be thinking of my God now?"

I didn't hear anything until a few months later. Out of the blue, I received a postcard. It was from America and signed by Willie Bell. He thanked me for my kind letter, and said that following his dismissal he went to America to visit friends. Those friends were Christians and they'd taken him and his wife to a prayer meeting, which in turn led to Willie and Mary giving their lives to Jesus. Willie signed off his card, promising that he would be in touch when he returned to the United Kingdom.

True to his word, after Willie was appointed manager of Lincoln City, he got in touch and invited Sylvia and I to their house in Lincoln. We went to see them for a couple of days and it was so gracious of them to give up their master bedroom so that we could sleep there. It was the height of luxury for us, especially the en-suite, which contained a huge round bath with steps leading up to it! The most wonderful thing, however, was to see Willie and Mary's sincere and simple faith. We visited their church on the Sunday, met their Pastor, John Shelbourne, who allowed me the privilege of preaching and sharing my testimony of faith in Jesus Christ. It was a lovely couple of days. We kept in regular contact until Willie quit football and went back to the United States, to live in Virginia where he studied at Liberty Bible College. The last I heard, Willie was taking teams of young footballers out to various parts of the world, to coach in schools and share their living faith in the Lord Jesus Christ.

Hot Chocolate sang, "It started with a kiss", but my friendship with Willie Bell started with a radio aerial outside the bathroom window. With God, you never know what seemingly innocuous incident he's going to use as part of his great plan of saving men and women. Even managers of the dreaded Birmingham City. Makes for an exciting life though!

For some years I'd been having painful infections in my left ear, often with an offensive, smelly discharge. Eventually it was decided that I should go into hospital for a couple of days, to have grommets fitted. Quite a routine procedure, often performed on children who suffer from what is known as 'glue ear'. My friend Dr. Gordon Coleman was quite interested in ears, and gained permission from the Consultant to sit in on the procedure - things did not go to plan however. A procedure which should only have taken a matter of minutes, turned into hours. When the knife went in, it caught my jugular-vein and I bled profusely for a considerable amount of time. I'm not fully aware of all that went on surgically, but what I was told afterwards was that, very unexpectedly, they found that I had an aneurysm on my jugular-vein, situated near to the left eardrum. Apparently when an aneurysm is situated on the jugular-vein it is referred to as a 'jugular bulb'. I was told that I could have been born with it, or that it had developed some time later in life. The best thing to do, was just to get on and live life and forget about it. That was hard at first, and it was really quite a chilling experience when the Consultant called us in, to tell us all about it. Since then I think we've taken their advice and just got on with life. As recorded in Psalm 31, my times are in God's hands and I commit myself to him each day, giving thanks for the fact that I'm alive and have breath in my body, to do good and to please God.

I was also enjoying working with Rev. Michael Blood, on BBC Radio WM. Once a month, I reviewed the latest Christian music releases. We'd do a 30-minute slot into a Wednesday afternoon programme, presented by the late Nicky Steele, a local disc jockey and fellow Aston Villa supporter. Apart from football, Nicky and I also shared a common enjoyment of soul music. These sequences would be edited and then go out as a segment in Michael's Sunday morning religious programme, A Word In Advance.

Over the years a number of recordings and artistes made an impact, none more so than Love Song For No. 2 by a Canadian duo, Mickey and Bekki. I played the title track, which had a kind of Carpenters' feel to it, giving it a big build up and calling all married couples to gather around their radios and listen to the words, because this was just for them. Of course I had no idea of the impact it was going to have, especially in one couple's relationship. Part of the song lyric:

"I'll sing you a love song that came to my mind,
It's not a typical love song because it's one of mine.
Now when I say I love you, you know that it's true
Even though you're number two.

For Jesus is number one in my life,
So second place will have to do for you
But I'm counting on spending the rest of my life in love with the two of you."

The week following the show going out, Michael received a letter from a teacher saying that the song Love Song For No. 2 had been used by God to save his marriage. He told how he and his wife had had a blazing row that Sunday morning, and he stormed out of the house, having packed his case, fully intending never to return. As far as he was concerned, it was all over. However, as he was driving away in his car, he heard me invite all married couples to gather around their radios and listen to the words. In his anger he pulled the car over to the side, parked up and listened. God spoke to him through the song and he turned the car around, went home and made things up with his wife.

Such is the power of music, to be able to speak to and inspire people. If God is working through the music too, then it's an incredibly powerful means of communication, reaching right into the spirit of men and women in a way that the spoken word doesn't seem able to.

I miss working on the radio. Even now, I'd love to have the opportunity to play music with a message for a few hours, over the air-waves and allow it to touch people deep in their hearts. An old Bible story tells of how King Saul, when he was deeply troubled in his soul, sent for the shepherd boy David to come and play the harp for him. As David played, Saul's troubled mind was eased. That's the way I would like to use music. To bring love, peace and joy into people's lives.

Although not specifically written as a Gospel song, I think Flying Without Wings by West Life is one of the most powerful spiritual songs I've ever heard. There's been times when I've been flat on my face, listening to it with the volume up and I've almost felt as if I was in Heaven. On another occasion, whilst travelling in the car alongside Sylvia with that particular song playing on the stereo, tears began to stream down my face as I felt profoundly grateful to be married to, and in love with, Sylvia. The words of the song that broke me up:

"Well, for me it's waking up beside you,
To watch the sunrise on your face
To know that I can say I love you
In any given time or place.
"It's little things that only I know,
Those are the things that make you mine
And it's like flying without wings
'Cos you're my special thing
I'm flying without wings.
"And you're the place my life begins,
And you'll be where it ends.

I'm flying without wings
And that's the joy you bring
I'm flying without wings"

(words and music by Steve Mac and Wayne Hector)

I looked towards Sylvia. As our eyes met, we knew what the other was thinking. Sylvia took her left hand off the steering wheel, for a moment, and clasped my hand - it was an incredibly tender, unplanned moment when no words were spoken, because the song said it all.

My job as an audio typist in Solihull was going well. The work was interesting; I worked for a really nice group of investigative tax Inspectors. No, honestly! We worked together like a tight-knit family unit. It helped me, that all of the Inspectors I typed for, were very keen on sport! especially football! Jim McMahon, a Scotsman, was an avid supporter of Motherwell Football Club. (Many English football fans have a favourite Scottish team and Motherwell just happens to be mine and has been, ever since I heard their name when I was a child.) Again, by way of coincidence maybe, during my ill-fated time with Torch, one of my deputation trips was to Motherwell. To a lovely couple, Louis and Kitty Howson. I was impressed by the way in which Louis ruled his house in a quiet, but firm manner. It was a privilege to stay in their home and sense the peace of God, in their family. Whilst there, I preached at Wishaw and Hamilton Baptist Churches, both on the outskirts of Motherwell itself.

Back to my tax inspector and his passion for Motherwell. Jim didn't usually arrive at the office until around nine, whereas I was usually in for 7.30am. On April Fools Day, I decided to play a joke and I left the following message on Jim's desk:

"Very sorry to hear about the fire at Fir Park and to learn that most of the Motherwell stadium has burnt down. Commiserations, John F."

At five past nine, my telephone rang. When I answered, I could tell it was a very upset Jim McMahon. I simply said, "April fool" and put the phone down.

Less than a minute later, the office door flew open. In stormed an enraged Scottish tax inspector, mouthing a load of expletives in my direction. For a fleeting few seconds, I thought I'd really gone too far, this time…it was only in fun however, and he very quickly turned it to laughter - it was his way of getting me back!

I had some good times at Chadwick House and was able to start a Christian Fellowship meeting, once a week in the building for those who wanted to meet for prayer, Bible study and mutual encouragement. We didn't have great numbers, but we developed some quality friendships and were able to support each other through some difficult times. Whilst the advent of this was undoubtedly worthwhile, I couldn't shake off the deep conviction that my primary aim in life was to serve my God in a full-time ministry. After all it was he who had called me, years earlier, when on the Wyrley Birch housing estate to "Launch out into the deep". I've since realised that that was not a one-off call to that housing estate, but is for the whole of life. On several occasions I spoke to my Elders at

Solihull Christian Fellowship about it and eventually, after I'd been back at the Inland Revenue for four years, it was agreed that I should resign my typing job in order to work full time for the Fellowship in a paid capacity. I was involved with leading one of the church house groups, available for outreach and counselling work within the church and also took up opportunities to speak in school assemblies and Religious Education classes. I was able to continue responding to preaching invitations, get more involved with local radio and of course, have more time to study the Bible and pray. Time working as an employee of the Solihull Christian Fellowship was financially, the most comfortable time of my life. They really looked after me. I was grateful to one of the leaders of the church at the time, Jonathan Wallis (son of the late Christian author and teacher, Arthur Wallis) who argued that people should be paid not according to their needs, but according to their worth. It was lovely one month, therefore, to get a most generous pay rise.

That said, there was still something which was not quite right. There was something missing. I didn't feel that I was giving the church value for money. I wasn't feeling fulfilled, spiritually. Alan Cameron, one of our Elders at the time and a dear friend, said I reminded him of a cricketer swinging his bat and not making connection with the ball. That was a pretty accurate analogy. I carried on for a while afterwards, swinging my proverbial bat as lustily as ever, until events took a surprising and to many of us, devastating twist.

I'd been made aware that things had become a little tense in the leadership of the church. It was all to do with the direction the church was going in. Our Eldership of eight fine Christian men were finding it difficult to reach agreement on a number of issues. Following one momentous church meeting, it transpired that four of the Elders were going to continue to lead the Solihull Christian Fellowship, whilst the other four would seek God as to the way forward for them and their families. The problem was, that these were our friends and it was one of the hardest things Sylvia and I have ever had to do, to choose which way to go. In the end, rightly or wrongly, we did what we have always done and followed our hearts. The result was that along with about twenty others, we decided to leave Solihull Christian Fellowship and many of our dear friends, including Bryan and Jenny, Alan and Heather and Gordon and Julia, with whom we had enjoyed such wonderful times. Not to be sniffed at, was the fact that we left behind the generous salary that the church had honoured me with. All I can say is that in everything, even when it has been later perceived to be a mistake, we have always tried to follow the leading of the Holy spirit and please God by our actions. I think it was then that I first discovered a verse in the Bible, in Psalm 84, that has come to mean so much to me:

"Blessed are those whose strength is in you,
who have set their hearts on pilgrimage."

After a cooling-off period, when a number of us didn't attend church for a few weeks, we were eventually drawn back together with a need for fellowship, praise and worship God and to hear from God together, about the way forward.

It eventually formed into a new church, initially called New Covenant Church, then New Life Church and finally, The King's Church. We were not destined to be part of this new venture for long, because we were about to 'launch out' once again.

Chapter Three

Cornwall Here We Come!

It had been an interesting nine years in Solihull. We had seen the birth of Ian, our only son, and the growth of our three girls, into teenagers. We had been the subject of two television programmes for Central Television, conducted a campaign to get pelican crossings installed outside the school where Allison was knocked over and set up the Aston Villa Christian Supporters Association. I had also initiated Ian into the joys of being a Villa supporter and over the years, enjoyed and endured some unforgettable times together, at Villa Park and around the country. Most importantly of all, we have had many quality times together, as father and son and that is priceless and irreplaceable. I would say that any time spent alone with my children has been precious, as too is time spent with my wife.

It was one of those precious times alone with one of my daughters, which indirectly led to our next major change of direction. Sara, one of the twins, now aged thirteen accompanied me on a three-day trip to London. I was attending a Christian conference in Kensington, on behalf of the breakaway group from Solihull Christian Fellowship. There was a preacher at the conference from the USA, by the name of Jerry Savelle. He was unknown to me at the time, but destined to become one of my favourite preachers. It was felt that he would have something to say which would be relevant to the way forward for us, as a group. Jerry was from the 'Word of Faith' camp, in terms of his theology and that was certainly an emphasis which was coming into the British Church at the time. I found what he had to say to be balanced and inspiring. Then and since, I have found Jerry Savelle to be a man of integrity, fully conversant with the British way of thinking; which cannot be said for all American preachers!

Whilst in London, Sara and I stayed with some good friends. Harry and Joyce Hughes first crossed my path when I was working with Torch, at the Millmead Centre in Guildford. Harry got on well with me because of our love for football. Not surprising really. Harry was an ex-professional footballer, playing many times for, and captaining, Chelsea in the 1950s. A rugged and uncompromising centre-half, I believe. Harry had become a Christian through the ministry of my good friend Peter Jackson, a few years earlier, and he also had the distinction of being baptised by total immersion in the River Jordan, whilst on a pilgrimage there.

Harry was great fun to be around, and handsome too; that's probably why Sara volunteered to come on the trip with me! All the kids loved Uncle Harry as they called him.

When Sara and I arrived in London, we had trouble at the tube station. She got through the ticket barrier first, whilst I was stuck on the other side, trying to find where I had to insert my ticket. For some reason Sara got an attack of the giggles, and couldn't get her words out to give me instructions as to, "where to put it" and the more I struggled the more she laughed. It sounds cruel, but it was one of those moments when you have to be there, to really appreciate the funny side of a simple situation. We went from there and asked a newspaper seller if he could tell us the way to Kensington.

He startled us by saying, "Which one?"

We didn't know there was more than one. This started Sara laughing all over again. "Is there more than one Kensington?" she said.

"Yes" counselled the man. "There's South Kensington and there's Kensington High Street…so which one do you want?"

Sara and I looked at each other. We decided to go for Kensington High Street. Thankfully, it turned out to be…the right choice.

Before going to Harry and Joyce's house, we decided that, as it was getting late, it would be too much to expect Joyce to cook us a meal, so we went to McDonalds. I was famished and went for a full meal. Sara just had a drink and some chicken nuggets. She too, made the right choice. When we arrived at our destination, as soon as Joyce opened the door you could smell the aroma of a cooked meal. Harry and Joyce made us feel completely at home, though as Sara and the others tucked into their roast dinner, there were a few wry comments made about my apparent lack of appetite. Sara didn't miss the opportunity to wind me up a little more either, when our hosts disappeared into the kitchen to get the apple pie and custard! It was a struggle, but I made it in the end. I know it would've been simpler to have just admitted that we had been to McDonalds, but typical of me, I didn't want to hurt Joyce's feelings.

Reminds me of a preacher I heard about, from Birmingham, who told this story about himself. He'd been staying at the home of an elderly lady for a couple of days, as he was the guest preacher at the church she attended. The only thing was, she gave him baked beans for every meal…breakfast, lunch and dinner. If he was on a diet, you could call it the F-plan! He hated baked beans, and come the final tea on the Sunday afternoon, once the lady left the room he scraped the beans off his toast and rolled them up in his handkerchief. About an hour later, he was preaching in church, when he began to sweat. He promptly pulled out his handkerchief to wipe his brow, only for baked beans to go flying everywhere! This is a true story. Can you imagine the look on the old lady's face, as she sat there in the front row! Goes to show, honesty is the best policy. Even if it does mean hurting someone's feelings for a moment or two.

Back to the conference in London and whilst the subject of my visit, Jerry Savelle, was very good it was somebody else who caught my attention for a completely different reason.

The Principle *[not his real name]* was a very inspiring preacher, hailing from the (American) State of Wisconsin. I'd never previously heard of him, either, but I was enraptured by his testimony of how God had brought him from his job as Dean of Students at the Christ For The Nations Bible Institute, in Dallas, Texas to establish a similar Bible training centre in Cornwall. Dr. Johnson said it was his vision to raise up men and women of passion, and equip them with the necessary gifts to go out as evangelists across the continent of Europe and further afield, to spread the gospel of the Lord Jesus Christ. I'm the first to admit that, up to that point I had been very 'anti' the idea of Bible College. Anything to do with school turned me off because of my negative experiences as a child. I don't think I had any particularly nasty experiences during my schooldays, but I couldn't wait to leave and get out into the real world. When it came to the matter of learning, I always felt that I wasn't very good at it. Taking exams turned me into a nervous wreck. From what I knew about Bible Colleges, they too seemed very academic. They were there for so-called clever people. That didn't include me.

What The Principle seemed to be conveying, however, was that the college he ran in Cornwall was for anyone who had a call from God to full-time ministry, and desired to be better equipped with a knowledge of God's word, thus going out with a greater confidence to do his will.

My interest was aroused. I was already intrigued by the fact that I'd recently been given some live worship tapes, which were recorded at Christ For The Nations Institute in Dallas. I'd also been to a seminar to hear Clifford Beasley and in his talk he had referred to a Gordon Lindsey, founder of the Institute.

Now, here I was in London and through The Principle I was hearing about it again and whereas before I had, only half in jest, said to Sylvia, "I wonder if God is calling us to go to Dallas, so that I can attend Christ For The Nations?" Now it had come to England.

On returning to Solihull, I duly 'reported back' to Steve Wood and the group about what I'd gained from the conference, as well as making available the tapes of the messages I'd brought back with me. I couldn't shake off the message from The Principle and there was a growing conviction within me, that God wanted me to attend The Bible College *[not it's real name]* in Redruth, Cornwall where The Principle was the Principal.

I didn't mention these thoughts to Sylvia because I didn't want to worry her unnecessarily, but as wives are prone to do, she picked up on the fact that something was playing on my mind. She quizzed me accordingly, asking what it was that was bothering me.

Hesitantly I began, "I think God may be calling us to move to Cornwall".

"You must be joking!" came the incredulous reply. "A few months ago it was Dallas, now Cornwall. So what's got into you?"

As calmly as I could, I explained to Sylvia how this had all come about. But I could understand if she was thinking, "Who is this *crazy man* that I'm married to?"

Sylvia, seeing that I was deadly serious about this said, "If this is of God, then He's going to have to show me, in ways that I can understand".

Over the next few weeks, God did exactly that. Firstly, the Avon lady called, saying it would be the last time we would be seeing her because she and her husband were selling up and moving to Cornwall, to run a Bed & Breakfast business. Then we went to visit some friends from another church, who we only saw very rarely. They told us that they had just booked a holiday; guess where? Cornwall. Finally, Ed Ryder (you remember the man who became a Christian at the meeting we held, with Willie Bell?) came to see us to let us know that he and his wife Mavis had decided to sell up and move to Cornwall. Even Sylvia had to admit that all of this was probably a bit more than just a coincidence.

Once Sylvia and I were agreed on our course of action, I decided it was time to share the idea with Christian leaders and friends. To my surprise, most of them didn't share in my excitement, but rather couldn't understand why I was prepared to take what they thought was a reckless step. Undeterred, convinced that God was in this, we decided to apply to The Bible College to see if I would be granted a place. I chatted on the phone with the Secretary and arranged to go down to the College for an interview. The meeting with The Principle and his wife Prin, went really well. They were warm and friendly and didn't see the fact that I was blind as being any problem at all. They said I could take my cassette recorder into lectures. Even sit my exams by whatever means was comfortable with me. I duly applied for, and was accepted on to a two-year Diploma course in Christian Leadership Training.

I'll never forget the touching response of our friends Brian and Janet Davis when we told them what we were about to do. They said, "We don't understand why you are doing this, but we want you to know that we support you, we love you and if it turns out that it all goes wrong and even if you lose everything, our home is your home and our possessions are your possessions and we will never say 'I told you so'…". That response was so liberating for us. It showed us what true friendship is all about.

Of course we discussed the matter with our children, who were all excited at the prospect of going to live by the seaside. Our house in Solihull sold within a couple of days and it necessitated Sylvia going down to Cornwall with my parents to have a look at some houses and make an offer on something which took her fancy. I trusted Sylvia implicitly to find something suitable, in the right location. She found a pleasant, modern three-bedroom house in Redruth. We put in an offer, had it accepted and the sale of our house in Solihull and the purchase of 60 South Park, Redruth, all went through without a hitch, enabling me to have a couple of weeks to settle in, before starting college.

Prior to our move, there was a major setback for us. My mum had been having some difficulty, for a few months, in swallowing her food. It would stick in her throat and she would have to cough until she could spit the food back out of her mouth. It was quite distressing for her. After eventually persuading her to see a doctor, and attend hospital, she underwent various tests which confirmed that she was suffering from cancer of the oesophagus. There followed a course of radio therapy. One hospital visit, dad and Sylvia were called in to be told by the Consultant that mum probably only had about six months to live. It was a devastating blow for all the family. Dad didn't want mum to be told that her condition was terminal and so we complied and respected his request. Of course, it made the decision to move to Cornwall all the more difficult to go through with. In the end, I concluded that because God is sovereign, what had happened with mum hadn't taken him by surprise. He knew about it all along. Yet he had still called us to Cornwall. We therefore went ahead with the move, entrusting mum and indeed the whole family, into God's caring hands.

The big move, 260 miles down to the south west corner of England, went really well. Beverley, Sara and Allison once again settled well into their new school, though it was a little harder for Ian at Trewirge Infants. He was only there for a few months before moving up to the junior school, where he got on much better and became a star pupil, especially excelling in sports. Ian captained the school football team, scoring one amazing goal from inside his own half, his long-range shot bouncing over the head of the diminutive goalkeeper. He went on to represent West Cornwall at various age levels.

The Bible College was situated in a village called Pool, which separated the two tin-mining towns of Redruth and Camborne. To get to-and-from college I either had to get a lift in the car from Sylvia, or catch a bus for the mile-and-a-half journey. Just over two miles away, was our nearest beach. This was Portreath and Sylvia loved to drive there, once the children had gone off to school and I had gone to college. In the winter time especially, she really appreciated parking up her car and glancing out to sea, when she occasionally lifted her head from reading the morning newspaper. All in all, we had some wonderful family times down at Portreath. Coming from a large industrial city like Birmingham, it was a novelty and a thrill to live near so many beaches with picturesque places such as Porthtowen, Perranporth and St. Ives within half hour's drive.

My first term at Bible College went superbly. I drank in all the lectures. The lessons were not as academic as I had imagined, but more like solid Bible teaching.

The college had about thirty five students from countries such as Ghana, Nigeria, India, Germany, USA and of course, the United Kingdom. We became very good friends with many of the students, and with many of them being single, they used to love to come to our home and be part of a family. One surprise attraction that we had, was a simple game called 'Ringboard'. This is the game when you have six small rubber rings that you throw and try to get them to hang on hooks on the board, which give you certain scores. As an adult you probably stand about two metres away and throw the rings one by one and see who could get the highest scores. This game really brought out the competitive edge in people and there were some really tense and exciting duals taking place. Such a simple game gave us so much pleasure. Some of the young men from Ghana became especially close friends of ours. It was not uncommon to see Alex, Seth, Osai or Samuel stroll into our house, take off their shoes and lie down on the settee and go to sleep. One night, they came round and made us an African meal which consisted of chicken in peanut butter soup, all placed in a big pot in the middle of the dining room table; then we all pitched in, dipping our fu-fu balls. The word 'scrumptious' didn't do this exquisite meal justice.

Everyone at the college was encouraged to live by faith, trusting in God for every penny. One day Alex came to me, saying in a deep Afro-English tone, "Brother John, I would be honoured if you would join me in prayer one Night, because I have a financial need".

I felt deeply honoured that Alex should ask me to pray with him. In my eyes Alex was a mighty man of prayer, as indeed were all of those students from Africa. I had a financial need too, which was causing me concern as our car was in need of some urgent attention. It was no small job. I was therefore very pleased to join Alex, one night. I guessed, knowing him, that we might be praying all night and so at 10.00pm, I said goodnight to Sylvia and informed her that I would see her in the morning.

When Alex and I started to pray, we were fairly quiet for a few minutes and then he got up off his knees and began to march up and down the room. He prayed using his gift of speaking in tongues. I arose from my chair and joined him pacing the floor. We were both speaking in tongues, then singing in tongues, and it was amazing to hear these two voices blending, as we called out to God in worship and placing our needs before him. It was an exhilarating time, as the songs and the prayers ebbed and flowed. Taking the occasional sip of water we were really going for it, until about 1.15am when Alex suddenly stopped and a great peace descended on the room. I followed his lead and sat down on a chair for a few minutes, before Alex broke the silence by saying, "Thank you brother, that was powerful".

"Yes it was, but why have we stopped?" I asked curiously.

"Because we got the breakthrough. Didn't you sense it?" he asked.

Well, I said I did, but in truth I didn't. I was glad Alex was happy however, and even more glad that I could unexpectedly go and join Sylvia back in our bed, much earlier than anticipated!

I was shocked and thrilled then, when a couple of days later I came home from college at lunchtime, for Sylvia to tell me excitedly that we had received a cheque for £1,000 through the post. She was a bit worried about the cheque, because instead of having a normal signature, it had a little squiggle where the signature should have been. She wondered if it was a hoax. To satisfy our curiosity I rang the Building Society, and they confirmed that the cheque was legitimate; it was simply that the donors wished to remain anonymous. We'd been taught the practice of tithing, so we decided to give £100 to my prayer buddy Alex (10% of what we had) and when I gave him the money he hugged me tightly and did a dance of delight in praise of God, because he said that that was the exact amount he had asked God for. Needless to say, we were able to put the rest towards our car repair, which cost us in excess of £500.

It was just one of many thrilling examples of praying with the Africans which I experienced during our time in Cornwall. Most Friday nights at the college, we had an all-night prayer meeting to pray for the nations of the world. They were truly powerful times. There was also a prayer meeting on weekday mornings before college at 7 o'clock for an hour, again to pray for the nations. It was a college which expressed God's heart for the world.

These early morning prayer meetings saw us praying for six or seven nations each day and by working to this outline, we would cover all the nations of the world in a month. One particular morning I had a remarkable experience. We were praying for what was then the Soviet Union (USSR), East and West Germany and South Africa. There were about six of us students praying and as we marched the floor of the classroom singing and praying in tongues I had a sense in my spirit of messengers from God going out to these nations and declaring "Jesus reigns". I became thrilled and excited on the inside and began to sing out boldly in tongues, something I don't do lightly or often, because I'm conscious of not having a very tuneful voice. As I sang, however, I was impressed by what sounded to me like a beautiful melody. Within myself I sensed that God was encouraging me to sing out in English and as I did, some words came. I was so amazed by what came out of my mouth in poetic form that I literally ran out to get the words written down. The words that I believe came from God in such melodic form were as follows:

"As the Gospel is preached
Many people they are reached
In every nation of the world Jesus reigns
Across the face of the Earth there is life and new birth
Don't you know in your heart, Jesus reigns
He is moving every hour
By the Spirit's mighty power
Sing and dance, clap your hand Jesus reigns
He is Lord of every nation, he is King of all creation

So I boldly now proclaim, Jesus reigns
He is moving in my heart
He is changing every part
I'm glad to say in me, Jesus reigns
Send me now Lord I pray, send me now Lord today
To the world to let them know, Jesus reigns."

How awesome and thrilling it was, a few months later when we heard the news about the break up of the Eastern Bloc, the Berlin Wall coming down and Germany being reunited as one nation. Within a few years, this news would be followed by the ending of apartheid in South Africa. The late 1980s were momentous and historic days. It was a privilege to have played a small part in all that through our prayers, along with millions of others no doubt, for the nations that God loves so very much. It seems to me that if you concern yourself with the nations, you touch God's heart in a very special way.

We'd been living in Redruth for a few months and I'd got my first term at college out of the way, when mum and dad came down to visit us. By this time, mum's radio therapy treatment had finished and though she was still having a certain amount of trouble swallowing, overall she was doing quite well in the circumstances. To our surprise, dad said that both he and mum would like to attend church with us. The Bible College had some very nice modern facilities, with lecture rooms and an auditorium which seated up to four hundred. Some years earlier they'd launched a church, Salvation Christian Fellowship *[not it's real name]*, which comprised the students plus families and individuals from the locality. The services were lively and inspiring, with time being made at some point for the sick to be prayed for. Mum and dad came to the Sunday service and though the style must have been alien to them, they coped with it pretty well and mum was prayed for by the assistant pastor, Mark Van Gundy. A nice guy, Mark was from Orlando, Florida and was married to Mary from just up the road in Camborne. Mark very kindly asked my mother if she would like him to come to our house, to pray. She said she would.

A few days later, Mark duly arrived. He prayed for mum in our lounge. He was gentle and compassionate, saying to mum that of course, one day, we will all die physically and stand before God. He described how important it was, that we were healed spiritually and that the Bible calls that 'being born again'. He simply explained the good news and quoted a verse from the New Testament to the Romans 10.13: "Everyone who calls on the name of the Lord will be saved". Mum had very little understanding of the Bible, but Mark explained things about as clearly as I have ever heard them explained. Mum indicated that she understood and wanted to call upon the name of Jesus to save her. Mark led her in a prayer of commitment to Jesus Christ. From that moment on I knew that mum, who I had prayed for, over eighteen long years, was now saved for all eternity.

Just under ten weeks later, on 23rd August 1986 Mum passed into the presence of God, to be with Jesus for ever. Her suffering was over. That morning, Ian and I were with mum in Birmingham. I had the privilege of praying with mum in the morning, before she went into hospital where she died that evening. Although it had no importance whatsoever, it was the first day of the new football season and Aston Villa lost 3-0 to Tottenham and a Clive Allen hat-trick. I mention that, not to be disrespectful but to recognise the fact was that mum had told dad to go to the match in the afternoon and leave her to rest. When dad returned to the hospital in the evening, she asked him how the Villa got on. Dad told her the score. A few minutes later, she breathed her last breath in this world.

Mum's funeral service was conducted by Pastor Morrison, our old Irish Pastor from the Kingstanding Elim Church. In a fine service, the Pastor gave a very inspiring gospel address and tribute to mum. One of mum's brothers, my Uncle Harry, was very intrigued by the message, having himself overcome bowel cancer, some years earlier. He said that he was a bit worried about me; on the day of the funeral he had seen me hugging several men, rather than the more-socially acceptable handshake. I explained to him that within the Church, it was not unusual to greet one another, be they male or female, with a warm and friendly hug. All this clearly left a vivid impression on my uncle. About two years after mum's passing, I received a phone call in Cornwall from Auntie Audrey, to say that Harry had been taken into hospital with a recurrence of his cancer problems. He wanted to speak with the Pastor who had conducted mum's funeral. My sister Susan was able to make contact with Pastor Morrison, who gladly went to visit my uncle in hospital and in so doing, answer some heart-searching questions that Harry had on his mind. Pastor Morrison was able to lead Harry and Audrey to Jesus. I took great comfort from the fact that mum had not only received the gift of eternal life, weeks before she died, but in her passing, it also led directly to her brother and his wife coming to the Lord also.

I was enjoying myself at College. The church side of things was going well, too. By way of a change of strategy, it was decided to introduce three 'house groups', meeting midweek so that people could come together for prayer, mutual encouragement and pastoral support. Sylvia and I were asked to lead a group in our home. Consequently, we played hosts to around fifteen people each week, including three of the African contingent, to add a bit of fervour. Adding to the cosmopolitan mix, were Daniel and Deborah Ng. Former students at the College, Daniel (originally from Hong Kong) and Deborah (Michigan) were now on the Bible College staff. They were good teachers in their own right. Daniel was also a fine worship leader. Though he was a qualified pharmacist and Deborah a teacher, nevertheless due to working at the College without a regular income, they lived in digs fairly frugally.

We'd been in Cornwall for about six months when we became aware that across the road from the Bible College, a new estate was being built. Out of interest, nothing more, we decided to go and have a look around the show house. As we entered it, I felt instinctively that this was the kind of house of which I dreamed. Not that it was a mansion you understand. When I was in Solihull and praying about the move to Cornwall, I had a definite idea of the kind of house, layout and style that I would like. Due to the fact that our house in Solihull sold so rapidly, however, meant we had to move quickly in order not to lose the sale. This meant, of course, that we had to buy somewhere pretty hastily and in that regard Sylvia - with mum and dad's help - did a great job in finding South Park. We were happy at South Park overall; other than it was a little on the small side, had night storage heaters which we really didn't like and there was that awkward little journey to and from college each day. Nothing major, but I did feel a stirring of faith for these new houses across the road from the college, on a small estate called Treloweth Gardens. There was a plot available for this soon-to-be-erected four bedroom house. We took away the details to mull over, but felt it was about £10,000 above what we could realistically afford.

The following night at our house group, we were drawing to a close and Sylvia went into the kitchen to make some drinks for the group. We were finishing off with a short time of music as Daniel gently played his guitar. Once again I had that experience of singing out in tongues and then finding the Holy Spirit prompting me to give the interpretation in English. I did it again as a song and the words were:

> "I want to do something crazy
> I want to do something good.
> I want to do something crazy for you Lord
> To love you, to trust you
> To depend upon your Word.
> I want to do something crazy for you Lord."

With that Deborah rushed out into the kitchen to tell Sylvia what I had just sung. She confided that she and Daniel were thinking about doing something crazy. They felt God was calling them to step out in faith and buy a bungalow, even though they had no money. Deborah pulled out of her bag some sales particulars, of a bungalow they were interested in and would you believe it? It was on Treloweth Gardens. Sylvia then produced our details and showed Deborah, resulting in Deborah and Sylvia embracing in fits of laughter at what seemed to be two crazy ideas!

Daniel and Deborah were greatly loved at church and college, and once news got around that they were looking to buy a property, we took up a 'love offering' one Sunday in church and raised enough money to enable them to have a deposit. Daniel picked-up a part-time job at a pharmacy in Camborne, and as a result they were able to obtain a mortgage and move into their bungalow.

In our case, were we ready to move again, only a year after moving from Solihull? Could we afford to do so? What would people back in the West Midlands think, if we moved again? When we prayed about the matter, it was as though God was saying, "If you've got the faith, I've got the house". No one we spoke to, said that the house was overly extravagant for a family of our size. It would have several advantages to it. Being at the College, we were surrounded by people of faith and the Word of God, and that made it so much easier to take steps that, ordinarily, might seem beyond us. So we decided to stretch our faith a little further and move from South Park to 25 Townfield, Pool, just two minutes walk from college and church.

Our first answer to prayer came when we were granted a mortgage, with me being a student and only having a limited amount of support from people around the country. Fortunately, the Building Society manager was a Christian and he was fully conversant with the term 'living by faith'. We decided we would take in a student to help us with the increased mortgage that we were embarking on. Once the paperwork had gone through and we knew we were actually buying the property, it was fun to visit the plot to see the house being built, brick by brick. The other astonishing thing about this, was that we didn't know until all the paperwork had been processed that The Principle and Prin, Principals of The Bible College had actually bought the property next door. How would they feel, having one of their students living next door we wondered!

As it turned out, they were absolutely fine about this and on the day of our move, we had some of the students give us a helping hand. Of all the houses we've lived in, this was my favourite, my dream house. It was detached, so I could play my records as loud as I liked without fear of upsetting the neighbours! We had a lovely big garden to stroll around, ideal for playing football, cricket and tennis whenever we liked; a double garage with plenty of room for storage, also leaving room for my car, should I miraculously get my eyesight back!

That word, 'miraculously'. It reminds me of something which happened to Sylvia while we were living in that house. Sylvia had been troubled with lower-back pain for a couple of years; there were times when it was very bad indeed. Most days saw her rolling out of bed in the morning and crawling around the floor, until her back loosened up.

A party of students were going over to a small church in Penryn, near Falmouth one night to watch a video of the American healing evangelist Benny Hinn. Sylvia agreed to take the car with me and three other students on board. We watched the video. In truth it was pretty amazing stuff and at the end of the service many people on the video testified to being healed by the power of God. The Pastor of that church, Patrick Stevenson, also taught at The Bible College and said that the same power that we saw displayed on the video, was present that night, to heal people in that little church in Cornwall. He invited anyone who needed to receive healing, to go forward for prayer. I could've gone forward, of course, but didn't. Rather, I was hoping that Sylvia would go forward for prayer because her condition was giving her far much more stress than my lack of sight was giving me. However, she stayed rooted to the spot and afterwards told me that even though what we saw on the video was pretty incredible, she remained dubious as to whether that same power could be transmitted to that little church in Penryn.

Next morning, I was downstairs when Sylvia called me from the bedroom. She had no back pain. It wasn't even stiff. Doubters that we were, we thought to ourselves, perhaps this was just one of those rare, good mornings. Nearly twenty years later, Sylvia's back is stronger than ever. She's worked for the past twelve years in nursing homes and a hospice. Much of that work is really heavy. She couldn't have done that kind of work, had God not graciously and miraculously healed her. I can only conclude that he did it out of his great grace and because he loves her so much, not because she had faith because, as she would tell you, she most certainly did not.

My first year at Bible College went brilliantly. I loved everything about it. The lectures were good and I did well in my exams. The church, Salvation Christian Fellowship was good too and we had the benefit of hearing some really fine speakers including Jason Peebles from Atlanta, Georgia and Robert Massbach, originally from Holland but now working in the UK. Our four children had all settled well into school and they were also enjoying church life, especially with there being so many young students. It was a happy time and we enjoyed taking our many visitors from back home in Birmingham, to some of the lovely seaside resorts around west Cornwall. In addition, Flambards' theme park, near Helston was always a big attraction for our own children as well as our visitors. Within the park, there is the Poldark Mine and I enjoyed the trip down there. *Poldark* had been the title of a hugely successful costume drama on BBC1, set in Cornwall, in the seventies.

In order to help us with the increased mortgage payments, we would have to take in a lodger. Our first student was Raid Thaglag, a Jordanian young man studying Aeronautic Engineering at the Cornwall College in Pool. Raid, a Muslim, was with us for nearly a year and was, on the whole, an ideal first lodger for us. He was always courteous, and out of respect, would never sit down at the meal table until I had taken my place. Although we said it was okay and he didn't need to ask, he would always request permission to turn on the television - except he never said it like that. He would say, "Please John, may I open up the television?" This always amused us. Our girls in particular, would pull his leg about it.

Meal times were lively occasions with endless chatter, debates and occasionally, arguments. One night Raid said that he would give anything to have a meal in silence, but he doubted that our girls could stay quiet for more than a few minutes. After some discussion about this, Raid said, "I'll give you £5.00 each, if you can stay quiet for ten minutes".

Well, no more incentive was needed and the deal was struck. We enjoyed the quietest meal we've ever had in our household that night, and Raid, true to his word paid out a fiver each to our kids, later that evening.

Raid was a good sport. He mixed well with the students from The Bible College. More than once, he felt as though he was part of a big family. When it came to say farewell to Raid, at the end of his academic year, we threw a party for him and invited a couple of his Muslim friends from college and a dozen or so of the Bible students. At the end of a lovely evening, we were able to pray for Raid and send him on his way with the Lord's blessing.

Our second student was a young lady. Carolyn Dowding from Guernsey in the Channel Islands was in Cornwall to take a qualification in Nursery Nursing. It turned out that she was on the same course as our own daughter, Allison. Just like Raid, Carolyn turned out to be brilliant. She became quite a good friend to Sylvia; almost a fourth daughter. She fitted in well with our family. It was a real pleasure to have her around.

It's hard to identify at which point things started to go wrong in Cornwall, but go wrong they did.

I was well into my second year as a Bible student, when my ear problem, which had settled down for a few years, suddenly flared up again. Sylvia noticed a disgusting smell coming from my left ear. A trip to the Doctors led to me being referred to hospital in Truro and then to another Consultant in Plymouth. I was having so much time off at that stage for investigations, that it was agreed that I would have the term off in order to concentrate on getting my ear sorted. I would then do that term again the following year. I cannot explain why this offensive smell occurred in my ear, but one doctor said it was like a dung heap in there. I underwent tests for cancer, which thankfully turned out to be negative and there was even talk of operating, but the dangers of facial paralysis were too great. It was decided to leave things alone. The anatomical structure inside the ear gave cause for concern, as I'd found out almost ten years earlier when they'd discovered the jugular bulb. Eventually, after much to-ing and fro-ing it was decided that I should attend Trelisk Hospital in Truro every Saturday morning, to have the ear cleaned under the microscope. It was a major inconvenience but at least it kept the foul smell away. A few years down the line, when back in Birmingham, a Consultant, John Campbell, performed a mastoid operation and with that he rectified the problem of the offensive odour and in so doing, also managed to improve my hearing on the left side too. Instead of weekly, I now only have to attend hospital for an ear check once-a-year, so that's a spectacular improvement. I will return to the God of the spectacular, later in the book.

During those months of uncertainty, particularly once the word 'cancer' had been mentioned as a possibility, an old fear started to invade my mind again. One night, I had a most vivid dream about my own funeral, and I awoke in the morning sweating and shaking with fear. I was relieved to find that I was still alive. I immediately got up and went downstairs to pray. I dropped to my knees and buried my head into the armchair as I cried out to God. "Please God, help me" I cried. "Deal with this...fear...and sort out the ear problem for me".

As I bowed there in desperation, I experienced another of those all-too-rare moments, when it's as though God speaks right into your heart. This is what I felt God was saying: "You can lie down and die, or you can stand up and live – the choice is yours".

It was sharp and like an arrow to my heart. I responded at once, by standing like a soldier to attention and I said back to God, "I choose to stand up and live". A Scripture came to my mind straightaway, from Psalm 118: "I will not die but live, and will proclaim what the LORD has done."

Ever since, it's been my watchword. I have breath this day, but only in order that I may declare the works of God. That is my primary purpose for being alive here on Planet Earth.

During the term I was off, things began to happen at The Bible College, of an alarming nature. Some members of staff walked out, whilst others were dismissed amid rumours of homosexuality and financial irregularities. We'd already picked up on certain things that were being said by other church leaders and Christians locally, but those things only confirmed misgivings that Sylvia had been having, for months. There was also a suspicion that one of the students was a paedophile. It was a big shock, because he'd actually become a good friend to us and our kids. A few years later, he was convicted and sent to prison.

The sad fact began to dawn on me, that I would not be able to go back to Bible College. I remember walking the streets around Treloweth Gardens and with a heavy heart, crying out to God: "Oh why has this happened? All I wanted to do was to study your Word."

By this time, Sylvia and I had become good friends with two young Lancastrian couples. John and Wendy Oldham and Phil and Christine Jenkins had come to Bible College from Rochdale and Oldham respectively. They'd been good friends themselves for many years. At that point, they had no children and we just hit it off together and our kids liked them too, which was a big plus. They'd also become concerned about a number of aspects within the college and the church. After some discussion between us, I decided to contact Steve Wood. Steve, you may recall I mentioned earlier, because I first heard him speak in Leicester. He was then the leading Elder at Solihull Christian Fellowship and was one of the four who had broken away over the issue of direction. Steve had since moved to the south west and was living in Wells.

It was agreed that John, Phil and I would travel up to Wells to chat and pray with Steve. We talked over our concerns with him, and spent a good deal of time praying together - Steve set out some things for us to think about and consider carefully. He added that, if we were to leave, then we should request a meeting with The Principle to explain why it was, that we could no longer be part of The Bible College or the church. Steve said that we owed it to The Principle, as a brother in Christ, to be honest and to walk in the light with him.

There was no doubt in our mind that we had to leave; somewhat naively, I went next door in the hope that I could chat with The Principle and Prin, as friends. I was told however, that I would need to make an appointment with The Principle's secretary and go through the official channels. I was saddened by this approach, but eventually got to make the appointment, though it was changed on a couple of occasions.

I attended with Sylvia and though I was nervous, I knew that I didn't want to cause trouble but simply share my heart. Despite all the flack that was flying around, I had a love in my heart for The Principle and Prin and no one was more upset than me, at the way that things were working out.

We entered the Principal's office. The Principle was sat behind a huge desk with his Dean of Students at his side.

"Come in John, and Sylvia; sit yourselves down…" The Principle said in his usual upbeat way.

With my voice already cracking I said, "Principle, can you come round from your desk and let me give you a hug?"

"No John, I'll be fine where I am, thank you very much" he responded, somewhat defensively.

I went on to explain the reasons why I couldn't continue as a student at The Bible College. Why it was that we, as a family, would be leaving the church. I stressed to The Principle that I'd really appreciated all of the good things that we, as a family, had received in the time that we'd been there. That we loved him and Prin.

The Principle was sorry he was losing us. How unfortunate it was that we "had listened to gossip". A brief handshake and we left The Principle's office, but not before a warning "not to steal his sheep". I assured The Principle that it wasn't in my heart.

Over the course of the next few months, one by one people continued to leave the church and the College. Some stayed of course, including our dear African friends who were on part-scholarships. We missed out on seeing them, because as we later found out, they were banned from coming to see us.

It was around this time that vile things started happening to us. Had it not been for the support of our friends who had all joined the exodus away from 'Salvation', I dare not think what may have happened to us.

It all began one morning, just after 9 o'clock. A ring on the front doorbell. I opened it: "Hello John, it's Florence Bailey; I'm here with a police officer because your Ian has been involved in an accident".

Time seemed to stand still. I didn't feel as if what I was hearing was really happening. Sylvia was at the top of the stairs, inquisitively wondering who was calling at that time of the morning. Once she heard the words "police officer" and "accident", she was down in a flash. Florence and the policeman came in. "Your son was involved in an accident with a bus, while crossing the road to school. He has suffered a head injury, but we do not know how serious it is. He has been taken to hospital in Truro, so if you would like to get your things together, we will take you".

By this time Sylvia was in tears, and being cuddled by Florence, whose son David was a friend of Ian's. All I knew to do, was to ask if we could pray before we set off for the hospital. Sylvia, Florence, the policeman and I stood there, all holding hands in a circle as I prayed for Ian, the bus driver and the staff at the hospital, that all would be well. I don't suppose the police officer will ever forget that moment. Neither will we.

Of all things, Ian had been listening to some Christian music - a tape of the U2 album *Rattle & Hum* on his personal stereo. He'd stepped out to cross the road to school, but had done so, in front of a park vehicle. Unfortunately, there was a coach coming past the stationary vehicle and it glanced the side of Ian's head, ripping his right ear almost completely off. Subsequently, all personal stereos, or 'walkmans', were banned in the school.

By the time we arrived at the hospital, Ian was already in the operating theatre. No time could be wasted, when it came to sewing the ear back on. Thankfully, the operation was a complete success and incredibly Ian was discharged in three days. One of the doctors at the hospital said to him, "Do you know, young man, that you are the first person I have met who has collided with a bus and lived to tell the tale?"

Shortly after, Allison was returning home from a night out with Matthew, her surfer boyfriend. They had a nasty experience on one of the coastal roads, when his van veered off the road and into a ditch. In the same period, Sylvia, who'd been driving for fifteen years by then, without a hint of an accident - had two in successive nights. On both occasions she was fetching lads, including Ian, from school football games; one in Truro and one in Camborne. On each occasion, Sylvia was waiting at traffic lights when someone bumped into the back of her. Thankfully, no one was hurt, but Sylvia was shaken emotionally and by now, we were all wondering what was happening to us. Not long after, we had a new car. But not for long.

From time to time I would receive invitations to preach in churches back in Birmingham, and other areas, including Rochdale and Oldham thanks to my friends John and Phil. Once, I was preaching at Castle Bromwich Community Church in Birmingham. Sylvia and the children stayed with friends in Solihull and attended Solihull Christian Fellowship, to try and meet up with old acquaintances.

After I'd finished preaching, I closed the service with a prayer. Before I could sit down, the Pastor came and stood alongside me and said that he wanted to pray for me. Before he did, he placed a set of keys into my hands. I said, "What are these for?"

He replied that these were the keys to our new car. It was another one of those déjà vu moments.

This was a very well planned manoeuvre. The whole of Castle Bromwich Community Church was in on this big surprise, and I was led outside of the Community Centre, where the service had been held. When out in the fresh air, I was taken to a beautiful blue Volkswagen Passat. I was told that this was now our family car, and when I asked incredulously how this had come about, I was told to speak with Dr. Gordon Coleman for the full story.

The Pastor drove me to Solihull, with his wife in their own car, following at the rear. We arrived in Solihull where a whole load of people, including Gordon and Julia, plus Sylvia and our four children were waiting to greet us. Sylvia had no idea what was going on - and it was left to me to have the joy of breaking this exciting news to her. So it was, that we had travelled up in an old Vauxhall Viva but were travelling back in a much more modern Volkswagen Passat. What had happened? Gordon became aware of our need for a more reliable car, and so he had contacted some of the local churches where I regularly preached, made the need known to them and asked if they would make a donation towards purchasing a newer vehicle. So the God of surprises had turned up again, just when we needed some encouragement after all the difficulties we had encountered in the previous few months.

The joy was short-lived however. By now, our three girls had left school and whilst Allison was at college, Beverley and Sara went into the retail trade. As teenagers do, they also got into the night life and very often, this meant Sylvia dropped them off, and more often than not, picked them up from somewhere late at night.

One particular evening, Beverley went into Camborne with her boyfriend, Ian, and because he could drive and we were, as we mistakenly thought, insured for any driver, we gave him the car keys to drive Beverley home. It avoided the necessity for Sylvia to go out late at night.

My wife had just gone up to bed at 11 o'clock, when the front door opened and Beverley came rushing in, crying hysterically. "Dad, Dad - I'm so sorry, I've crashed the car." She could hardly get her words out for sobbing.

Sylvia ran down the stairs to find out what had happened. Apparently, on the way home Ian had asked Beverley if she wanted an impromptu driving lesson. With her agreement Ian drove into the car park of Cornwall College, before allowing Beverley to take the steering wheel. How it happened I don't know, but I think Beverley put her foot on the accelerator instead of the brake pedal, causing the car to mount a verge, go over the garden area and into a brick wall.

Beverley then ran home to tell us what had happened, leaving Ian to try and clear up some of the mess.

Sylvia went to the scene of the accident with Beverley and, together with Ian, managed to get the car off the garden and back around the corner to our garage. It was only later, after I'd broken the news to Gordon, that I found out that the car was only insured third party, whereas previously we'd always insured our cars fully comprehensive any driver. So it was that our lovely new car had been written off within a couple of weeks, but the overriding and important factor was that nobody had been hurt. The car was gone. But we still had Beverley fully intact. A painful and expensive lesson had been learned, not for the first time, or the last by the Flanner family.

One of the quirkiest, but still distressing things to happen to us back then, was the fact that a £200 gift from some friends just apparently vanished into thin air. We wouldn't have known about it had these friends not telephoned, slightly embarrassed, to say that it was unusual that we hadn't acknowledged an amount of £200 that had been paid into our bank account. I had to say, that I hadn't acknowledged it because I hadn't received it. They double checked their account and found that the money had gone out and I checked my bank accounts, even visited the bank and established that no money had been paid into my account from that particular couple. The mystery has never been solved.

After leaving The Bible College, we had a total break from church for a month or two. Eventually we visited a couple of local churches. At that point, however, I had to conclude that we were beaten, battered and bruised by events. We were mostly happy to stay at home. Together with our friends John and Wendy, Phil and Christine and Daniel and Deborah however, we did meet together for prayer and arising out of that, we decided that we would organise a Gospel concert in the area, featuring an artiste we all admired, Bryn Haworth. Bryn's a magnificent exponent of the slide guitar, and has featured on many hit albums and singles, not least *Baker Street* by Gerry Rafferty.

We wrote to Bryn to check out his fee, to see whether he would be willing to come to our area. He was keen to break new ground in west Cornwall, and so we agreed to go ahead and arrange the concert. We booked the main hall at Cornwall College and after a slow start, the tickets sales really picked up so that on the night we had over two hundred people in, for what was a memorable evening. Bryn and his wife Sally stayed with us in our home, indeed they even had our bed, but sadly the mantle of being a great guitar player didn't rub off on me, in any way, shape or form!

In publicising the concert for Bryn, it gave me the chance to make contact with BBC Radio Cornwall and even take part in an interview. Later, I also had the chance to co-present a 'Country Gospel' programme on the station with their regular Country music presenter in those days, Chris Phipps. It was great to get involved with radio once again. Another little surprise was about to turn up.

On leaving the studio, I was told that a lady by the name of Rosemary Noakes had been on the phone and she wanted me to contact her. She lived in St. Berrian, near Penzance. It turned out that she was very interested in my surname. Rosemary had developed an interest in family trees and, in looking back into her family history, had come across the name of Flanner. Intrigued by this rare surname, she investigated further and the deeper she dug the more interesting it became. In all, she had done the Flanner family tree back to the 17th century and discovered that we originated from a family of Austrian flan makers. She was, as you might imagine, really excited to hear a Flanner on her local radio station. Sylvia and I were to visit Rosemary and her husband Norman, at their home in St. Berrian where she gave me a copy of the Flanner family tree.

By now, our next door neighbours The Principle and Prin had gone off to America on an extended preaching tour. In their absence we were all surprised to learn that The Bible College was closed down, along with Salvation Christian Fellowship. Rumours were rife, and subsequently proved to be accurate, that a new Bible College was opening in Manchester. I understand that that too, has now closed.

With the fall out from Salvation there were a lot of Christians going nowhere as far as church was concerned. A few of us did meet in our home to start with, and, then in Redruth Community Centre on a Sunday afternoon. Around thirty people were joining us.

We were blessed in having some excellent musicians among us. Daniel played guitar, as did Wendy and Christine, who could also sing. John was a gifted drummer and then we were joined by Ian and Jackie Langridge. Together with their three young boys, they were one of the families who'd attended the church at Harvest. Jackie was an excellent pianist and played other instruments as well. We had several gifted speakers in our midst as well including Phil and Deborah. So all in all we had a pretty strong nucleus of solid Christian people. For practical reasons we gave ourselves the name of Redruth Community Church, and I do believe that things could have taken off and God could have raised up a pretty significant local church in that area. Perhaps it had all come just a little bit too soon, after the recent major disappointments.

The events outlined above were certainly taking their toll on our marriage. Rows became the order of the day, often with the kids involved and our once-happy home began to resemble a war-zone rather than a loving Christian family. Then came the hammer blow. Sylvia announced that she was leaving as she couldn't take any more. At that point she didn't know if she was leaving for good, or just for a break. All I know is that she was going to live with her parents back in Birmingham for a while. The day Sylvia left, I remember being overwhelmed with a sense of grief and failure. I wrote a poem, or perhaps it was a lament, that had three verses to it. I think it would've made a good lyric for a country and western song. The first verse, which is all I can remember now, went as follows:

"Doom, gloom and despondency fill my heart today
Twenty years gone out the door, my baby's gone away.
Never knew she was leaving me, thought we were doing fine
But now doom, gloom and despondency overwhelm my mind."

After the first couple of days, which felt really strange, I actually started to enjoy myself. It was quite nice, being able to do what I wanted to do without having to think about anyone else first. I know it sounds selfish, but that's how it was. I had time for me. I did have the kids of course, but Beverley, Sara and Allison were pretty independent by now. Ian was very little trouble. I think, on reflection, it was a very precious time for us all, and I don't know how long we would have stayed in that state, had not God intervened once again.

Out of the blue we received a cheque for £200 through the post from New Life Church in Solihull, suggesting that we use it to book a place with them at the Wales Bible Week, to be held a few weeks later in Builth Wells. I spoke with Sylvia on the phone to explain what had happened, and within a few days she returned to be with us, back in Cornwall. Ultimately the time came around and we did go off to the Bible Week and spent a week in a tent. It was just Sylvia, Ian and me, as the girls stayed at home to carry on working. We weren't alone in our tent, however, because Pat and Josie Stevenson, who had given up leading their church in Penryn to teach full time at the Bible College, came with us, along with their two children. The Stevensons had been unceremoniously dumped out of the College and were understandably feeling at a very low ebb.

Just a few days after Sylvia had returned, we'd spent a lovely day on the beach at Portreath, soaking up the sunshine with the Stevenson family. It was whilst chatting, that Pat told us that some of the events of the previous two years had affected him to the point where he had almost felt like giving up. He said ruefully, "I think I need to be literally picked up and dropped in the middle of a large worship meeting. Maybe then, the flame will be rekindled.".

I heard the cry of Pat's heart. It saddened me to see this man of God, normally so full of joy, as crestfallen as he was. Later that day I was on the phone to Steve Wood in Wells, talking about another issue altogether and as our conversation drew to a close, Steve said, "Oh by the way, how are Pat and Josie doing?".

"Funny you should ask" I said, and went on to relate what had happened to them and our conversation on the beach, earlier in the day.

A few days later a very excited Pat Stevenson came on the phone, saying that they'd received a generous cheque from Steve Wood's church in Somerset - with the suggestion that they attend the Wales Bible Week, with the Flanners. So it all happened in a very short space of time and there we were, as two families, sharing a tent in Builth Wells.

Sylvia found it one of the hardest weeks of her life, attending all these joyful meetings and seeing all these people, when on the inside she was feeling so emotionally distressed. For all that, we did have plenty of laughs, especially in the tent at night. The Stevensons were clearly amazed by the week and by the warmth of the friendship they experienced from those on site. As we lay on our beds, divided by curtains, we chatted long into the night trying to fathom out where things had gone wrong at College. We'd been chatting a long time one night. Pat said, "It must be getting very late, anyone got the time?"

I responded, "Hang on, I'll just have a feel".

This quite natural comment of mine, or so I thought, brought a spontaneously-loud burst of laughter from Pat and it was so infectious, that Josie and Sylvia started as well! It seemed as though the more Pat thought about what I'd said, the more he laughed. The more he laughed the more others laughed, too. It went on for a while, until someone from an adjacent tent came out and sternly asked us to be quiet, out of respect for others. For the record it was half past midnight.

The week was memorable for Pat and Josie's teenage son, Darren. Along with many other young people, Darren had attended some seminars to watch and listen to the highly acclaimed American mime artiste, Todd Farley. From that week onwards, Darren knew exactly what he was to do with his life. He was truly smitten by the art of mime. Subsequently, Darren went to study at Todd's college in the States, married a girl called Heather and now they run a very successful ministry, Push Theatre Co. They perform their own sketches across the United States, as well as now having their own school of mime and dance. Amazing to think that it all began with a seemingly innocuous conversation, on the beach at Portreath.

On returning home from the Bible Week, family life was more peaceful, though there was a growing sense that our time in Cornwall would soon be at an end. Sylvia and I decided to go up to Wells, to spend a few days at Beckington Cottage with Steve and Jeanne. The Woods' home at the top of a hill, overlooked the quaint historic city of Wells, with its cobblestone streets and majestic Cathedral. We spent a pleasant couple of days there, talking over our situation and tapping into their wisdom. At the end of it, we were all of one mind. That is, that we needed to move back to Solihull in order for me to find employment, to be back among family and friends, and most important of all, for the good of our marriage.

Our decision to leave Cornwall led to an exodus of our friends, too. John and Wendy and Phil and Christine went back up north to their former churches, whilst Daniel and Deborah moved back to Michigan in the United States, where Daniel began working for a pharmacy within a large hospital. Currently they live in Virginia and they have three children. We're still often in touch, especially by email. John is now Pastor of Emanuel Christian Fellowship in Rochdale, whilst Wendy is working as an audiologist. They have three kids. I have the privilege of going to preach there, about times a year. Phil and Christine, after a few years back home, decided to up and move once again and currently live in Bradford-on-Avon. They have three children too! They attend Bath City Church, where Steve Wood is now one of the Elders. Ian and Jackie, with their three boys who've now grown up, stayed in Cornwall and attend Truro Vineyard Church.

Our own family had mixed feelings about us leaving Cornwall. Beverley had just moved away from home. She'd moved to Dursely in Gloucestershire, with her then boyfriend Ian. He was working for a Building Society, whilst Beverley had a job as a sales assistant with River Island. Allison was settled into her Nursery nursing course, and decided to stay to complete that, and we did find that hard, leaving her behind in that way. Sara, then working for Texas Homecare, decided that she'd give that up and go back to Solihull with us. Ian was just excited at the prospect of being closer to Aston Villa once again – clearly destined to be a man after my own heart!

I found it very difficult, putting our house at Townfield, Treloweth Gardens up for sale. It was my dream house and I loved it there. It had to be done, as it was well over a year since I'd left the College and I hadn't been able to get myself so much as a sniff of a job interview. Again, as on the two previous occasions we sold very quickly, but in looking for houses in Solihull, it soon became apparent that we were going to pay a big financial penalty for our move back to the West

Midlands. Taking into account the costs of our moves, Bible College fees, financial support we had given to various students, plus the church building fund, in all we reckoned it cost us in excess of £20,000. In the four years we'd been away property prices in Solihull had gone up at a far greater rate than those in our part of Cornwall. Just maybe therefore, with all that had gone on, the people who said we shouldn't move to Cornwall in the first place, were right after all. Even with the benefit of hindsight, however, I still cannot say whether it was the right or wrong thing to do. What I do know is that our motives were pure in wanting to serve God and in doing that, we have learned some very valuable lessons - albeit at a price.

After unsuccessfully attempting to buy property in other parts of Solihull, we eventually gravitated back to Damsonwood and bought a house about two hundred yards from the one we'd sold. Draycote Close is a quiet little cul-de-sac, where at least I know my way around and am familiar with the bus-routes and shops.

There followed a two month gap between selling our house in Cornwall and being able to move into Draycote Close, so rather than risk losing the sale, some friends of ours very kindly agreed to put Sylvia, Ian and me, up for a while. We spent eight weeks in the home of Richard and Audrey Akers and their two boys, Stuart and Graham. Very pleasant it was too. We ate out a lot, particularly at a pub called The Orange Tree, located in a village called Chadwick End. Sara joined us too, for those treats as she was living with my sister Joan, who also resided in Solihull.

When we eventually got to move into 16 Draycote Close, there was hardly any work needed to be done to it. It helped us settle in, all the more quickly. No cheeky bathroom wallpaper at this Solihull house!

After quite a bit of soul-searching, we decided to go back to Solihull Christian Fellowship, rather than New Life Church. This was hard on Richard and Audrey, because they were at New Life and could reasonably have expected us to go there, in light of the love which they'd shown us. What clinched it in the end, though, was probably a visit from one of the Solihull Christian Fellowship Elders, Dave Wort. Dave made it clear that it was lovely to have us back in the area, and if we were still looking for a church then we would be most welcome back at the Christian Fellowship, where we had a lot of friends and there would be no pressure. We would just be free to relax and enjoy the love of God. It sounded good and in truth, it was, for quite a few years.

When it came to me finding a job, this was proving more difficult. Since I last worked in an office things had moved on, as far as technology was concerned. No longer the manual typewriter, or indeed the electric typewriter. No, in the short time I'd been away many offices had now gone over to personal computers, or 'PCs' as they were increasingly being referred to! After discussions with my Disability Officer at the local Job Centre, it was decided that I should apply to go on a Business Administration course at Queen Alexandra College in Harborne, Birmingham. This was a specialist college of further education, offering a wide range of courses for people, not just with visual impairment, but also a number of other disabilities, too. Within a couple of weeks of applying, I'd been accepted and started soon afterwards. The course involved me learning a number of skills including telephony, reception work, brushing up on my audio typing skills and what was to become very important to me, word processing with the aid of speech-based, screen-reading software. I wasn't using *JAWS* then, but a system called *Hal* which was (and still is) produced by a company called Dolphin. This was also pre-*MicroSoft Windows* and I was using *WordStar* in DOS format. It was amazing to me to be using screen-reading software and even though it was a synthesised voice, its monotonous robotic tone didn't bother me at all. I loved the extra freedom to be able to listen to, and correct, my own documents the synthesiser gave me.

I thoroughly enjoyed my year at Queen Alexandra, achieving good grades in all of the modules I studied, but I especially did well at, and loved, word processing. Queen Alexandra possesses a great reputation for high standards of education and, I have to say, the food in the dining room wasn't bad either! Often we were literally spoiled for choice. I travelled in each day by public transport, so I only got to taste the dinners, but the boarders of which there were many from this country and overseas, got to reap the benefits of three cooked meals a day!

Towards the end of my year I attended two weeks' work placement, at the Birmingham Housing Department. That was fun. Following that, on my return to college, our head of department, Theresa Napier mentioned that the college had received an invitation from a local Rotary Club to attend one of their fundraising dinners. At the dinner, they wanted to hear from two or three of the students; about which course they had undertaken, what kind of employment they were looking for. Theresa wondered if I'd be willing to give the final talk of the evening, summing things up for about fifteen minutes. Of course I agreed, saying I would consider it an honour.

I'd never been to a Rotary-type dinner before. It was quite an experience, with a number of distinguished people being applauded to their tables – we weren't among them, I hasten to add!

The whole occasion added to my education. The five course meal added to my already-expanding waistline. I was very pleased the way my talk went. I was able to pay apt tribute to the work being done by the staff at Queen Alexandra College, as well as place myself in the proverbial shop window for any would-be employers. It worked a treat too. After the dinner, as we mingled with other guests, I was approached by one of the businessmen.

"That was a pretty fine speech" said the man, as he shook my hand warmly.

"I have a vacancy for an audio typist, if you're interested. I run an Estate Agents' business in King's Heath."

Needless to say I was all ears. "My name's Peter Cariss. I'd like to arrange for you to visit my premises, so that we can talk – if you're interested in the job, that is?"

In the absence of other offers of work, it transpired that I left college one Friday in the July, and walked straight into the job as an audio typist/word-processing operator with Cariss Residential, on the following Monday.

I was basically typing-up the sales particulars on a variety of properties and, all in all, it was very interesting work. Peter was a good employer and occasionally, would take his staff to auctions and that included me. It was something that Peter didn't have to do, but I enjoyed it and it helped us all to feel a part of the business as a whole. Sadly for us, the company ran into financial difficulties and after six months working at Cariss Residential, I, along with other full time staff, were told we would have to reduce our hours to become part time. I couldn't agree to that, with a mortgage and other financial commitments. So I allowed Peter to make me redundant.

I was only out of work for a few days. On the off-chance I decided to pop into the Inland Revenue office in Solihull, where I'd previously worked in Special Office. God's perfect timing? I discovered that there were two vacancies for audio typists, was able to grab an application form, fill it in there and then (with someone's kind assistance) and apply. A couple of days later I received a phone call inviting me for an interview and thankfully, I got offered a job. Praise God, the Inland Revenue had come up trumps for me again. I was destined for a longer period of service, than the two previous occasions.

I worked in an office with about six other people, ladies of course, and a typing manager, which was a new experience for me. Among them was Samantha, who used to be at school with my daughter Beverley. She was also an avid Liverpool supporter. Her knowledge of football certainly rivalled that of anybody I knew. Sam married a tax inspector and though football was not his number one passion, Sam soon got him travelling with her up and down the M6 to Anfield, as a Liverpool season ticket-holder. Another of the girls was Lynnette, reminiscent in some ways of Doris Day. Perhaps 'Calamity Jane' would be more appropriate! Lynne loved tap dancing, and one year she was persuaded to undertake a spot of tap on one of the desks, in order to raise money for *Children in Need*. Sam and Lynne were just two of the many kind ladies I worked with, then. Of course, they always looked after me with cups of tea or coffee, at the appropriate times of the day. Perhaps the most interesting manager I worked for in those days was Pat O'Kelly. I wasn't with Pat for long, as she took a redundancy package with the demand for typists starting to diminish, but she was a truly wonderful personality. Her partner was a professional comedian, part of the management of Kings Nightclub in Great Barr, Birmingham and though I never met him, they must have made a great couple, if Pat was anything to go by! Pat was also the brother of Richard O'Kelly, the former Walsall footballer and West Bromwich Albion coach. Fact!

This was a great place to work, because on good weather days I could walk to-and-from work, a distance of about two miles. It was my attempt to reduce the aforementioned expanding waistline. A lovely, peaceful walk, around the back of Solihull Hospital and along the path at the side of Solihull School. On that journey, I had many talks with God about all kinds of people and situations.

One such walk home saw me caught totally unawares. When I left the office at about 4.30pm, it felt like a warm, balmy evening. So I began my trek home at a fairly gentle pace. I'd been walking for about ten minutes when I felt a few spots of rain. Followed by a distant clap of thunder. For a moment I thought about going back and getting the bus home, but in the end decided to press on, at a much quicker pace. It now began to look distinctly dark, even to my eyes! The rain became heavier and heavier. The thunder drew ever closer. It seemed as if I was the only person walking that afternoon, because I didn't pass another soul on that journey. As the rain lashed down, I became drenched through to the skin and I could hardly walk because of the rain running into, and irritating, my eyes. I began to feel quite distressed, that I had lost my way. I couldn't locate the alleyway that I was supposed to go down. The rain was so loud, and my senses were so dulled with the cold and the wet, that I became hopelessly disorientated.

After about a twenty-minute downpour, the rain subsided as quickly as it had come and I was able to find my way home. I just remember getting in, cold and wet to hear Sylvia say sympathetically, "My love, you're soaked!".

"Indeed I am" I thought, "thoroughly soaked".

It turned out to be quite a profound moment for me. God spoke to me. He said that this was kind of a parable. God showed me that he wants his people, that is those who love him, to be soaked in his Holy Spirit. He pours out his Holy Spirit like rain, and he wants us to be drenched even to the point where we become disorientated, just as I was. He said that we rely too much on our own abilities and not enough on his. People are far too content with a touch of God in their lives, instead of allowing him to consume or soak them. I'm sure you get the analogy. For me, it was a defining moment.

Things were going quite well at Solihull Christian Fellowship. I was leading one of the house groups, centred on Damsonwood where we were living, along with seven or eight families. There were two Elders serving in the church, Alan Cameron and David Wort, two long-standing friends of ours. It was a surprise to me, when I was invited to prayerfully consider becoming part of the Eldership of the church. I say it was a surprise, because I didn't consider myself the type to become an Elder. My experience had been that Elders were a serious-minded, cautious type of person whose children were all 'good' and regularly attending church. I certainly didn't fit that image. I love to be spontaneous; can occasionally be flippant; have a *Carry On*-type sense of humour - and following the debacle in Cornwall, my children rarely went to church. I talked about my misgivings, especially with Alan and in so doing, asked what it was they felt I would bring to the Eldership. I was told that I would bring qualities such as faith, inspiration and love to the church. Along with a wealth of experience. After careful consideration, and talking it through with Sylvia, I eventually agreed and was duly brought into Eldership, along with another friend of many years, Pall Singh. Pall, as his name would suggest, is from a Sikh background and was converted in his late teens in the Handsworth area of Birmingham. Pall and his wife Joy are now actively involved in supporting people from an Asian background, who are seeking to live out their lives as Christians.

Shortly after becoming an Elder, it became apparent that something phenomenal was happening in the wider Christian Church. It got labelled the 'Toronto Blessing'.

Toronto Airport Vineyard Fellowship met for worship, one Sunday evening in January 1994. That night, God turned up in an amazing way and began to touch lives. Obviously it was one of those times that is hard to describe, even if you had been there, but there are plenty of reports of what happened at that time. Lives were changed for good. God's presence became so real in that gathering, that nobody wanted to leave. The Pastors of what is now called Toronto Airport Church, decided that if God wanted to meet with his people then they should continue to gather together, night after night and that is what has happened ever since. Initially, it was just members from that church who met, then people from nearby churches started to join in, but as news of what God was doing each night spread further, people started to travel from all over Canada and North America. Gradually, the phenomena spread across the globe as people travelled to Toronto. Of course, being at an airport allowed the phenomenon to be an international one. In the presence of God, many testified to being greatly 'refreshed'; having a deeper understanding of the Father heart of God; were emotionally and physically healed. To date hundreds of thousands of people have travelled from across the world and met God afresh, or even for the first time, in that seemingly insignificant church at Toronto Airport.

One night a Christian friend, Elizabeth, said she'd heard a taped message which had had a profound effect upon her. Clearly enthused by what she'd heard, Elizabeth dropped the tape into our porch one afternoon. A tape of a message given by Ellie Mumford, wife of London Pastor John Mumford. Ellie (who sounds a bit like the Queen) was describing her visit to Toronto and the impact it had on her.

Sylvia isn't really one for listening to tapes. But on this occasion she said, "Let's have an early night and listen to Ellie Mumford in bed".

An offer I couldn't refuse. We listened with baited breath; hanging on to Ellie's every word. We found ourselves laughing heartily and at other times, the tears were streaming down our faces as the love of God touched our hearts. It was beautiful and we didn't sleep well that night because in our hearts, we were so exhilarated. We decided we would play the tape at our house group meeting, in our home, a couple of nights later. We had no idea the incredible impact it was going to have.

There were ten of us gathered in our lounge that night and it was soon time for me to introduce the tape. It isn't always easy for people sitting around in someone's lounge to listen to a cassette tape. I stressed that it was something very special and it only lasted for half an hour or so. As soon as Ellie began to speak you could tell that folk were right with it. Just as with Sylvia and me, a couple of nights earlier, there was laughter and tears. At the end of the message Ellie asked people to stand for prayer. Immediately, everyone in our lounge stood up. Ellie began to pray and I heard a thud, as one of the ladies in the group fell to the floor. I obviously looked concerned, but Sylvia reassured me that everything was okay. Then Colin, one of our dear friends, began to laugh infectiously (so unlike Colin, to draw attention to himself in that way!) One by one, around the room different people began to be touched by the Holy Spirit, including Eileen, a lady in her seventies from a very strict wing of the Christian

Church - she began to shake from head to toe. It was an astonishing evening, when God turned up in a way that I'd never known, before or since. We *usually* wound things up around 10.30pm, but nobody wanted to leave. It was midnight before we were able to persuade the last person to go!

All Ellie does on the tape is talk about her visit to the Toronto Church and the impact it had upon her. It seems as if everywhere that tape is played, similar things happen, in that God turns up and blesses people. That indeed is a characteristic of the 'Toronto Blessing', in that if you've received something then you receive an ability to give it away to others. The more you give it away, the more you get back.

A man in our church, John, had suffered on-and-off from depression for many years. He asked Dave Wort, Sylvia and I to go and pray with him. We went to his home. The moment we reached out to pray for him, he fell on the floor and began to roll around, laughing like a baby. He laughed and laughed with his legs in the air. It was so funny, that we all laughed along with him! His wife Audrey said that she'd never known him laugh so much. Apparently, in the years that followed he never suffered from depression again.

Around that time I was invited to preach at Birches Green Evangelical Church in Birmingham, where I'd preached on many occasions before. It's a small church that's known better days and the folk there were definitely in need of encouragement. I therefore rang the pastor, John Usher to ask if I could bring my house group and another couple along, to share with the church what God had been doing in their lives. Pastor John agreed enthusiastically and after a couple of hymns, I testified as to some of the unusual events we'd been experiencing since listening to the Ellie Mumford tape. Different ones told their story, especially John, of his release from depression. After all the talking we said we would like to pray for anyone in the church who wanted to be refreshed and encouraged.

We began with the Pastor and his wife. They both received a clear touch of joy from God, as they lay on the floor soaking in God's presence. Now I knew what the Lord was talking about when I got soaked in the rain, coming home from work that day. Everyone in the church got prayed for that night, receiving a touch from God, through people who normally wouldn't have done *that type of thing*. Truly amazing.

Back at the Fellowship, it was decided to invite Steve and Jeanne Wood up from their home in the south west to come and talk to the church one Saturday, following their visit to Toronto. We wanted to know first-hand from people that we knew well, what was going on over there. This turned out to be another watershed. Steve, in particular, was clearly different. His words had previously carried conviction and clarity and now they were mixed with a gentleness and compassion. The tears flowed from Steve at different points as he shared, out of weakness, and again when Steve and Jeanne moved out to pray for people.

The floor once more resembled a war zone, with bodies prostrate on the floor, meeting with God. I promise you, this wasn't your normal middle-class English church. Not any more.

Sylvia was certainly affected by this move of God. She moved into an area of spiritual sensitivity the likes of which she hadn't known before. She experienced a lot of emotional healing from her past, and God did it with Sovereignty, and gently, in a most quiet and unassuming way. Albeit with bucket-loads of tears.

So many people were being touched by this move of God, we decided (as a leadership) to begin a Sunday evening service, enabling people to come and meet with God and be refreshed. Sunday night meetings hadn't been a regular part of the life of Solihull Christian Fellowship since its inception in the early 1970s. So it was hard to get people out. We decided that no pressure should be placed upon anyone to attend these Sunday night gatherings. If God 'turned up' then things would happen and people would hear about it. We started with about twelve people and as more and more people were touched by God, the numbers increased. At it's height, we were getting around sixty attending those Times of Refreshing, and a few people even visited from other churches, after their Sunday services had finished.

Inevitably with something like this, there was criticism. Indeed the whole Toronto blessing phenomena has attracted masses of criticism. Many respected theologians have been divided on the issue of whether this move has been of God, or Satan. I've no doubt that whilst there have undoubtedly been excesses in terms of some of the so-called 'manifestations of the Spirit', that primarily this has been a move orchestrated by God himself. Through this 'outpouring' (remember my soaking?) God has come close to people in intimacy, with his kiss and with a fresh revelation of his Father heart.

As Elders of Solihull Christian Fellowship, we received criticism from inside and outside the church for allowing such self-indulgent behaviour. These comments were given serious consideration and after much debate and prayer, it was decided that the Times of Refreshing meeting on a Sunday night would undergo a change of emphasis, and would become more of a traditional-style prayer meeting, where we would concentrate on praying for the needs of those outside the church. It sounded good and spiritual, but something in my heart was ill at ease with this change of direction. As I saw it, God was still working in people's lives and it was like turning the power off in the middle of surgery; people would be left to bleed to death.

This whole debate became very stressful for me. I was getting lots of headaches and feeling very nauseated. Eventually I went to see the Doctor who told me that my blood pressure was very high and that I needed to go on medication. I didn't have the courage of my convictions (without cracking up physically) to say to Alan, Dave and Pall on behalf of the church of which I was an Elder, that I believed categorically that we should continue with the Times of

Refreshing. With my continuing sense of stress, however, allied to my feeling of being 'out of step' with my fellow Elders, there was no alternative as I saw it but for me to withdraw from Eldership and ultimately continue my pilgrimage elsewhere. It was a hard decision to come out of Eldership and an even harder one to leave Solihull Christian Fellowship a second time. It was difficult leaving behind friends and also the sense of disappointment that they may feel in Sylvia and me going. However, as I said earlier in my story I had by this time discovered that wonderful verse in Psalm 84: "Blessed are those whose strength is in you, who have set their hearts on pilgrimage."

The Bible makes it clear that that which is not of faith is sin, and sometimes you have to make painful decisions just to get back into a place of faith, rather than just going through the religious motions. Better to be a God-pleaser than a people-pleaser, though admittedly it's nice if you can do both...

Chapter Four

Ian: the agony and the ecstasy
(August - September 1996)

Shortly after the 'Toronto Blessing', as a family we were hit by another thunder-bolt. Our son Ian was taken ill. I can best relate the story by reproducing the diary of events which I kept at the time.

DIARY OF EVENTS: August - September 1996

Thursday 22 August

Ian arrives home early from work complaining of headache and feeling sick. Goes to see doctor, who diagnoses a virus and recommends pain killers.

Friday 23 August

Ian still off work and feeling no better. Goes out in the evening for a drink, but feels very unwell and is sick many times throughout the night.

Saturday 24 August

We telephone the doctor's surgery to explain the situation and are told to go there immediately. Ian arrives there with sick bowl in hand feeling very un-well. Dr Smith gives Ian an injection in the leg, which is intended to stop him being sick; she also prescribes antibiotics. Ian arrives home, and tries to sleep but is frequently being sick.

By the afternoon his condition is worsening so Dr Smith is called in again. After a thorough examination, during which she notices a swelling around the left eye, she decides to admit him to hospital. Arrive at Birmingham Heartlands at about 6.00pm and eventually, Ian is admitted to the Infectious Diseases Unit.

Sunday 25 August

Ian connected up to various intravenous drips and condition being regularly monitored. He still has headache and some sickness.

Monday 26 August

Having shown no signs of improvement it is decided to give Ian a lumbar punc-ture. This proves difficult as Ian is very tense but eventually at the fifth attempt fluid is drawn from his spine. Within a short time viral meningitis is diagnosed. In the evening Ian seems much brighter and he has actually managed to walk to the toilet.

Tuesday 27 August

Disappointed to find that Ian has regressed in the sense that he has become very drowsy and aggressive when he is roused from sleep. We express our concerns to a nurse who says that Ian is sleeping because he is bored and he will be out within 48 hours. We feel angry at these comments and continue to be very concerned over Ian's condition.

Wednesday 28 August

On finding Ian to be no better, Sylvia consults the Staff Nurse who calls for a doctor. A doctor arrives and is sufficiently concerned about Ian's condition to request that a brain scan be done.

Sylvia phones John at work and he immediately arranges to go to the hospital. On his arrival at hospital around 3.45pm Sylvia informs John that there are serious complications and Ian has a bleed in the brain. A doctor explains to us the seriousness of Ian's illness and says that he will be transferred to the Walsgrave Hospital, Coventry where he will be admitted to the neurosurgical unit for a possible brain operation. On the advice of the medical team, we telephone our daughters in Newcastle and St Agnes respectively, informing them of the gravity of the situation and saying that we would like them to be with us, if at all possible.

The ambulance heads off with Ian to Coventry whilst we follow by car. Shortly after arriving at Walsgrave we are told that Ian is being taken for an MRI scan and we are sat in a room and given a much-needed cup of tea.

Two hours later Ian is brought back from his MRI scan and is taken straight to the Intensive Care Unit. A doctor calls us into his office and says that they will only operate in a life or death situation because they wish to await the results of other tests done at Birmingham Heartlands. Ian has severe swelling and bleeding in the brain. He is suffering from something called Encephalitis and his chances of pulling through are regarded as 50-50. The next 48 hours are crucial and he will remain in Intensive Care for as long as necessary.

We go and visit Ian in Intensive Care. He is sleeping peacefully but he does have to be awakened at regular intervals by the nursing staff, for observation, blood pressure readings, etc.

At approximately 11pm Beverley arrives from Newcastle at the same time as Allison, Sara & boyfriend Steve arrive from Cornwall, followed by our friend Dr Gordon Coleman. After hugs, kisses and prayers, it is decided that Allison and I will stay the night. Allison reads from the Gideon Bible Psalm 139 and tells John that on the way up the M5 from Cornwall she was praying for Ian and when she opened her eyes there was a rainbow stretching from one side of the motorway to the other. She took that as a sign from God that Ian would be okay.

Thursday 29 August

Having been encouraged by Allison's "Rainbow story" we begin the day by reading again Psalm 139 and then go to Ian's bedside at about 6.30am. The nursing staff tell us that at about 1.00am some young people came to visit us. They said they were part of Solihull Christian Fellowship youth group and they had been praying for Ian. They left an envelope for us and when Allison opened it, inside were the words of Psalm 139 that she had read to me a few minutes earlier. We are told by a nurse that Ian has had a good night. He is still relatively peaceful. During the day close family visit Ian and when he does come around, albeit drowsily, he amuses and embarrasses all concerned with his comments, colourful language and sexual innuendo. Again the nursing staff are very reassuring saying that this kind of conversation is quite common from people who are suffering from the kind of thing that Ian is going through. Sylvia and Allison stay at the hospital through the night.

Friday 30 August

Beverley & Phil do the day shift. Very much the same as before, though Ian is awake for slightly longer periods. He can remember little and is very confused. He has not eaten for a week now, and is starting to look very thin, especially in his surgical stockings! A friend from church takes John, Sylvia and Allison to the hospital. John & Sylvia stay overnight.

Sadly Beverley & Phil have to head home to the North East as work duties beckon.

Saturday 31 August

Another friend takes Allison to the hospital, he then take Sylvia & John home. Sara & Steve arrive for the day time stint. Ian's condition remains much the same, though he has now passed the critical 48 hour period. In the afternoon his level of consciousness does drop to a level which causes some concern. For that reason it is felt wise that Sylvia & John should stay one more night.

Sunday 1 September

Ian wakes up feeling really grumpy. A nurse responds by trying to explain to Ian how ill he has been and how fortunate he is to be alive. This seems to jolt Ian and we have the best conversation with him for a week or more. Encouraged by this we do a swap with Allison, Sara & Steve. We head off for church feeling very encouraged and give a testimony to the fact that Ian is recovering. We thank people for their great expressions of love and faithful prayers. It is all very emotional.

In the afternoon, it is time for Sara, Steve, Amy & Allison to head off home to Cornwall. It has been wonderful to have our family around us at this very difficult time. We really appreciated their love and support. It was so good to be together.

On our visit to the hospital in the evening we find Ian continuing to improve and enjoy reasonable conversation with him.

Monday 2 September

Great news! Ian leaves the Intensive Care Unit having won the biggest battle of his life so far. On visiting him, we find him in pretty good shape although he is nagging the nurses for a 'rooney' (cigarette to the uninitiated!) Although still on a couple of drips, his appetite is gradually returning.

Tuesday 3 September

Ian is now fully awake, getting bored and expressing a desire to go home.

Wednesday 4 September

We visit hospital in the morning in order to keep an appointment with the Consultant, Mr. Sakas. Gordon, Julia and Jonathan Coleman are present with us and while we are sitting around Ian's bed a message comes through to Gordon that Jonathan has been accepted into medical school at St Andrews. Joy fills the air and it is good that as two families we are together at such a poignant moment. Ian, though somewhat bemused by it all, is aware that something good is happening.

We leave Ian's bedside for a while to hear what the Consultant has to say and during that interview we have it confirmed by Mr. Sakas just how dangerously ill Ian has been and that he has now made a "spectacular recovery" and the outlook for a full recovery is now very good indeed.

Sylvia, together with the Colemans, goes off to see the results of the various brain scans whilst John stays with Ian.

Thursday 5 September

Happy 18th birthday Ian. Not where he would have wanted to spend this special day but he's alive and on the mend and that is what is really important. There are many birthday cards and 'Get Well' cards, but they are nearly all at home as Ian has requested it that way.

He is a little down today, perhaps understandably so, and he cannot wait to get home. Ian is now asking more and more questions about his illness.

Friday 6 September

Another brain scan is taken to assess how the swelling is reducing. Ian is also given some glimmer of hope that he may be coming home today. However this hope is dashed when he is informed that he will be going back to Birmingham Heartlands before his eventual discharge. Ian is now becoming very frustrated with his confinement and he is now frequently heard uttering those 'immortal' words "Ah, we'll see won't we!"

Saturday 7 September

Sylvia back at work on an early shift.
Ian's last day on a drip his arms and hands, like pin cushions, breathe a loud sigh of relief. Ian is cheered during the afternoon as Aston Villa go two up against Arsenal. His condition deteriorates slightly when Arsenal pull a goal back only to have a total relapse when an equaliser is scored late in stoppage time!

That night Ian and his pals on the ward enjoy a late night curry from a local Indian take away, while Maurice goes walkabout.

Sunday 8 September

After attending church in the morning we go to see Ian on the afternoon and with the permission of the nursing staff we take him out for a McDonald's tea, at a nearby restaurant. Obviously Ian is very weak and a little disorientated but he enjoys his tea and appreciates the break from routine.

Monday 9 September

John back at work. Go to hospital at around 4.00pm and although Ian has been told he can be transferred back to Birmingham, no bed is available on this day. Tomorrow is more hopeful. Ian is cheered however by the arrival of Beverley, Phil & little nephew Elliott.

Tuesday 10 September

Beverley & Phil visit Ian during the day and wait patiently for an ambulance to transfer him back to Birmingham. Eventually Ian says goodbye to the staff at Walsgrave at about 6 pm and we all meet up again for visiting time at 7 pm on the ward in Heartlands where the adventure began more than two weeks ago. Ian is convinced that he will be home tomorrow.

Wednesday 11 September

Telephones ring at both the Prince of Wales Nursing Home and the Inland Revenue office, in Solihull, "Hello, this is Ian here, I'm coming home". The news was received with great joy and relief of course. Phil and Beverley have the privilege of driving to the hospital and bringing Ian home. Sylvia and John each leave work early, and arrive home to emotional hugs and kisses, before sitting down with Ian for a couple of hours, opening cards and presents. It is a wonderful time and now together we can really begin the process of seeing Ian through to a complete recovery.

During this most anxious of times, we received wonderful support from our friends at Solihull Christian Fellowship, at work and in churches around the country. On Radio WM, Michael Blood on his Sunday morning programme, asked people to pray for Ian's full recovery. No wonder I shed a tear or two at Wembley Stadium, when we sang *Abide With Me* at the FA Cup Final of 2000. It wasn't because Villa lost to Chelsea – I was just thankful to be there with Ian, to share in that momentous day.

By this time Sylvia and I were just about getting used to the idea of being grandparents. The first time it was a bit of a shock, because (I suppose a lot of people go through this) we felt too young to be called 'nanny' and 'granddad'. At the time of writing we currently have nine grandchildren, five boys and four girls. We adore them all.

Sylvia, after many years of being at home for the children and undertaking a variety of cleaning jobs, then became a care assistant. After three or four sorties into a variety of caring situations, she found a job that she loved at the Prince of Wales Nursing Home, in Solihull Lodge. After being very nervous about going back into regular employment, Sylvia took to this kind of work like a duck to water. She found it personally rewarding. Sylvia also loved working at that home because of the superb way it was run by the Matron, Anne Barry, a former nurse at Solihull Hospital.

Sylvia developed a particular rapport with people who were dying and also in comforting relatives. More than once it was put to Sylvia that she would make a good nurse in a hospice situation.

Sylvia doesn't take to change that easily, though being married to me she has had plenty of practice over the years! As there's a Marie Curie Hospice, Warren Pearl, quite near to where we live, she decided to ring up and request an application form. Within days of submitting the application form she was asked to attend an interview. Sylvia was successful. She went to Warren Pearl as an auxiliary nurse, or as the new name decrees, a health care assistant. Anne Barry, now a good friend, was sorry to see Sylvia go. But she knew that she'd fit into life at Warren Pearl like a hand in a glove.

Not only have I been excited at what Sylvia has achieved since working at the hospice, I am in awe at the wonderful work carried out by so many of the nurses who undertake this vocation. My wife has found considerable fulfilment and self-worth in caring for people in this way. Once, with a group of nurses she abseiled down one of the largest buildings in the centre of Birmingham to raise funds for the hospice. Ever since then she's been keen to get a group together to undertake a fundraising tandem parachute jump, but to date this hasn't materialised. I wouldn't rule it out, however!

Another time, Sylvia and other members of staff were caring for a fanatical Birmingham City supporter. She contacted the club manager, Steve Bruce, to see if anything could be done for this fan to give him and his family a massive morale boost. She was thinking of maybe, a signed shirt or football. However, one day there was a phone call for her. She was convinced it was me, as she picked up the receiver.

"Is that Sylvia?", the man asked.

"Yes" wondering who it was.

"Hi Sylvia, this is Paul Devlin and I'm ringing from the Blues training ground. I have your letter to the manager, and I would like to come and visit Warren Pearl this afternoon. Is that okay?"

Sylvia was thrilled and excited. The news that Paul Devlin (one of the more popular players) was coming caused a real buzz about the place. When Paul arrived he was accompanied by another player, Curtis Woodhouse. They went in to see the gentleman concerned, who by this time was joined by his family. They presented him with a signed shirt, which he immediately put on. Photographs were taken of this happy scene and the terminally-ill man declared that it was one of the happiest days of his life. As an Aston Villa supporter, it pains me to say this, but the two players were a credit to themselves and to Birmingham City. Within 72 hours of their visit, the gentleman had passed away and he was later cremated in the football shirt. The family were so grateful, for a gesture which had meant so much. A local newspaper printed an article and picture about the event with a headline that read, "My Blue heaven".

Through Sylvia's passion for her work I've taken a keen interest in the thinking Behind palliative care. I've read about the life of the founder of the modern hospice movement, Dame Cicely Saunders, who died in July 2005 when she was well into her eighties.

Dame Cicely had to fight tooth and nail to get funding and the go-ahead to form the first hospice. She believed firmly that a person when faced with a terminal illness had the right to be cared for physically, emotionally and spiritually. Each of those areas was important in their own right and Dame Cicely strove to maintain those values all through her nursing life. She wanted people to be free from pain and emotionally at peace as far as possible in order that they may consider their eternal destiny. I am led to understand that she was happy if people had given serious thought to the existence of God and then concluded that he did not exist, unlike herself who as a Christian, had thought about these things and concluded that through a personal faith in Jesus Christ, it was indeed possible to receive the gift of eternal life. What Dame Cicely hated was the thought that people would go to their graves never having considered the issue of where they would spend eternity.

Sylvia often comes home and weeps with me, over her patients. We have some precious times praying together for them. Down through the years, Sylvia has supported me so much in my work and what might be termed as 'flights of fancy', but now it's my very great privilege to support her in this work of caring, which I know touches the heart of Jesus in a very special way.

As far as churches were concerned, at this point in our lives, there were two in the Solihull area that were still 'flying the flag' for the Toronto Blessing. As far as we were concerned this was the biggest thing to hit the Christian Church, maybe in our lifetime. We wanted very much to be part of it. For a time we went to Arden Church, about four miles out of Solihull Town Centre, in the village of Knowle. We were quite happy attending services there, without making any long-term commitment. Then, as he often does, God took a hand.

I was invited by friends, Phil and Christine to visit their church in Middleton, Lancashire for a weekend to talk about what the Holy Spirit was doing in the British Church as I understood it. Sylvia and I thought about the weekend, and the more convinced we became that we should invite Steve and Jeanne Wood from Wells to accompany us and take the lead part, as they had first-hand experience of what was going on, in and out of Toronto.

Having cleared this with Phil and his fellow church leaders, we duly contacted the couple who responded enthusiastically to our invitation to join us. Suffice to say that we had a wonderful time and God moved powerfully in people's lives. A major thing that came out of it was that two local churches decided to reform as one body and so pool their resources. On the way home, Steve told us that he was due to be preaching in Solihull the following week. He would like it if Sylvia and I would join him, so that we could be available to work as a team once again, when it came to praying for people. We readily agreed. The church Steve was preaching at was the other one in Solihull still running with the 'Toronto Blessing'. It was where Richard and Audrey attended (who we'd stayed with, when we came back from Cornwall) along with quite a few others who'd left Solihull Christian Fellowship with us, all those years earlier. I think that is why we didn't attend The King's Church initially. It was on our doorstep. But I guess we just didn't want to have to humble ourselves again and say, "Will you take us back?".

So it was that we accompanied Steve and Jeanne that Sunday. Quite a morning it was too. Steve preached powerfully. At the end of the service, most of the congregation (about 50) started coming forward for prayer. As we laid hands gently on people, it was clear that God was touching lives. Some laughed, some shook and some cried. Some did all three. These were special moments. Not least because in nearly thirty years now as a Christian, since giving my life to God in Westminster Chapel, I'd only rarely witnessed stuff like this. I'd read about it happening in far off lands. Now it was happening in our back yard. It was thrilling.

Leaving Solihull Christian Fellowship had been very painful for us; apart from leaving great friends behind, it also left us open to criticism, which may or may not have been justified. Whatever, it was difficult, but what we were experiencing now, was what we'd moved on for. We wanted to know God in a deeper and more intimate way. The Toronto experience had made this possible and we wanted to run with it, for as long as we possibly could. We didn't want to go back to doing church as we'd always done it and known it.

Hence we attended The King's Church. A part of New Frontiers International, a worldwide family of churches which, over the years became synonymous with the Bible Weeks at Stoneleigh in Warwickshire. Until recently over 20,000 people would gather at the end of July each year, over a two week period to hear inspirational Bible teaching.

King's Church had three Elders, Graham Pearce, Stuart Webb and Paul Crabtree. They seemed to complement each other well. They'd been to Toronto together, experienced the 'Blessing' first hand and they led the church in a very relaxed, laid-back manner, simply allowing God to 'flow' through them; or at least, that's how it seemed to us. At the time three other families made the switch from Solihull Christian Fellowship, for the same reasons.

During an early visit to Kings', Paul, one of the Elders (with whom we were to become close friends) simply told us to, "Chill out and enjoy God". This we did for a short time and probably would've continued doing, had we not been put on the spot somewhat.

One particular Sunday morning, a young couple named James and Suzanne were invited to the front of the church by Graham, one of our Elders. Graham then came across to Sylvia and me, and asked us if we would go out to the front and pray for the couple. Suzanne was one of the worship team and also a daughter of Elder Paul and his wife Carole. Other than that we knew little about them and that's obviously why Graham asked us to pray for them. As we stood in front of James and Suzanne, quietly praying, I became aware that Sylvia was struggling with something. I said to Sylvia "Do you have something you want to say?"

"Yes", she said with stammering lips "...but it seems crazy".

Sylvia, with a great deal of nervousness: "I feel the Lord is saying, don't worry for it will all be done and dusted by September."

James and Suzanne looked at each other knowingly and then hugged us tightly, as if we were close family friends. Little did we know then, but we were about to become exactly that!

Later in the day, after a nice Sunday roast, the telephone rang. It was Suzanne. Were free to go round to their house for tea, as there was something they wanted to tell us? By 5 o'clock, we were sitting at their dining table enjoying a selection of sandwiches, cakes and cups of tea.

Eventually the conversation got around to what they wanted to tell us.

"That was amazing this morning, wasn't it James?" said Suzanne.

James nodded his agreement.

"You couldn't have known what we were thinking, Sylvia" continued Suzanne.

The couple had been feeling a little bored. Both were about as far as they could go in their present jobs; James a teacher and Suzanne lecturing in law at a Wolverhampton College; they wanted to do something a bit different. Suzanne had seen a job advertised in the Cayman Islands for someone to lecture in law. It fitted her qualifications perfectly. The contract was for two years, and the job would start later that year – in September, just as Sylvia had said. James would have to get a teaching job, but they'd been praying about whether this course of action was right for them. They'd been asking for guidance. Then Sylvia, who didn't even know them, goes and says it "will all be done and dusted by September". It was God's confirmation to them.

Sylvia, of course, was greatly encouraged by this, as indeed we all were. They decided to proceed and James applied for a job and got one without any hassle at all. It was indeed, just as Sylvia had prophesied. Done and dusted by September. James and his wife talked this through with their respective parents, but within a few months they were nicely settled into their luxury apartment on the beautiful island of Grand Cayman.

Chapter Five

I still believe in fairy tales...

As we stepped off the Boeing 777 and descended the steps onto the concrete runway, it was immediately apparent we were somewhere exotic. The hot, gentle breeze upon the face and the fragrant smells in the air were an instant reminder, if we needed one, that this was to be no ordinary holiday. Could it really be that the Flanners, who, for most of their married lives had struggled to raise the money for a week in Blackpool or Torquay with their four children, were now embarking upon a week in the luxurious Cayman Islands? Apart from a little pocket money, it wasn't costing them a penny! It was a gift from friends. How they first heard about the offer of this gift, actually stretches back to a telephone conversation at home one evening.

Telephone rings and John answers -

"Good evening! Can I help you?" (Professional telephone manner, even at home)

"Hello John, this is Carole. How are you doing?"

"Fine, thanks" I said cheerily.

Carole went on. "Have you and Sylvia booked a holiday this year?"

"Yes we have," I said, "we're going to Scotland for a week in July - it's something we've wanted to do for years."

"Oh I see", Carole said, with a note of disappointment in her voice. Before going on to say, "Well, would you like another holiday?"

"Yes of course - wouldn't we all?" I replied with a hint of laughter in my voice.

"No! I'm serious," said Carole. "Paul and I would like you and Sylvia to go to the Cayman Islands, to visit Suzanne and James."

Carole went on to say that the happy couple had asked for us to go and visit them, and as Paul and Carole had some air miles, they wanted to treat us. They booked the flight and everything. It was simply amazing.

Having come to terms with the initial shock, told the news in the office and arranged the Leave situation, it was all systems go! Our knowledge of the Cayman Islands was negligible. So we took to reading travel books and watching a video about the place.

There are three small islands which make up the Caymans. Little Cayman, Cayman Brack and the largest (which is still not very big) and where we would be going, Grand Cayman - the capital of which, is Georgetown. The Islands are situated between Jamaica and Cuba; a British colony in the Caribbean with a great deal of wealth. The climate is definitely on the tropical side. The temperatures (when we were there) were around 90 degrees Fahrenheit, with a fairly high humidity.

I counted the days down like a little child waiting for Father Christmas. I was so excited. We took a 4.30am coach to London Gatwick, in order to catch the 11am flight to Grand Cayman. It was such an adventure.

The eleven hour flight (surpassing our previous longest trip by some seven hours) was a source of fascination for us, in itself. We were like two children, wide-eyed at a couple of lovely meals, a free bar service and some good movies. We were no-less curious about having to stop for people to get off at Nassau in the Bahamas, and for re-fuelling and then, on for just over an hour, to land at Grand Cayman.

Having collected our luggage, Suzanne and James were there to greet us enthusiastically, with hugs all round. Then by car, for the twenty minute journey to the flat they're renting for the two years they're out there. A mixture of excited conversation, catching up on news from home and eyes looking out of the window, not wanting to miss any of the scenery, with palm trees very much in evidence across the flat landscape. Driving takes place on the left-hand side of the road, though most of the vehicles are left-hand drive, imported as they are, from America.

Our hosts arrived at a complex called Flowers Apartments - about thirty spacious, luxurious two-bedroom flats, served by an open-air swimming pool which was to be quite a haven for us, in escaping from the blazing sun!

The Cayman Islands were six hours behind our British Summer Time. The air-conditioning in the flat was superb, as it is throughout the Island, so we had an excellent first night's sleep.

Our hosts went off to work early the next morning. We showered, had breakfast and planned our day. On Radio Cayman, temperatures were expected to be 87 degrees with cloudless skies, for several days. Now the fairy tale could really take shape.

Within a fifteen minute walk of the apartments was a tiny beach called Smith's Cove, so we headed for that. Within minutes we would be dripping with sweat. We walked down Webster Drive, with its sprawling *Dynasty*-like mansions either side of the road, with their long, sweeping drives up to the impressive entrances. The trees were tall, beautiful and fragrant; with colourful exotic birds, including parrots, nestling in the branches. Pausing to take photographs along the way, we eventually arrived at the beach. Weaving our way through the trees and down a short hill which became increasingly sandy, we were suddenly confronted with a most breathtaking view of this small cove with its white sandy beach, a handful of people dotted about under the many palm trees, and the beautiful Caribbean Sea, stretching out calmly before us. The sun was beating down from a clear blue sky; the sea to reflecting a variety of magnificent colours.

We paddled for ages in the warm water, sat around on the sand and took in the idyllic scene. Not for the last time we were to say "Can this really be happening to us?"

Later in the week, we visited two more beaches which were much bigger but equally beautiful in their own ways. Rum Point was gorgeous. It was there we took to sunbathing in a double-hammock with the ever-present sound of reggae music playing gently in the background - very romantic! We followed this with a visit to the most aptly named Seven Mile Beach, which gave the impression of what it might be like to be on a desert island. It was about 6pm, the sun was going down and there weren't many people around, as the stunning landscape once again captured the emotions.

No holiday is ever complete, especially for the ladies, without a shopping trip. One morning we went into Georgetown, with its many banks and other financial institutions. We discovered that on a daily basis thousands of American and Canadian tourists pour into the gift shops of Georgetown as they come off the luxury cruise liners, for a few hours' sightseeing. Jewellery shops are very much in evidence and extremely expensive, but diamonds and especially black corral proved very popular with the wealthy tourists. We walked a little and sat a little, because it was so excruciatingly hot. Often we would nip into the shops just to enjoy the refreshment of the air conditioning! We took in some other kind of refreshment once we'd set eyes upon a Kentucky Fried Chicken restaurant. After all, it was coming up to 12 noon, lunchtime for any self-respecting Englishman!

A few surprise happenings took place, which were like icing on the cake. James had been doing some voluntary work at a Christian radio station, Heaven 97, and as a result I was invited to be the subject of an interview about my life and faith.

Following the radio interview I received a call asking me if I'd go and preach at a church the next evening. An amazing experience - It was an all-Jamaican Church, we were given a wonderful welcome, the worship was vibrant and I thoroughly enjoyed preaching there. Afterwards the men came up and shook my hand but the women came up and showered me with hugs and kisses - Sylvia was most gracious. Especially as the Church gave us a very generous gift of $137 (approximately £100) as a token of their appreciation!

Another bonus came my way. Friday evening, James saw in the local newspaper that one of their bars would be screening a live Premiership football game on Saturday morning at 9am - did

I want to go? Of course I wanted to go! Even more so when I learned that the match in question, was Aston Villa against Charlton Athletic from Villa Park, Birmingham. We rose early on Saturday morning to get to the Sportsman's bar about five miles away; even at that time of the morning, the temperatures were in the 80s and it was strange to arrive at the bar and to see on the screen that in Birmingham, it was pouring with rain. I felt sad, for a fleeting moment because my son Ian would be at the match and getting very wet! The game turned out to be thrilling, though we were the only Villa fans in the bar. We lost 3-4, but I'll always have the memory of watching that particular match. As Sylvia said to me, "God really is good to you, isn't he?"

"Yes, but I wish he'd helped the Villa to win!"

Anyone who knows me would realise that no holiday would be complete without me bringing back at least one CD. This was no exception and I picked-up one containing a reggae song, *Cayman Islands*, which was being played in shops as we walked around. The song really captures the laid-back atmosphere of the place. One other CD was by a guy called 'The Barefoot Man', featuring his big hit *Viagra*. James and Suzanne said that I just had to hear this song and so they took me into a music shop, put the headphones on me and said I must listen to the words. I could hardly stand for laughing, it was so funny. As indeed is most of the CD, and once we were back in the UK, it was much in demand!

Eventually, it was time to put away the sun cream and head back home. Armed with a bag-load of goodies, including presents for the grandchildren and souvenirs to remind us of the fairy tale, we arrived back in Solihull.

*

Does lightning strike in the same place twice, or do fairy tales repeat themselves? For us they do. Two years later, we returned to the Cayman Islands accompanied on this occasion, by Paul and Carole. On this holiday we really became great friends. We got on so well and it was a totally different type of holiday to the first one, when we basically stayed with the beaches and the restaurants.

Paul hired a car and drove us around the Island, to visit some of the most gorgeous places. We took in the lovely, fragrant Queen Elizabeth II Gardens, took a boat trip to Stingray City and even though Sylvia and I are non-swimmers, were able to get out of the boat and have the thrill of playing with the hundreds of stingray. For me, as a blind person it was simply magical just to touch these incredible fish. I was impressed by the smoothness of their skin and very strong backbone. We had the joy of meeting up with a lady doctor friend whom we knew who had moved out there to work, from Solihull. We sampled some of the local cuisine including, of course, jerk chicken and red snapper fish, which Sylvia especially appreciated. A highlight of the second trip came when Paul taught Sylvia to snorkel. We were based at the lovely Smith's Cove and as Carole and I sunbathed under the palm trees, Paul managed to persuade Sylvia to go snorkelling. She was a bit nervous, but she was up for the adventure. As they made their way out to sea, a distance I think of about

50 feet, Paul managed to encourage Sylvia to trust him and put her head under the water. What she saw was so moving, the experience will stay with her for the rest of her life. Even though the waters were still fairly shallow, she saw the most awesome array of fish which were a kaleidoscope of magnificent colour. Sylvia and Paul went out a little further to witness more of the spectacular display of colourful fish. When they returned to where Carole and I where, Sylvia removed her goggles and began to sob, overcome with emotion at the beauty of what her eyes had just witnessed.

Belinda Carlyle sang the hit song, *Heaven Is A Place On Earth*. For us, Grand Cayman was a little bit of heaven on earth. Paul and Carole had certainly become wonderful friends to us and though we haven't been to the Caymans again, they've greatly blessed us with some other lovely holidays, including Florida.

Our friendship with Paul and Carole is enhanced on our various holidays together. But it's deep in the sense that we talk a lot together about the joys and sorrows of family life. The Christian faith which we share in common, means that we can pray for, and with, each other with a genuine feeling for what the other is going through. Following a particularly wet week's holiday in Marbella, I wrote the following ode as a tribute to our friends:

ODE TO PAUL & CAROLE

We went with Paul & Carole for our holiday in the sun
And though it didn't work out like that, we still had lots of fun.
The weather did its best to dampen down our frolics
And I have to confess that lesser mortals may have become alcoholics.
There was G & T and San Miguel and the occasional glass of wine
So "Happy Hour" at the Tapas Bar ensured we did just fine.
All things in moderation though, is what the people say
So day by day we drove about even though the skies were grey.
Up the mountain and round the shops we went with vim and vigour
And the amount of food we ate did no good for the figure.
With prawns and sword fish and juicy, succulent steak
This fine cuisine is going to be, a very hard habit to break.
Sitting up at night and watching a movie became a bit of a thing
Hard to believe that in a few days, back in the groove we'll swing.
We'll be early to bed and early to rise
Going back to work so we can take to the skies.
With our hard-earned cash we'll be looking for the sun
Together with our friends having great fun.
Our God is so good he has blessed us together
With friendship made deeper by the inclement weather.

So all that remains for us to say
Are thanks for your kindness and may God we pray.
Bless you abundantly with lots of good cheer
So that together we can drink the wine and the beer.
In celebration of him who does all things well
His name is Jesus, our Lord, Emanuel.
So lift up a glass and raise up a toast
To the Father, the Son and the Holy Ghost.
Now in closing this ode, I'm sure Sylvie agrees
Thanks for all the firsts, especially 'blue cheese'.

In our walk of faith, at every stage, God has given us at least one or two couples that we could get really close to, for mutual encouragement. I appreciate every individual and couple that God has put in our path. Thankfully, though we have all moved on in our journey, I'm still in touch with nearly all of them either by email, letter or telephone. I regularly thank God for every person who has added something to my experience of life.

Things had been ticking along quite nicely at work, though it came as a bit of a shock when the office I was working in, near to Solihull town centre, was closed down and most of the staff, myself included, were relocated back into the centre of Birmingham. I was placed in a large typing pool on the third floor of a twelve-storey building, City Centre House. I was one of only two typists moving from Solihull to Birmingham and it was quite difficult going from a pool of six people, to one of sixteen. Even more difficult than that however, was the trip from my desk to the toilet. It was quite a long walk down a corridor, through several swing doors and down some steps. When in the vicinity of the gents I had to make sure I counted the right number of doors, in case I ended up in the ladies', kitchen or even the mop room.

I was well used to travelling into Birmingham over many years, so the journey didn't bother me, it was just a case of getting started earlier to catch the bus to the train station and then hopping on a regular train into Brum. All went well for a couple of years. Then came the accident.

Chapter Six

Accidents will happen

The train was just pulling into Moor Street station. I was a little late going into work, due to a doctor's appointment. The train slowed down, almost to a standstill. I got up from my seat and made my way to the exit door along with a handful of other people. The doors opened. I followed a couple of others and stepped off the train, white stick in hand. What happened in the next second or two remains a painful memory to this day. I'd probably become a bit blasé when it came to getting off trains, having done it successfully for many years. Either way, I didn't put my stick down on the platform first. I simply stepped off the train like everyone else, but my right foot missed the platform and went down into thin air; pulling me off balance out of the train and causing my left ankle to be trapped under the weight of my body. Apart from the actual shock of what was happening to me, the pain of having my ankle trapped under the weight of my 14-stone frame was excruciating as I hung there, half-on and half-off the platform. Fortunately, a young man had the presence of mind to pull me clear of the train and carefully take off my left shoe, as I screamed out, "It's my ankle, it's my ankle! The pain's unbearable…"

Soon, I heard the sound of the ambulance siren. I was then on my way to the City Hospital. Although my left ankle had swollen up to about twice its normal size, x-rays confirmed no break; but there was some soft tissue and ligament damage, resulting in me taking a couple of weeks off work, until I could a put a little weight on to the ankle again. Several years have elapsed since the accident; I don't think my ankle has ever felt totally back to normal, as it frequently swells up.

I entered into some fairly lengthy correspondence with Central Trains. I was concerned that someone my size could actually slip so easily down the gap between train and platform. It could easily have been a child or a frail, elderly person and more serious injuries than the ones I sustained could have incurred. Where there's a gap like that, the driver should announce this, to passengers, before opening the exit doors as a clear safety warning.

The train company would not admit any liability, stating that the gap came within the safety regulations. I made the point that, in that case, the safety regulations should be tightened up. As a "goodwill gesture", Central Trains offered me two train tickets for a day trip anywhere in their area…

Returning to work, my manager advised me that she'd been told of a scheme, Access to Work. A Government run scheme, which enables disabled people to have a taxi take them, to and from work and the individual has to pay only what it would normally cost them, using public transport; the rest is funded from the scheme. I'd known about it previously, but much to the astonishment of my colleagues, had chosen to ignore it and travel by public transport. I enjoyed the experience of travelling and meeting interesting people to chat with, on my journeys. I much appreciated the flexible working hours scheme that operated at the office, and I didn't want to lose that, by having to have set times for my taxi. In the interests of safety and job security however, I was persuaded to give it a go. I was to make some unlikely friendships and allay a few more fears along the way.

My initial contract under Access to Work was a local taxi company, which lasted a few weeks. They were looking for bigger contracts and didn't like waiting for their money. The firm in question, put me on to a taxi driver who occasionally did some work for them. Noor Hussain quickly agreed to take as my regular driver. We just as quickly became good friends, though I was apprehensive at first, possibly due to ignorance. Hussain, like me in his fifties, was a very religious man - a devout Muslim. Occasionally he would ask me if he could pull over to the side of the road, so that he could pray for a few minutes. I would agree but still felt a little uncomfortable. Rather than sitting there passively, I decided I would pray, too. I therefore prayed in tongues to the God of Abraham, Isaac and Jacob, the God and Father of our Lord Jesus Christ. Picture it: here were two very sincere men praying to God in a taxi, but were they praying to the same God?

When he collected me from work in the evenings, Hussain would often tell me of a particular bargain he'd bought that day. He'd rarely purchase something at face value, but usually bartered to get the price down (a bit like my friend Gordon Coleman) and one day he amused me with the story of how he bought a whole fish for a huge knock-down price. He was thrilled, like a little boy in a chocolate factory. I named Hussain 'the bargain man'.

We started our little tradition that on the way home each Friday, just before I got to the taxi, I would pop into McDonalds' and pick up two fillets-of-fish. Hussain would bring two cans of pop. We would have our own little party. One day, Hussain said he wanted to take another contract and it would mean that he'd pick me up fifteen minutes earlier in the morning and it would take me fifteen minutes longer to get home in the evening. This was a schools contract. A carer would escort a child, to and from school. The first day of this new arrangement - which started in the afternoon - I arrived at the taxi to be told by Hussain that the lady in the back was named Ann. I got into the front passenger seat. I heard the lady exclaim, "Oh no, I don't believe it, it's John Flanner!"

I must have looked puzzled. "You do remember me, don't you?"

"I know your voice".

"I should hope you do, Sylvia used to look after my twin boys…" she said with a growing sense of frustration, at my inability to recall the name.

The penny dropped. Ann Shirley was at Solihull Christian Fellowship when we were, first time around. For the whole of that school year, Ann joined our many discussions on a whole range of subjects, as well as our Friday night fillet-o'-fish parties. Ann also took Hussain's daughter Amner, for after school English lessons.

Hussain would sometimes take a short break from taxi driving, or go back to Pakistan/Kashmir for an extended holiday. During those times other Asian drivers looked after me, and I got to know Sarfraz, Abid and Zubair. The driver I have travelled with most, is Mohammed. Now that Hussain has gone home on a more-permanent basis, Mohammed is my regular driver. He's a young man with a wife and three daughters.

We've become firm friends and we help each other out, wherever we can. Although the Friday parties have now stopped, we do treat each other occasionally, though I think Mohammed is leading the way on the generosity stakes, because he often greets me from work with some freshly-cooked samosas, to try out.

Prior to the scheme I cannot remember ever encountering any Muslims, let alone having them as friends. The guys I've come to know have all been delightful in their own way, but in Hussain and Mohammed I've found two men both generous and kind. The way they care for each other, within their extended families, is a real challenge to us in the West. We've had many discussions about our differing religious beliefs. But in the end we respect each other. If I'd been brought up in Pakistan, who knows - would I believe as they do? I can't say. I do make the point, however, that I do not believe in the Lord Jesus Christ as my personal saviour because I was brought up to do so; instead I came to an understanding at the age of 21 that Jesus died for my sins, and he rose again from the dead to give me, not only forgiveness, but also the free gift of eternal life.

Chapter Seven

Face to face with fate

My son Ian and I share not only a love of sport, but also enjoy similar music. Don't laugh, but among our favourites are the Bee Gees and John Denver. In the case of the former, we went together to Wembley Stadium to see the Bee Gees in concert on their 30th anniversary tour. It was to celebrate Ian's 20th birthday. We had a magical day together, singing along to many of the great tunes composed by the Gibb brothers. As darkness fell over the old stadium, over 50,000 adoring fans fully extended their vocal chords on numbers like *Stayin' Alive* and *Night Fever*. For sheer spine-tingling excitement, it rivalled any football match.

When I first heard the news that John Denver had been killed when the plane he was piloting crashed, I rang Ian at McDonalds restaurant in Solihull, where he was working at the time, to break the news. He was grief-stricken and ran out of the restaurant in floods of tears and disbelief. It sadly brought back memories to me, of when three of my other heroes, Buddy Holly, Jim Reeves and Otis Reading, all died in plane crashes.

One of Denver's hits is *Some Days are Diamonds*. The chorus goes:

"Some days are diamonds/some days are stone
Some times the hard times/won't leave me alone."

I think particular years can be like that. Some years are wonderful and like diamonds, whereas by comparison, some years are like stone. 2003 was like that. On new year's day, the phone rang.

Ian was calling from the beautiful Trout Inn, situated in the heart of the Oxfordshire countryside. He was working as Relief Manager there, alongside his wife (of six months) Clare.

"Hi Dad, it's Ian here. I just rang to wish you and Mum a happy new year."

Though the greeting was meant to be a cheerful one, there was nevertheless a sombre tone in Ian's voice and I responded with "Thanks Ian, but how are you and Clare?"

Ian hesitated for a moment before saying, "We have a bit of a problem… Clare's walked-out on me and gone back home to her parents".

I was stunned by this news. We had no idea that there was any problem in their relationship. They'd enjoyed a wonderful wedding day a matter of months earlier. Both families were so proud as we celebrated a wonderful occasion. Clare had gladly given up a career in office work, to join Ian and train together in pub management. Now, it appeared that the long hours of working together professionally, and then slumping into bed exhausted in the early hours, had taken its toll on their fledgling marriage.

There was no reconciliation. Clare, who we had a lot of time for, is now with someone else and has a baby son. Ian too, is now in a happy relationship with a lovely lady at Flo-gas, his employer latterly. He is now out of the pub trade, as he doesn't want to contribute towards another relationship break-down.

A few weeks later in this year of stone and Leber's Optic Atrophy struck again in our family. My sister Joan, not in the best of health and divorced from her husband Neil, had to come to terms with a crushing blow. Her oldest son, Matthew, aged 18, awoke one morning to find that he couldn't see very well out of one eye. A hospital appointment was quickly arranged. The same old scenario was about to be replayed. First, the eye deteriorated followed by the other, a month or two later. Almost all of the sight is gone. A series of vitamin injections slowed down the deterioration and possibly prevented a complete loss of sight, but the loss was still dramatic and devastating for the entire family. Matthew is now in his twenties and went on to gain a place at Birmingham University, to study Philosophy.

More tragedy was to hit the following month. My brother Paul had been idyllically married to Sue for nearly twenty years. Even though Paul has been registered blind since the age of 17, he still held down a job in a factory for over twenty five years until taking redundancy. Sue had worked as a laboratory assistant in a school. Unfortunately, she had an accident when a bottle of sulphuric acid fell out of a cupboard and went all down her, leaving her physically and emotionally scarred. The trauma seemed to bring on arthritis. Slowly, over the years the arthritis spread further around her body. Sue was never one to complain. She had a wonderful sense of humour and the couple enjoyed some wonderful trips out on their narrow boat around the canals of the West Midlands.

Sue underwent numerous operations and injections of various drugs to try and reduce swelling and pain in her joints. In the March of our year of stone, she developed breathing problems, was admitted to hospital, where she subsequently died after a brave fight. Sue was 42 years of age and the story goes that she and Paul never had a cross word in all their years of marriage. They were devoted to each other. As a family we were all crushed by this loss.

Many months later, while Paul was still grieving, he began to search for consolation in the Internet and corresponded with others experiencing similar bereavements. He corresponded with several ladies, following the loss of a beloved husband. One lady in particular grabbed his attention. Amazingly, the lady concerned was also named Sue, and her late husband was called Paul - after emails and lengthy phone calls, they eventually met and later married.

In the midst of grief and sadness came a phone call in the early hours from our daughter Allison, still living in St Agnes, Cornwall. There's always a sense of alarm when the phone rings after midnight, and on this occasion, our concerns were well founded. Sylvia fumbled in the dark to pick up the receiver. Allison's trembling voice gave it away immediately.

"I'm really sorry Mum, to have to call you at this time. But Sara has been badly beaten-up by Tommy". *[Tommy is not his real name]*

Sara was living just a short distance from Allison, and her boyfriend Tommy, was known to have a temper and a particularly jealous and possessive side. If you have ever seen the film Sleeping With The Enemy there's certainly some similar traits.

Sara had received kicks to the face and other parts of her body, sustaining several broken teeth and many bruises, both physical and emotional: although the physical bruises have since healed. Like so many cases, Sara took him back, accepting his tears as an apology. Again history repeated itself and ultimately Sara had to flee from Tommy, whilst he was out at work one day. There's a lot more I could say about this, but that's for Sara if she chooses. It highlights what was happening to Sylvia and me and how we dealt with it. I'm a great believer in forgiveness. I preach it all the time, believing it to be the most wonderful word in the dictionary. One of the worst things I hear in life, is when someone says, "I will never forgive them".

I believe that I need to forgive anyone who offends me, for the sake of my own health. Unforgiving eats away on the inside, like a cancer; causing bitterness of spirit, leading to misery and depression. Finding the grace to forgive leads to freedom, health and joy on the inside. I have come to realise that unforgiving does more harm to me, than it does to the person who offended me.

I also need to forgive others because in the Lord's Prayer it says, "Forgive us our sins as we forgive those who sin against us". It's an awesome thought that if I don't forgive others for what they've done to me, then God cannot forgive me for the many times I have offended him. Jesus himself upon the cross cried out,

"Father, forgive them, for they know not what they do". Jesus is my example and now as a Christian, he lives inside of me and works out his purposes through me. I therefore have the grace to forgive. Having said that, to forgive Tommy for what he did to Sara, was one of the hardest things I have had to do. It happened again. Not just with Tommy, but Sara moved into another relationship and the cycle repeated itself. She and we had to find the grace to forgive all over again. My kids have all found the ability to forgive and for that I'm very grateful. Because it's a truly beautiful quality.

For the record, I'm glad to say that, since then, Sara has entered a relationship with a very nice Irish lad and Allison herself, has met a male student at College in Falmouth.

During our year of stone, I did a lot of reflective thinking. Inevitably the whole issue of life and death came under my contemplative microscope. I seriously questioned my Christian faith, as to how relevant it was to me and people around me, in light of all this suffering.

On the morning that Sue, my sister-in-law died, I sat in an armchair feeling perplexed and angry. I wanted to play some music. Nothing particular came to mind. I walked across to my CD cabinet, pulled out a disc from the top shelf (what I usually call a 'lucky dip'; it has to be when you can't see) placed it on the deck and when it began to play that I realised it was Boyzone. I skipped the first three tracks, but as soon as track four began, I knew this was the one. I put it on to repeat and sat down to listen. It was the song No Matter What. As I listened, a fresh surge of defiant faith filled my heart and these words came to my mind:

"No matter what they tell me/No matter what they do/No matter how tough life gets/I'll keep on loving you".

My world, and that of others was being shaken, but I needed to make a quality decision that, no matter what, I was going to go on trusting and loving God with all my heart.

*

The whole issue came sharply into focus once again, when the news came through of the sudden death of Maurice Gibb, founder member of my beloved Bee Gees. I began to feel a deep sense of sadness about people who die without knowing God; yet they have given so much pleasure in their lives to so many people. I wanted all good people to go to Heaven and live for ever. My emotions were bombarded with questions.

I thought about decent people who don't believe in God and have Humanist funerals. I admire their honesty, their lack of hypocrisy. I've often puzzled as to why people who had no time for God in this life, then went through (no pun intended) the sham of a religious funeral. Or was it a sham, after all? Perhaps it is as some say, that all people who have tried to live a good life go to Heaven anyway. Is there a Heaven? Is there a Hell? Does it really matter, when all is said and done? We have no say in where we go. Or do we? It was really bugging me.

Then what about my Muslim taxi drivers. Where will they go when they die? Is their religion the right one? Are there several 'right ones'? Do all paths lead to God?

We live in a heightened awareness of terrorism. We see the effects of it daily, on our television screens. The human race, however, faces one common terrorist. None of us can escape. The name of this terrorist is *Death*. The thought of death and dying strikes terror into the hearts of millions of people worldwide. The subject is one avoided by many people today. I once asked my son-in-law Phil, what his thoughts were about death and he replied that he was too busy struggling to live, to think about death and it was a subject that he and Beverley never discussed.

Arising out of my months of thinking, I put together a talk which I presented at churches called 'Putting Death Back On Life's Agenda'. I think it was quite well received with many people, even Christians, coming forward for prayer as the thought of death held them in fear. I truly believe that death is something the human race needs to start talking about, once again. Instead of different religions fighting each other over issues that separate them, they should, along with everyone else, start loving each other and genuinely seek the answers for the important questions. One thing is certain. When we die, the truth will be known. We'll have fallen asleep for the last time, or we'll discover that there's a God, after all. We'll either then, all be in Heaven (if that's what it's called) or some will be in Heaven, and others, Hell. Didn't someone once say, "What's it all about, Alfie?". Not one of my favourite songs, but Cilla Black's version was pretty good. Before we get onto Michael Caine films, what's it all about then, whatever your name is? Every person needs to face the issue for themselves and find some answers. Along the way, if we find some things which help us to clarify the mystery of facing our common terrorist – Death - then surely, out of genuine love, we should pass on what we've learned.

It may be simplistic, but here's what I understand:

1. I believe in God as creator of all things. When I look at the vastness, intricacies and beauty of creation, I find it easier to believe that a magnificent, loving person is behind it all, than to believe that a whole series of explosions in the atmosphere led us to where we are today.

2. I believe that this God is pure and holy. That he set many laws into motion, one of which is that there is no redemption without the shedding of innocent blood. God hates sin; he cannot look upon it and so has to do something about it. Because all of mankind was full of sin, God took action. He decided he would, out of his own genius, make himself totally vulnerable by coming to Earth, as a seed and in a way known only to him (our God) he planted himself deep inside the womb of a young woman by the name of Mary.

3. Jesus (God) was born of a virgin, therefore totally without sin. He grew up in a normal family and submitted himself to his parents for around thirty years. He then went out teaching and preaching the Kingdom of God. He also healed the sick, raised the dead, did many mighty miracles and taught his followers to do the same by using their faith.

4. Jesus made many claims about himself, including several mutually exclusive ones such as "I am the light of the world", "I am the resurrection and the life", "I am the way, the truth, and the life. No-one can come to the Father except through me." I agree with C S Lewis who argued that you cannot therefore, label Jesus simply as a 'good man'. He was either mad, bad, or who he claimed to be. If Jesus lied, then he it misled millions and tricked them

into following him. If Christ actually spoke the truth, then he is who he said he is. None other than God Himself.

5. Religious leaders were incensed by Jesus' claims. Roman authorities were upset with him. So Jesus was arrested and crucified on trumped up charges. God knew this would happen; it was all in his plan to shed his totally innocent and pure blood for the sins of the entire human race.

6. In accordance with the many words spoken by the Prophets, Jesus was then raised from the dead on the third day and he spent a further forty days with his disciples, being seen on numerous occasions during that time, by a variety of people. The disciples, hiding away out of fear for their own lives, were totally transformed by the resurrection of Jesus and following the day of Pentecost, when they were filled with the power of the Holy Spirit, went out with incredible boldness proclaiming the message that Jesus was alive - and they did extraordinary miracles in his name.

7. Jesus (God the Son) then returned to Heaven and sat down at the right-hand of God the Father, from where he has all rule and all authority. God the Holy Spirit was sent into the world to fill every believer with power to live for God and demonstrate his love throughout the world.

8. God's own sinless blood therefore has been shed for the remission of all sin. So will everyone be saved and go to heaven? I think not. In many places the Bible (which I believe is God's Holy Word) states clearly that only those who believe in and put their trust in Jesus Christ as their Lord and Saviour will be 'cleansed' by the blood and accepted into Heaven. Some classic verses which helped convince me are:

"For God so love the world that he freely gave his one and only son, so that whoever believes in him will not die, but will have everlasting life" John 3:16

"All have sinned and come short of God's standard. The wages of sin is death, but the free gift of God is eternal life" Romans 3:23 & 6:23)

"Whoever calls on the name of the Lord will be saved" Romans 10:13

"God is not willing that any should perish, but that all should come to repentance and eternal life." 1 Peter

9. God is passionate about all of his creation; loving every boy and every girl, every man and every woman. People often remark that a loving god would not send people to Hell to burn in the lake of fire. That is true. The lake of fire is made for Satan and all his demons, but clearly there are people who will reject God and the salvation he offers and will end up following Satan to that

place of eternal torment. It is absolutely vital that we consider the Gospel (good news) here and now, and make an informed decision as to whether we are going to put our trust in Jesus Christ, or not.

Look at it this way. If you wanted desperately to attend a particular concert, then you really have to decide well in advance to get your ticket. It may be too late trying to gain entry on the night without a ticket; you may manage to squeeze in on the night, if you're early enough...but even then, it's cutting it fine. You may love the artist in question, but either way, without a ticket you're not going to gain entry.

Whilst it's not a perfect analogy, it highlights the point. If you seek eternal life, to live forever in paradise with God where there are no tears, no sickness or disease, no war but love, peace and joy in abundance, where even the streets are paved with gold, then you need to decide, here and now, while you are still alive to put your trust completely in Jesus Christ; to apply his blood to your sin-stained life so that when you stand before Almighty God, on the great day of judgement, he will accept you because your sins have been washed away by his own perfect blood. It will have nothing to do with how good or how bad you have been. But it will have everything to do with Jesus and the fact that he has paid the price for your total salvation. Phew! No wonder I love him! I trust you will come to love him also!

I can understand it from a legal and intellectual standpoint. It seems like a reasonable faith to have, and the story has stood up to historical scrutiny: the power of its message has changed millions of lives down through the centuries, from all walks of life. Ever since I first opened my heart to Jesus all those years ago at Westminster Chapel, I've never seriously doubted his presence with me. don't always know his perfect will for my life, and I still have many questions, but I've felt his closeness and known his touch so many times that I'm convinced that if I should drop down dead today, I would wake up safe in his presence. Quite literally, I'd stake my life on it.

I don't know of any other religious figure through history who has dealt with the question of sin (mine and yours) and the issue of eternal life in the way that Jesus has. My dear Muslim friends do not believe that Jesus even died on the cross for our sins, but that Judas Iscariot took the place of Jesus. If that were the case, who has paid the price for my sin and what about God's eternal law, "Without the shedding of innocent blood there is no remission of sin"? Also, if Jesus did not die and rise again from the dead, how come all of those Apostles were transformed from fear-filled into people of great boldness and power? Many were martyred for what they preached and for refusing to deny the resurrection.

If I'm ultimately proved wrong then so be it. I'm certainly having a great time being 'deceived' in any case. I'd urge anyone reading this book to take time out to think very seriously about the terrorist called death, and start searching for some answers…another verse from the Bible says, "If you seek me you will surely find me, when you seek me with all of your heart." Please do not make the grave mistake (pun intended) of leaving it until it's too late. Your research, just may lead you to a different conclusion to the one I have come to; but at least you'll have given the most important question, some quality consideration.

Chapter Eight

Journeys of the heart

It's now been a while since I commenced this journey in print. True to the story of my life so far, it's been a rollercoaster of a ride in itself. Perhaps you'd expect nothing less!

At the point when I started this book, my Dad, now eighty five, was taken ill and subsequently suffered a burst duodenal ulcer. Along with other members of the family, I was called to his bedside at Good Hope Hospital in Sutton Coldfield; we were told it was unlikely he would live through the night, following an operation during which his heart actually stopped beating. Incredibly, Dad pulled through. During his rehabilitation period, he fell and broke a hip, necessitating a further operation and period in hospital. Dad was later diagnosed with dementia and became a resident in a care home not too far from us, in Solihull.

Things have continued to go well at work and after twenty-three years as an audio typist, I'm now settled into life working as part of the Open Case Clearance Team at HM Revenue and Customs. I wasn't pleased when I was told that I was being transferred (no fee involved!) from the typing team to the open case team. This change, for me, felt uncomfortable and unnecessary, but like so many people these days, I wasn't exactly given a choice. As with lots of changes in life though, it's turned out for the better.

I'm on a team with some really friendly people, including one or two men, which is unusual for me; I haven't worked alongside too many male typists in the past. Secondly it excites me that I'm part of a team of about twenty visually-impaired people, working around the country for HMRC, being trained on this open case tax work. Thanks go to Dave Yates, who has become an expert in understanding how Job Access With Speech (JAWS) works, and has written a multitude of helpful scripts to enable JAWS users to navigate around various screens, thus making it possible for the visually impaired person to be able to cut and paste information, solely by the use of the keyboard. One of the other trainers, Penny Hilton, has been awarded an MBE for her work done in this ground-breaking initiative. Dave and Penny are just two of the dozen or so people who have brought their skills into this very specialised arena and through their tremendous dedication, have created job opportunities for blind people, that just a few short years ago, would have seemed unthinkable.

During my early training, one experienced tax officer said, "I don't mean to be disrespectful, but you are never going to be able to do this job without sight. The screens are too complicated."

I replied, with a smile on my face, "My aim is to be able to do your job with my eyes closed!"

A couple of months later, I issued my first form to an employer without any assistance whatsoever. I was smiling from ear to ear, especially when someone collected the form from the printer and said it was absolutely perfect. "I feel like I've just scored the winning goal in an FA Cup Final", I said.

With that, my aforementioned disbelieving colleague spoke up, "You've done it then! You can now do my job with your eyes closed."

I think HMRC deserves a huge pat on the back. There probably isn't another government department - or indeed any other business - in the United Kingdom that's doing so much to create and encourage new working practices for those with a visual impairment. I haven't been paid to say that, either!

When starting work on this team, one person I quickly got to know was Heather Jacob. Heather, I soon discovered, is a committed Christian. She's part of a worship band, Vision, itself part of Coton Green Church in Tamworth, Staffordshire. Heather informed me that the band visit Swinfen Hall Prison in Lichfield, once a month, to lead the Sunday morning service in the chapel. Heather loves these times and explained how the young men, offenders between the ages of 18 and 25, really entered into the worship. I hadn't been involved in prison work for over twenty-five years, but said to Heather how much I would love to start again.

Shortly after, following Heather putting in a word for me, I entered Swinfen Hall and shared something of my story with the men, as part of the morning service. Leading them in prayer afterwards, it was such a joy when two young men came over to speak to me. They'd prayed along with me, to commit their lives to Jesus.

I went to prison again a few weeks later, and again it was a joy to be able to share the good news about Jesus and then witness two more men giving their lives over to God. There is no joy in life quite like that, but the icing on the cake for me is to be able to sit and listen to the Vision band as they play their selection of traditional hymns and modern Gospel songs, with a very Celtic feel to their sound. I'm now a regular member of the team, with the privilege of going into Swinfen Hall prison to share my message of hope with the men.

*

At this stage in my life, I'm hoping to re-fire into a whole new orbit and this book will be just a small part of that. I'm still convinced that God's word to launch-out into the deep is ongoing, and will be, until the day I die.

Therefore, I'm deeply grateful to John Dolan, the Area Director, who first expressed appreciation of my writing, and then encouraged me to go on Breakthrough.

I'm also grateful to Linbert Spencer for writing the Breakthrough Programme and for putting it together, in the way that he did. It truly has been the most powerful personal development programme I've ever undertaken and it's definitely helped transform my life. I believe that if the lessons in Breakthrough could be taught in our senior schools, many young people would discover their destiny, rather than wandering aimlessly through life and getting caught up in the binge-drinking and drugs culture.

I'm also grateful to the many people who have encouraged me over the past few years inside and outside of the office, and in particular, to all of those who have e-mailed me, following my Diversity Awareness presentations.

At this stage of my story, God had another massive surprise up his sleeve for me.

2006 saw the inaugural Civil Service Diversity & Equality Awards. Not that I particularly aware of them, in spite of being a civil servant. Imagine my surprise therefore, when I received a letter stating that I had been nominated for an Outstanding Achievement award and had reached the finals, to be held in London at Lancaster House.

Several people had put my name forward as a nomination. The one which carried weight was from Nick John, with whom I've become really good friends. I used to undertake audio typing work for Nick when he was a leading Tax Inspector in the Birmingham office. Nick was also on the same Breakthrough programme as myself; he was one of the mentors. At various events, Nick had also heard my Fear, Fun & Faith presentation. He was keen to put my name forward, citing my presentation as the reason.

Nick did a really thorough job and spent many hours putting his nomination together. I was so impressed with what he'd written about me, I would have chosen myself for an award!

The great day came for the finals and Nick and I travelled down to London by train. We arrived at the imposing and historic Lancaster House and after registration, sat down for pre-lunch drinks. Nick did a great job of describing the architectural style of the building, together with many of the murals and paintings that decorated the walls. There was a real excitement about the place, as people gathered from all over the country. After being called to lunch we found our seats and continued our buzz of conversation.

Nick began a conversation with me, on spiritual issues and particularly around the issue of proof for the resurrection of Jesus. I said that I'd seen a series of programmes screened on BBC1 a short while beforehand, the *Miracles of Jesus*. The series of four programmes on Sunday evenings were absolutely brilliant; I'd learned so much from them and I'd encouraged friends to watch and write to the BBC in appreciation. The series astonished me all the more because it was written and presented by Rageh Omaar, known as the BBC's man in Baghdad, for his courage on the war in Iraq, who is a practising Muslim. To attempt such a programme was a very courageous thing to do on Rageh's part, and I wrote to the BBC, to tell them so.

There I was, eulogising to Nick about the journalistic skills of Rageh Omaar, when suddenly Nick tapped me on the knee and said in a somewhat incredulous tone, " You're never going to believe this!"

"Believe What?"

"I think Rageh Omaar is standing right behind you," said a still disbelieving Nick.

"You're having me on…"

"Excuse me John", said Nick again. "I'm just going to creep around and have a look at his name badge".

I sat alone as other people chatted around the table. After a couple of minutes there was a tap on my shoulder. Nick said, "John I've got someone here, who wants to meet you. Stand up and meet Rageh Omaar."

I shot to my feet, excited and amazed that the very person I had been enthusing about, was now right behind me. I reached out and grabbed Rageh's hand as if he was a long lost son and squeezed it tight.

"Rageh, I'm so thrilled to meet you! I was just talking to my friend about you, and the series you did for the BBC, the *Miracles of Jesus*".

Rageh responded very warmly. It was indeed, a very challenging programme for him to do and he described it as a defining moment in his life. We chatted together like old friends for a few minutes, before he was called away. I sat down feeling utterly gob smacked. I don't like that phrase, but it conjured up the exact impression of how I felt. Nick too, was absolutely freaked out with the very person we'd been talking about, suddenly appearing before our very eyes. This was proving to be a good day - and we hadn't had lunch yet!

It seemed like no time at all that we were into the awards ceremony. I listened attentively to the citations for each award, and marvelled at the contributions being made by so many people, right across the Civil Service in celebrating the diverse nature of our workforce.

Eventually, it came to the category for which I had been nominated, 'Outstanding Achievement'. The citations for the three finalists were read out. Then the words, "And the winner is…." were spoken by the Master of Ceremonies: none other than Rageh Omaar, of course. After an eternity, when my heart was beating fast, the words came.

"John Flanner".

In that moment, I felt like I'd been raptured into Heaven. I almost floated to the front of the stage to collect my award from Rageh, who tapped me on the shoulder and said, "Well done mate. I'm really proud of you". I then shook hands with Sir Gus O'Donnell, head of the British Civil Service. He presented me with a framed certificate and an engraved paperweight to celebrate my victory. I had the privilege of posing for photographs and meeting with other leading civil servants, including Paul Gray, then Acting Chairman of HMRC.

Paul congratulated me. I said I was surprised that I was the only person from HMRC to get into the finals, as an individual. I asked Paul if this was indicative of apathy within HMRC towards Diversity & Equality issues. He said it wasn't the case at all. HMRC had more nominations than any other government department; 178 in all. The fact that I had been the only one, along with two other teams, to get into the finals reflected so well on the Diversity project which I'd undertaken, my presentation.

On the back of this award, I continue to travel the length and breadth of the country making my presentation. Not just to colleagues within HMRC, either. I've spoken to staff at the Cabinet Office for instance; taken part in a forum at the House of Commons; been interviewed on radio. I've also launched my own company, Perfect Vizion.

Through Perfect Vizion I'm aim to offer my *Fear, Fun & Faith* award-winning Diversity presentation to people in the wider business world, along with other motivational talks. I have a dedicated business website, which contains all the necessary details and I'm also available as an entertaining and inspirational after-dinner speaker.

There is no time to retire, because in 're-firing' there are many people in need of the kind of encouragement and inspiration I attempt to bring.

John's dad, Francis Flanner passed away, on 19th October, 2008.

A challenge

This book tells the story of my life, up to the moment when I entrusted my existence to Jesus Christ; and the ongoing tale of what has happened to me, following the momentous decision to 'invite Him in' to my life, on every level.

Such a choice was not taken lightly. Ever since, this preferred lifestyle of mine has been challenging, difficult and costly. Not that I regret my course of action - rather, I wholeheartedly and urgently recommend that you, the reader, consider making such a decision in your own life, if you've yet to do so. Your own background and experience of life, up to this point, will inevitably be different to mine. But I believe that God, as seen in the person of Jesus, knows every detail about you already, and longs to enter into a relationship with you - if you will allow it. If you have yet to make such a choice, the 'thing' which separates you from receiving unconditional acceptance from God, is your sin.

If you wish to change this state of affairs, and entrust your life to Him, you are encouraged to pray sincerely, along the following lines:

"Heavenly Father, I recognise that you sent your son Jesus into the world to make it possible, through His death on the cross, for you and I to enter into relationship. We do not have to be distanced from each other.

"I recognise that I am a sinner, and that I have previously alienated myself from you, by the many wrong things I have thought, and said and done.

"I recognise that I have often known what the 'right' thing is - and have chosen not to do it.

"I recognise that at other times I have done the 'right' thing, but for the wrong motives.

"I recognise that I will probably sin again in the future.

"Heavenly Father, I am sorry for the sin in my life and turn my back on it, entrusting my life to you. Please enter in, as you promise to, and by your Spirit help me to live according to your good purposes. In the name of Jesus Christ, amen."

You may find that after you have prayed such a prayer, you initially feel no different. But if you sincerely mean it, you will still have taken the most profoundly important step you can ever take, in life.

Once a person has taken it, I encourage them to tell other Christians about it, so that they can advise further. If you don't know any, perhaps you may be able to contact a local church, possibly your parish church. I'd love to hear about it too, and I'd welcome the news: you can reach me at **john@flanner.co.uk**

Acknowledgements

Special thanks to my parents, for so lovingly bringing me into this world, to enable me to enjoy life as much as I do; to my brother Paul and sisters Joan and Susan, for their encouragement.

Thanks to my children Beverley (and Phil), Sara, Allison and Ian for their love and belief in their dad - even when I have made it hard for them.

Most importantly of all, very many hugs and kisses to my beloved Sylvia, who has lived through most of this with me, and without whose love I would not be, what I am today. Thanks for your patience, darling!

Finally, to God be the glory, great things he has done. in the words of the great and delightfully-named blind hymn writer of the 19th century, Fanny Crosby:

"This is my story, this is my song
Praising my Saviour all the day long."

For more information on John Flanner, please go to **www.flanner.co.uk** or contact Perfect Vizion at **www.perfectvizion.com**

TORCH TRUST
Torch Trust are still providing a magnificent level of support to visually-impaired people in the UK and around the world. Their Christian-based books and magazines are distributed in Braille, large print and audio-books in ever increasing numbers. There is always a need for volunteers to learn how to transcribe books into Braille and to read them onto discs. There are many other ways to support this invaluable ministry of serving blind and partially-sighted people.

If you would like to contact Torch for further information, please write to them at:

Torch Trust for the blind
Torch House
Market Harborough
Leicestershire
LE16 9HL

e-mail: **info@torchtrust.org**
Website: **www.torchtrust.org**

JOHN CHEEK

Also an HMRC employee, in Southend, Essex, John is a writer in his spare time and has written for Christian publications such as Third Way, as well as secular titles including Record Collector. He has contributed to two books on U2, Walk On and U2: A Diary, as well as the Hope 08 Resource Manual and a forthcoming title on Street Pastors.

He regularly gives radio broadcasts as part of the religious programming of BBC Essex, and each year helps to run the Press Office at the Greenbelt Christian Arts Festival; as well as handling press and publicity for the inter-church organisation, Love Southend **www.lovesouthend.org**

John is married to Fiona. They live 'just over the border' in Rayleigh.